CW01669724

Francis Frith's
WILTSHIRE

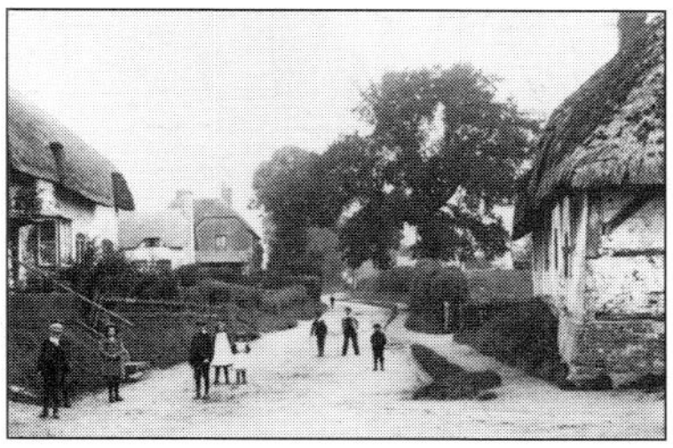

PHOTOGRAPHIC MEMORIES

Francis Frith's WILTSHIRE

Dennis Needham and Les Moores

FRITH BOOK Co

First published in the United Kingdom in 1999 by
Frith Book Company Ltd

Hardback Edition 1999
ISBN 1-85937-053-5

Paperback Edition 2001
ISBN 1-85937-277-5

Reprinted in Hardback 2002

Reprinted in Paperback 2002

British Library Cataloguing in Publication Data

Francis Frith's Wiltshire
Dennis Needham and Les Moores

Frith Book Company Ltd
Frith's Barn, Teffont,
Salisbury, Wiltshire SP3 5QP
Tel: +44 (0) 1722 716 376
Email: info@francisfrith.co.uk
www.francisfrith.co.uk

Printed and bound in Great Britain

As with any historical database the Frith archive is constantly being corrected and improved and the publishers would welcome information on omissions or inaccuracies

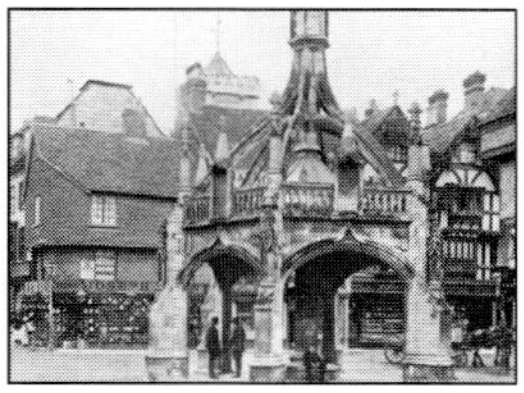

Contents

FRANCIS FRITH: *Victorian Pioneer*

FRANCIS FRITH, Victorian founder of the world-famous photographic archive, was a complex and multitudinous man. A devout Quaker and a highly successful Victorian businessman, he was both philosophic by nature and pioneering in outlook.

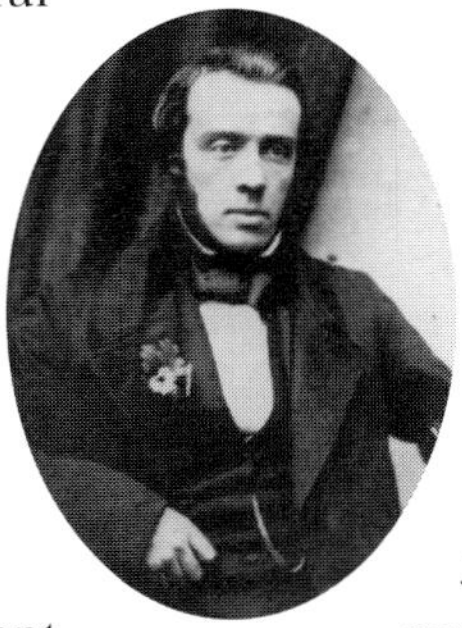

By 1855 Francis Frith had already established a wholesale grocery business in Liverpool, and sold it for the astonishing sum of £200,000, which is the equivalent today of over £15,000,000. Now a multi-millionaire, he was able to indulge his passion for travel. As a child he had pored over travel books written by early explorers, and his fancy and imagination had been stirred by family holidays to the sublime mountain regions of Wales and Scotland. 'What a land of spirit-stirring and enriching scenes and places!' he had written. He was to return to these scenes of grandeur in later years to 'recapture the thousands of vivid and tender memories', but with a different purpose. Now in his thirties, and captivated by the new science of photography, Frith set out on a series of pioneering journeys to the Nile regions that occupied him from 1856 until 1860.

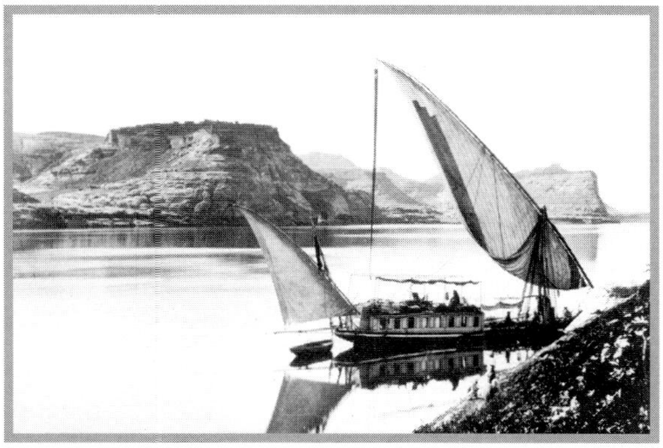

INTRIGUE AND ADVENTURE

He took with him on his travels a specially-designed wicker carriage that acted as both dark-room and sleeping chamber. These far-flung journeys were packed with intrigue and adventure. In his life story, written when he was sixty-three, Frith tells of being held captive by bandits, and of fighting 'an awful midnight battle to the very point of surrender with a deadly pack of hungry, wild dogs'. Sporting flowing Arab costume, Frith arrived at Akaba by camel seventy years before Lawrence, where he encountered 'desert princes and rival sheikhs, blazing with jewel-hilted swords'.

During these extraordinary adventures he was assiduously exploring the desert regions bordering the Nile and patiently recording the antiquities and peoples with his camera. He was the first photographer to venture beyond the sixth cataract. Africa was still the mysterious 'Dark Continent', and Stanley and Livingstone's historic meeting was a decade into the future. The conditions for picture taking confound belief. He laboured for hours in his wicker dark-room in the sweltering heat of the desert, while the volatile chemicals fizzed dangerously in their trays. Often he was forced to work in remote tombs and caves where conditions were cooler. Back in London he exhibited his photographs and was 'rapturously cheered' by members of the Royal Society. His reputation as a photographer was made overnight. An eminent modern historian has likened their impact on the population of the time to that on our own generation of the first photographs taken on the surface of the moon.

Venture of a Life-Time

Characteristically, Frith quickly spotted the opportunity to create a new business as a specialist publisher of photographs. He lived in an era of immense and sometimes violent change. For the poor in the early part of Victoria's reign work was a drudge and the hours long, and people had precious little free time to enjoy themselves.

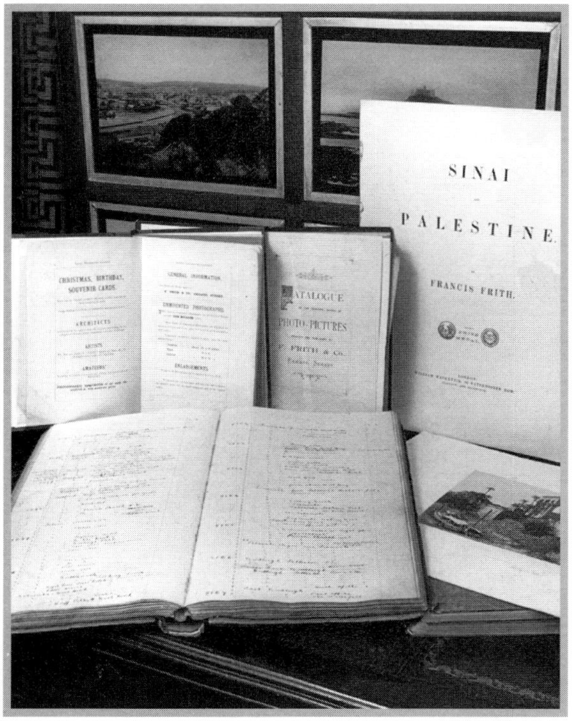

Most had no transport other than a cart or gig at their disposal, and had not travelled far beyond the boundaries of their own town or village. However, by the 1870s, the railways had threaded their way across the country, and Bank Holidays and half-day Saturdays had been made obligatory by Act of Parliament. All of a sudden the ordinary working man and his family were able to enjoy days out and see a little more of the world.

With characteristic business acumen, Francis Frith foresaw that these new tourists would enjoy having souvenirs to commemorate their days out. In 1860 he married Mary Ann Rosling and set out with the intention of photographing every city, town and village in Britain. For the next thirty years he travelled the country by train and by pony and trap, producing fine photographs of seaside resorts and beauty spots that were keenly bought by millions of Victorians. These prints were painstakingly pasted into family albums and pored over during the dark nights of winter, rekindling precious memories of summer excursions.

The Rise of Frith & Co

Frith's studio was soon supplying retail shops all over the country. To meet the demand he gathered about him a small team of photographers, and published the work of independent artist-photographers of the calibre of Roger Fenton and Francis Bedford. In order to gain some understanding of the scale of Frith's business one only has to look at the catalogue issued by Frith & Co in 1886: it runs to some 670

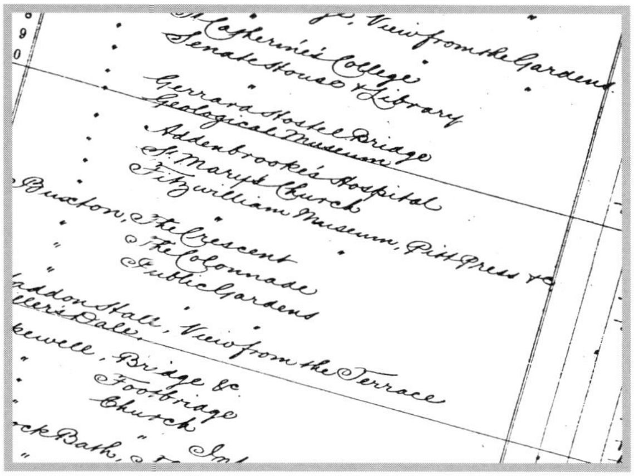
St Catherine's College
View from the Garden
Senate House & Library
Gerrard Hostel Bridge
Geological Museum
Addenbrooke's Hospital
St Mary's Church
Fitzwilliam Museum, Pitt Press &c
Buxton, The Crescent
The Colonnade
Public Gardens
Haddon Hall, View from the Terrace
Millers Dale
Bakewell, Bridge &c.
Footbridge
Church

pages, listing not only many thousands of views of the British Isles but also many photographs of most European countries, and China, Japan, the USA and Canada – note the sample page shown above from the hand-written *Frith & Co* ledgers detailing pictures taken. By 1890 Frith had created the greatest specialist photographic publishing company in the world, with over 2,000 outlets – more than the combined number that Boots and WH Smith have today! The picture on the right shows the *Frith & Co* display board at Ingleton in the Yorkshire Dales. Beautifully constructed with mahogany frame and gilt inserts, it could display up to a dozen local scenes.

Postcard Bonanza

The ever-popular holiday postcard we know today took many years to develop. In 1870 the Post Office issued the first plain cards, with a pre-printed stamp on one face. In 1894 they allowed other publishers' cards to be sent through the mail with an attached adhesive halfpenny stamp. Demand grew rapidly, and in 1895 a new size of postcard was permitted called the court card, but there was little room for illustration. In 1899, a year after Frith's death, a new card measuring 5.5 x 3.5 inches became the standard format, but it was not until 1902 that the divided back came into being, with address and message on one face and a full-size illustration on the other. *Frith & Co* were in the vanguard of postcard development, and Frith's sons Eustace and Cyril continued their father's monumental task, expanding the number of views offered to the public and recording more and more places in Britain, as the coasts and countryside were opened up to mass travel.

Francis Frith died in 1898 at his villa in Cannes, his great project still growing. The archive he created continued in business for another seventy years. By 1970 it contained over a third of a million pictures of 7,000 cities, towns and villages. The massive photographic record Frith has left to us stands as a living monument to a special and very remarkable man.

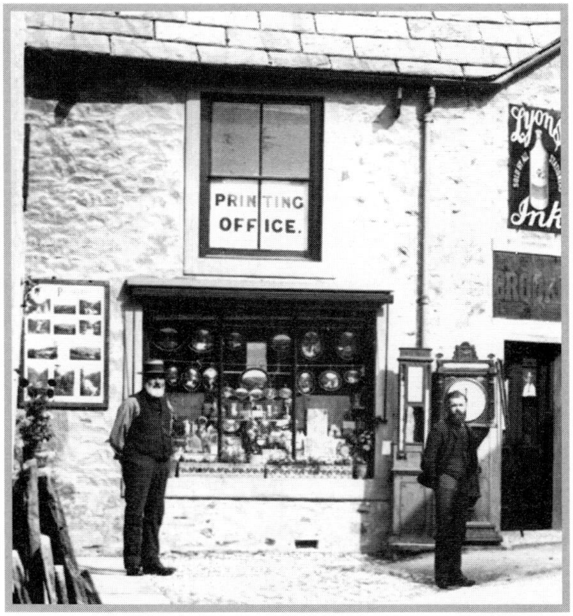

Frith's Archive: *A Unique Legacy*

Francis Frith's legacy to us today is of immense significance and value, for the magnificent archive of evocative photographs he created provides a unique record of change in 7,000 cities, towns and villages throughout Britain over a century and more. Frith and his fellow studio photographers revisited locations many times down the years to update their views, compiling for us an enthralling and colourful pageant of British life and character.

We tend to think of Frith's sepia views of Britain as nostalgic, for most of us use them to conjure up memories of places in our own lives with which we have family associations. It often makes us forget that to Francis Frith they were records of daily life as it was actually being lived in the cities, towns and villages of his day. The Victorian age was one of great and often bewildering change for ordinary people, and though the pictures evoke an impression of slower times, life was as busy and hectic as it is today.

We are fortunate that Frith was a photographer of the people, dedicated to recording the minutiae of everyday life. For it is this sheer wealth of visual data, the painstaking chronicle of changes in dress, transport, street layouts, buildings, housing, engineering and landscape that captivates us so much today. His remarkable images offer us a powerful link with the past and with the lives of our ancestors.

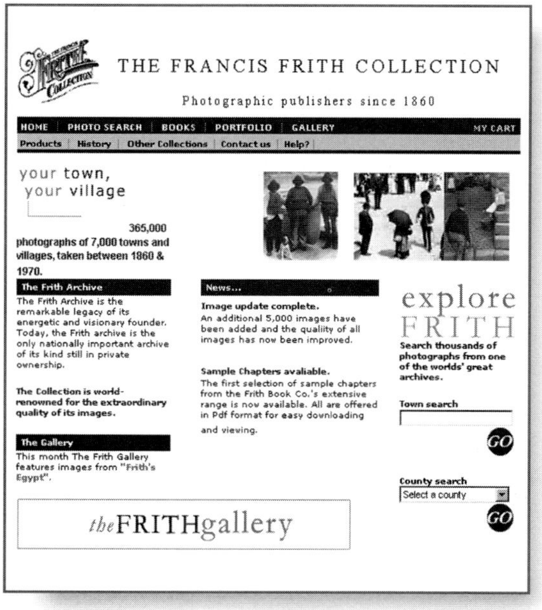

See Frith at www.francisfrith.co.uk

Today's Technology

Computers have now made it possible for Frith's many thousands of images to be accessed almost instantly. In the Frith archive today, each photograph is carefully 'digitised' then stored on a CD Rom. Frith archivists can locate a single photograph amongst thousands within seconds. Views can be catalogued and sorted under a variety of categories of place and content to the immediate benefit of researchers. Inexpensive reference prints can be created for them at the touch of a mouse button, and a wide range of books and other printed materials assembled and published for a wider, more general readership - in the next twelve months over a hundred Frith local history titles will be published! The day-to-day workings of the archive are very different from how they were in Francis Frith's time: imagine the herculean task of sorting through eleven tons of glass negatives as Frith had to do to locate a particular sequence of pictures! Yet the archive still prides itself on maintaining the same high standards of excellence laid down by Francis Frith, including the painstaking cataloguing and indexing of every view.

It is curious to reflect on how the internet now allows researchers in America and elsewhere greater instant access to the archive than Frith himself ever enjoyed. Many thousands of individual views can be called up on screen within seconds on one of the Frith internet sites, enabling people living continents away to revisit the streets of their ancestral home town, or view places in Britain where they have enjoyed holidays. Many overseas researchers welcome the chance to view special theme selections, such as transport, sports, costume and ancient monuments.

We are certain that Francis Frith would have heartily approved of these modern developments, for he himself was always working at the very limits of Victorian photographic technology.

The Value of the Archive Today

Because of the benefits brought by the computer, Frith's images are increasingly studied by social historians, by researchers into genealogy and ancestory, by architects, town planners, and by teachers and schoolchildren involved in local history projects. In addition, the archive offers every one of us a unique opportunity to examine the places where we and our families have lived and worked down the years. Immensely successful in Frith's own era, the archive is now, a century and more on, entering a new phase of popularity.

The Past in Tune with the Future

Historians consider the Francis Frith Collection to be of prime national importance. It is the only archive of its kind remaining in private ownership and has been valued at a million pounds. However, this figure is now rapidly increasing as digital technology enables more and more people around the world to enjoy its benefits.

Francis Frith's archive is now housed in an historic timber barn in the beautiful village of Teffont in Wiltshire. Its founder would not recognize the archive office as it is today. In place of the many thousands of dusty boxes containing glass plate negatives and an all-pervading odour of photographic chemicals, there are now ranks of computer screens. He would be amazed to watch his images travelling round the world at unimaginable speeds through network and internet lines.

The archive's future is both bright and exciting. Francis Frith, with his unshakeable belief in making photographs available to the greatest number of people, would undoubtedly approve of what is being done today with his lifetime's work. His photographs, depicting our shared past, are now bringing pleasure and enlightenment to millions around the world a century and more after his death.

WILTSHIRE – *An Introduction*

WILTSHIRE is a greatly underestimated county. To most people it means Stonehenge and Salisbury, or somewhere that appears on a sign as travellers rush up and down the M4 motorway, heedless of what is around them.

To the aficionado, the seeker of beauty or the traveller willing to do more than simply scratch the surface, Wiltshire offers a surfeit of enchantment: rolling downland, towns steeped in history, and glorious rivers - many of Southern England's best known rivers either rise in or pass through Wiltshire.

It covers some 800,000 acres of land and is bounded by Swindon in the north, Salisbury to the south-east and Trowbridge in the west. The Somerset Avon rises in Gloucestershire and heads south to enter the county near Malmesbury, and passes through Chippenham and Melksham on its way to Bath, and the Thames passes through the county on its way to Oxford, Reading and London. The Hampshire Avon, one of England's best known trout streams and famous for its beauty, rises near Devizes and passes through Salisbury en route to the English Channel at Christchurch. Another popular trout river is the Kennet. This rises on Marlborough Down and heads east to the Thames at Reading. It is also navigable for part of its length, sections of it having been canalised as part of the Kennet and Avon Navigation.

In many respects, Wiltshire has for centuries been two counties, divided by the great Salisbury Plain. On the plain itself and to the south of it, and on the Downs to the east, there is rolling open chalk downland countryside which used to support a huge population of sheep, the home of wealthy farmers and many well-endowed churches. To the north and west are the relatively flat and enclosed fields of the clay and greensand vales, with their small dairy farms, textile mills and a strong nonconformist conscience among the people. This contrast between 'chalk and cheese' and between 'church and chapel' can be traced in many other aspects of life even today, from building materials and dialect to employment and shopping patterns.

Agriculture plays a major part in the economic activity of the county. Large fertile plains around the Vale of Pewsey are well cultivated, the upland areas less so. Sheep are the main farming activity here, although the army uses some of the most attractive areas on Salisbury Plain to practice their tank manoeuvres. Paradoxically, because of the limited public access and land use of these areas, many of them are now important sites of interest for wildlife conservation. The Marlborough Downs are popular with racehorse trainers; the well-known training town of Lambourn is only a couple of miles over the county line in Berkshire.

The main centre of industry is Swindon. Until comparatively recent times, Swindon was a centre for heavy industry and engineering, as the Great Western Railway had its locomotive works here. Some of England's most famous steam engines were made in this factory. As railway services contracted, a major rationalisation in the 1980s saw the unthinkable happen - the Swindon works closed. But out of adversity came opportunity: the town is now a commercial centre, with computers, finance and motor cars offering plenty of employment. Trowbridge, on the other hand, seems to specialise in satisfying the inner man. Pies, bacon and other meat products have long been associated with the town and Ushers still brew beer there, despite the increasing rationalisation of the brewing industry.

If Wiltshire's towns are pleasant, the villages are breathtaking. Lacock is probably one of the finest in the county. The whole village is owned by the National Trust. It was presented to them in 1944, and the Trust has been ruthless in preserving the 'olde worlde' charm of the place. The buildings date from the 14th century and blend well together. Yet Lacock is not a sterile place. There are pubs and tea rooms and a thriving village life, and also much to attract overseas visitors, to whom it is the quintessential English village. But perhaps the biggest blight of life in Lacock is the fact that almost every period drama for television or the cinema that needs period atmosphere is filmed there. This can cause severe disruption to Lacock's inhabitants.

There are other popular destinations in the county for film makers. Castle Combe, for instance, another superb village with its old Manor House and thatched cottages clustering around the Market Cross, looked very different in 1966. Then, the set decorators transformed the village into the seaport of Puddleby-by-the-Marsh. The river was widened, harbour walls and jetties built, creating a set for 'Dr. Dolittle'. It is even more amazing that the village was returned to its original state after they had finished. The Beatles filmed 'Help!' at Stonehenge, the Jane Austen classic 'Sense and Sensibility' used Mompesson House in the Cathedral Close in Salisbury. 'Pride and Prejudice', 'Far from the Madding Crowd' and 'The Madness of King George' are just a few of the others to be filmed in Wiltshire.

Apart from exemplifying 'village England', Wiltshire also has more than its share of grand houses. The castles of Wardour and Longford, the great houses of Wilton and Biddesden, all add grandeur and elegance to the county. Perhaps the most famous of Wiltshire's great houses, Longleat, seat of the Marquess of Bath, was one of the first to be opened to the public. It was built in 1580 on the site of an Augustinian priory that was sold after the Dissolution. The gardens were laid out by Lancelot Brown in the 18th century, and an orangery and terrace were added at this time. Today, that landscape is most famous as a safari park where lions and other animals roam freely. Lancelot Brown's proper name may be somewhat unfamiliar, but his nickname - Capability - is known to most people. He acquired it by telling potential clients that he could see their properties had 'capabilities'. He was responsible for many of England's finest gardens: Blenheim, Kew and Stowe are the most notable. Brown also worked on the park and gardens at Longford Castle, to the south of Salisbury.

Although nominally a house, Wilton is built on a grand scale. The family seat of the earls of Pembroke, it was also constructed on the site of a religious establishment that was disbanded by Henry VIII. The first building was destroyed by fire in 1647 and the current one, designed by Inigo Jones, built to replace it. Wilton is also famous as the birthplace of English carpet manufacture. The Earl of Pembroke encouraged this industry and it still operates today.

But if the secular is grand, the sacred is spectacular. Salisbury Cathedral is unique in many respects, not least because it is the only English cathedral built in one architectural style throughout - the Early English style. It was built in 1258, with the tower and spire added later. At over 400ft the spire is the highest in the country, and took nearly thirty years to complete. It is the landmark around Salisbury, visible for miles and famously captured on canvas by John Constable. Over the years, the tower, which has foundations only 6ft deep, started to lean; when the great architect Sir Christopher Wren was called in to look at it, he found it had moved almost 30 inches from plumb. His solution was to straighten it with iron rods; when these were replaced in 1951, no further movement was found to have taken place. Wren, incidentally, was a Wiltshire man, born in the village of East Knoyle south of Warminster in 1632.

The interior of Salisbury Cathedral is built in the grand manner. It has a high vaulted nave and graceful columns of Purbeck stone, and there are many carved stone monuments and effigies. All this can be seen more clearly than in some other cathedrals because of the large number of windows. The associated buildings are many and equally impressive. The Cathedral Close is all set within a walled square, the largest in the country.

Yet the city of Salisbury did not exist before the cathedral was built. Two miles north is a low hill, standing alongside the Avon. This was originally an Iron Age fort, built around 500BC, discovered by the Romans when they arrived. Realising its defensive potential, they built Sorviodunum here, which became Old Sarum. When the Normans arrived, they built a cathedral and a royal castle on the site. However, there were constant problems, particularly with water supplies. The site was also very exposed. Bishop Herbert Poore decided to build a new cathedral on a different site, close to a sound water supply. The present site by the River Avon was chosen, and the former cathedral dismantled and abandoned. There is still much to see within the great earthworks of Old Sarum. The site is maintained by English Heritage and is open all year round. Because Salisbury was first built all at one time, the streets were laid out in a logical grid pattern. When the noted diarist Samuel Pepys visited in 1668 ('...guided all over the plain by the sight of the steeple') he noted that 'the river runs through every street'. This was a system of small canals provided for water and drainage.

The other major antiquity in the county is the world-famous Stonehenge. Over the centuries, learned scholars have pondered the reason for this massive construction. Stonehenge has been reliably dated to between 1800 and 1500BC. This pre-dates the Siege of Troy, although the pyramids were already a thousand years old. Will the exact purpose ever be discovered? Theories abound, some more likely than others. Two of the more sustainable theories are that it was a temple to the sun or a seasonal clock. Another major prehistoric henge monument, in some ways even more impressive than Stonehenge, is Avebury. Much of it pre-dates Stonehenge; Wiltshire is most fortunate to have these two exceptionally important antiquities within its boundaries.

THE VILLAGES

WILTSHIRE is nothing if not a rural county. With only a single city and a scattering of market towns, village life until the end of the last century was exactly that. Not until the all-pervasive influence of the motor car was felt did the rural backwaters of Wiltshire enter the modern age. Was change a good thing? Most people who live in rural areas today are thankful for mains electricity, piped water and sewage disposal. But they mourn the destruction of their communities that ease of transport has brought.

As even a cursory glance at the photographs in this chapter will show, much has been lost of a simple way of life. Yet it is all too easy to look at these pictures through rose-tinted spectacles: the quiet streets empty of cars, trees growing everywhere, and a profusion of trim cottages - often with thatched roofs - look picturesque. But the camera can lie. The photographer rarely ventures forth in the depths of winter. Low light levels, short days and no foliage on the trees made photography - especially in the early days - difficult at best, and often impossible. So we rarely see these rural idylls with unpaved streets ankle deep in mud, or their inhabitants chilled and saturated through a complete lack of waterproof clothing. Thatched roofs are pretty, but what if they leak? The cob or wattle and daub of which the cottages were built would disintegrate in the wet, and great chunks of the walls literally fell down.

Fire was another danger. The greatest hazard of all to thatch is the open fire below. There was no central heating then, certainly no gas and probably no electricity. Cooking, heating and lighting all came from an open flame: a sure recipe for disaster. People disposed of their own rubbish and waste, for no corporation dust cart called once a week. If the village was big enough, it employed a night soil man to empty the earth closet - not the most pleasant job on earth. Unquestionably, life was hard . But as many of these valuable old pictures show, people lived and worked in what we today would consider intolerable conditions. Thomas Hardy describes these times in his Wessex novels: Salisbury, for example, was Hardy's 'Melchester'.

It is possible that the relatively uncomplicated life these people led brought an inner contentment that we find difficult to comprehend today. There was no television, radio or cinema to show that there was another - possibly better - life elsewhere. Generally, a person was born, lived and died in the same parish. An air of peace and tranquillity seems the common denominator of the many villages we visit during the next few pages. Avebury with the village children on the street, shopping in Wilton in 1919, market day in Wootton Bassett, even the centre of that village in 1960 - all these convey the same impression. But whatever is the truth about life in rural Wiltshire, one thing is unarguable: the scenes captured by these pioneering cameramen record an England that is forever lost. Whether this is a good or a bad thing depends on your own point of view.

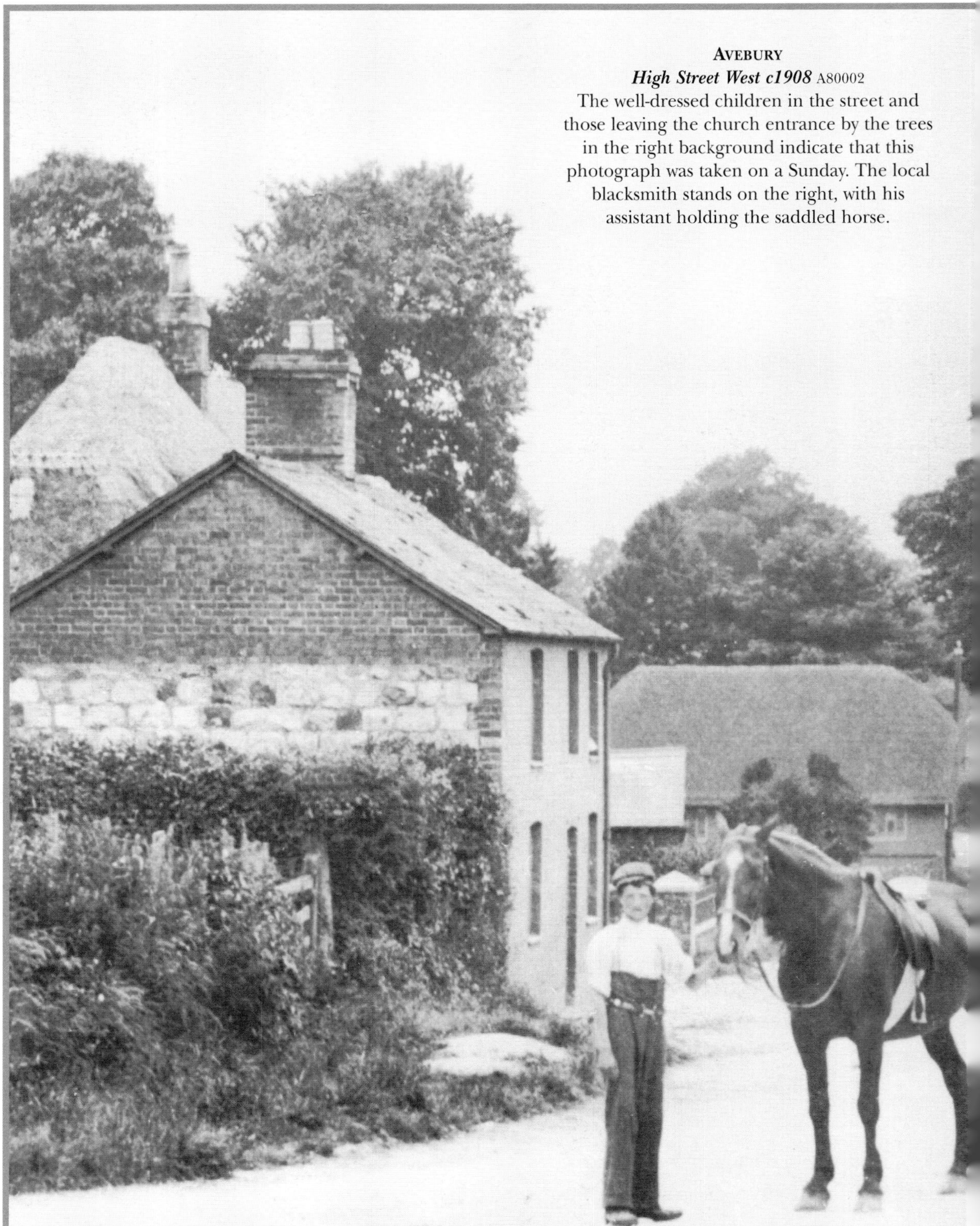

AVEBURY
High Street West c1908 A80002
The well-dressed children in the street and those leaving the church entrance by the trees in the right background indicate that this photograph was taken on a Sunday. The local blacksmith stands on the right, with his assistant holding the saddled horse.

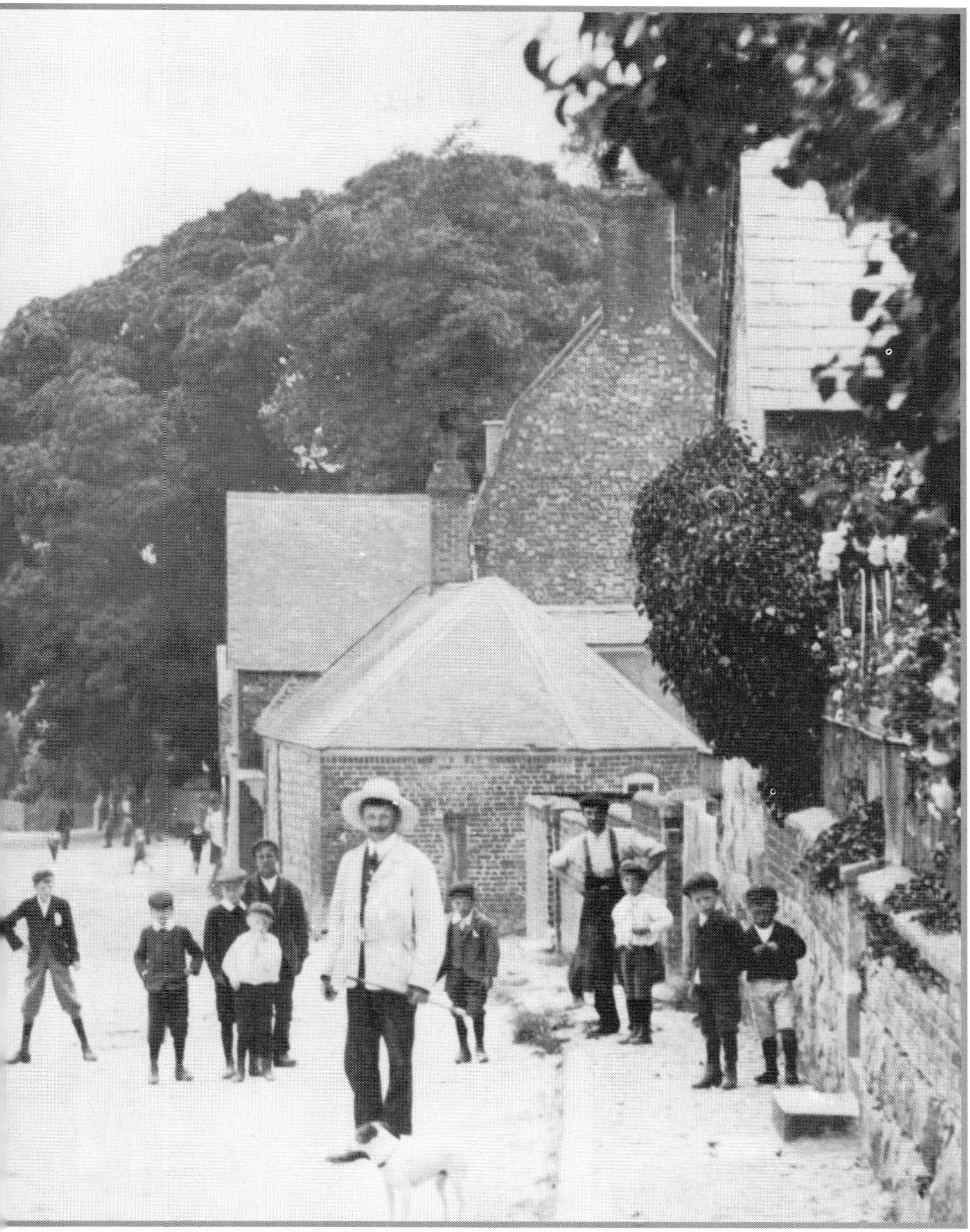

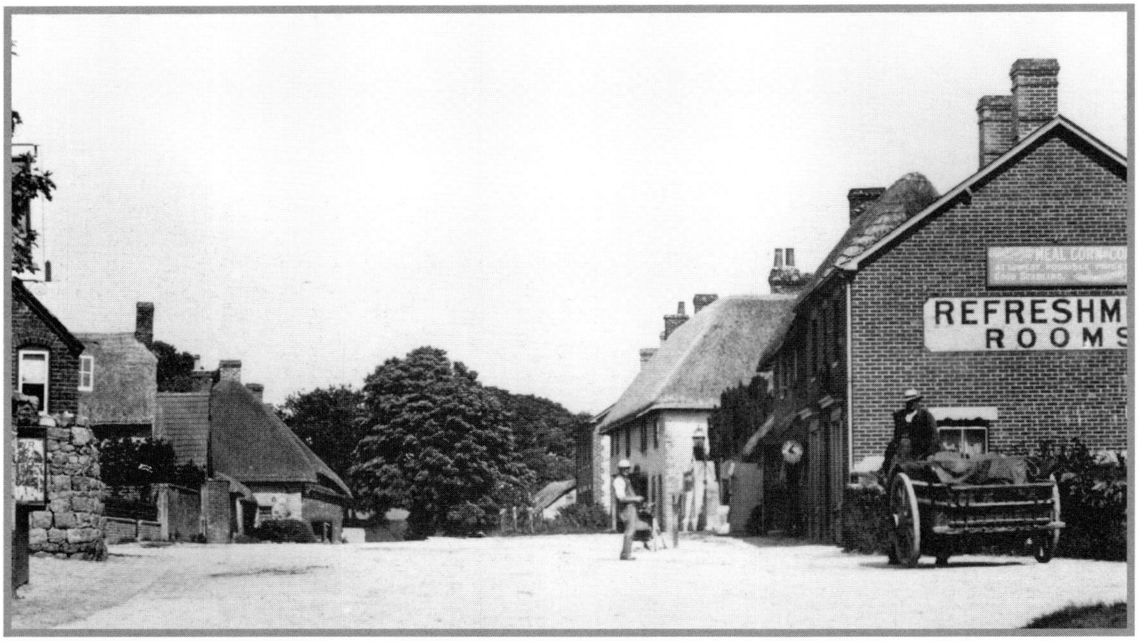

AVEBURY, HIGH STREET EAST c1909 A80004
The Devizes to Swindon road veers to the left just after the public house, which still trades today as the Red Lion. A variety of building materials are evident, from thatched and tiled roofs to brick and stone walling. The refreshment sign indicates that as early as 1909 the Avebury stone circle attracted visitors.

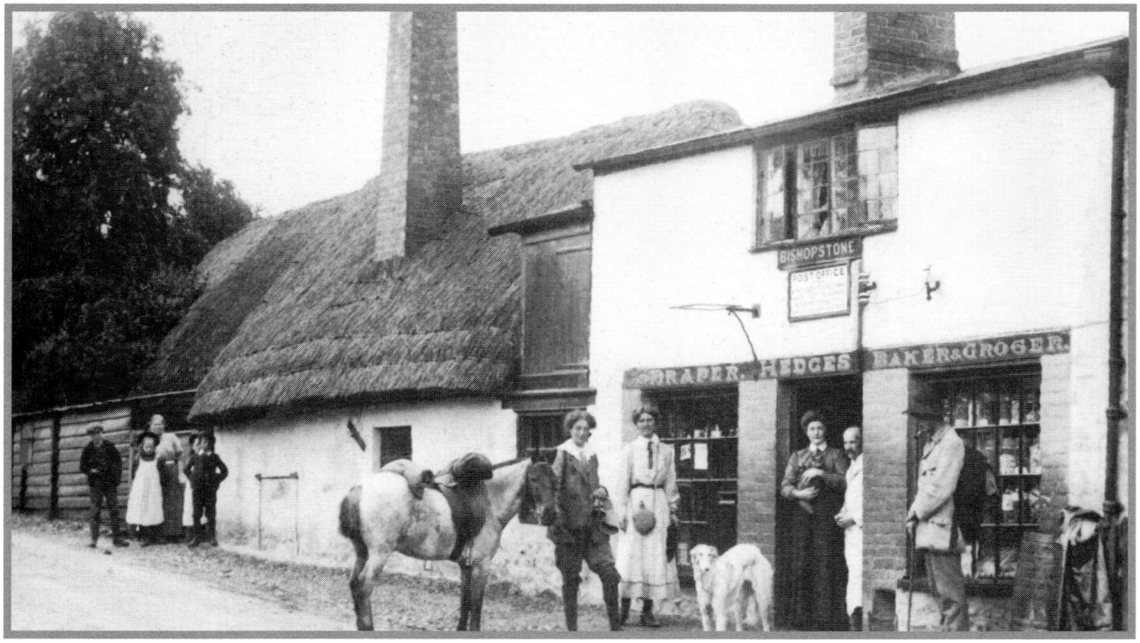

BISHOPSTONE, THE POST OFFICE AND STORES 1908 B298001
Unusually for this era, there is a walker with a back pack. He has stopped at Hedges' shop to replenish his stores. Note the cottage's tall chimney, creating the draught necessary to produce a good fire. The shop is baker, grocer and draper; as it was probably the only shop in the village, it needed to carry a broad range of goods.

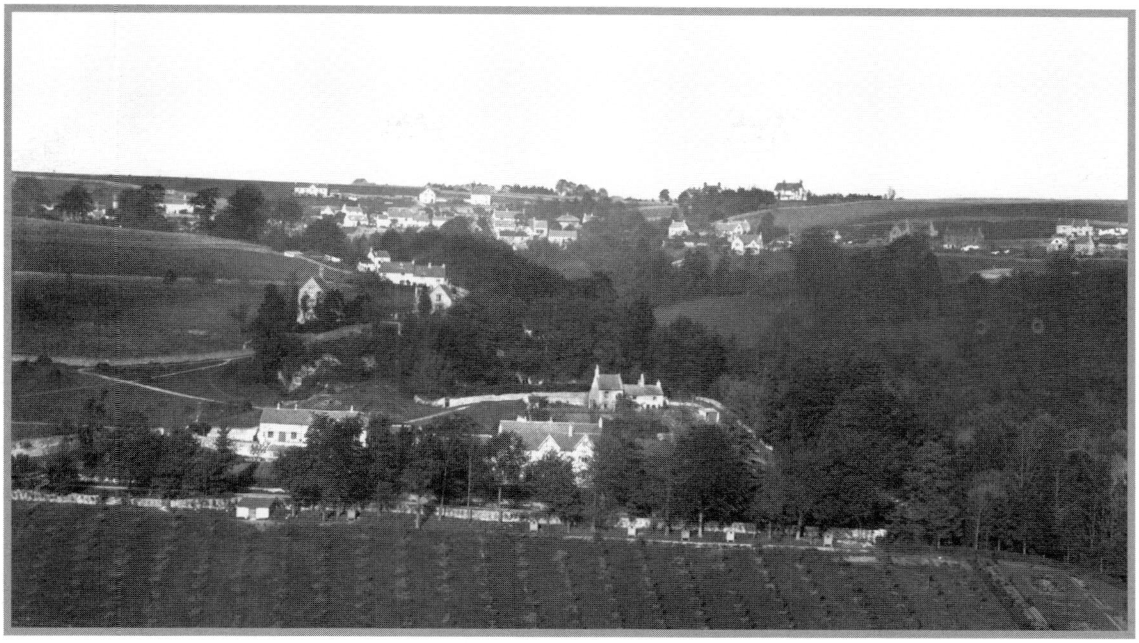

Box, General View 1904 53128
Scar Hill and Box. The village straddles the A4 trunk road, and is the location of a superb railway tunnel. Box is the last village on the A4 and the railway in Wiltshire, and Bath is just five miles away.

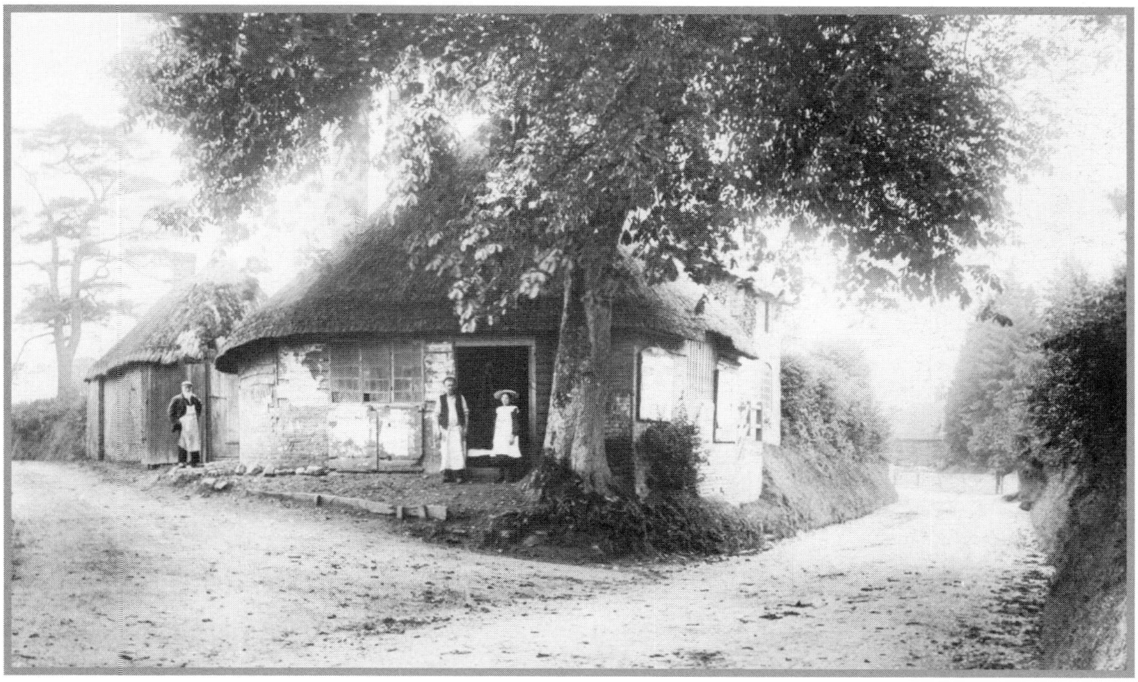

Burbage, The Village Smithy 1907 57209
The village blacksmith was then an important member of the community. Horses were still the main form of motive power, and the skill in keeping horses well shod and farm implements in good repair was vital to the local economy.

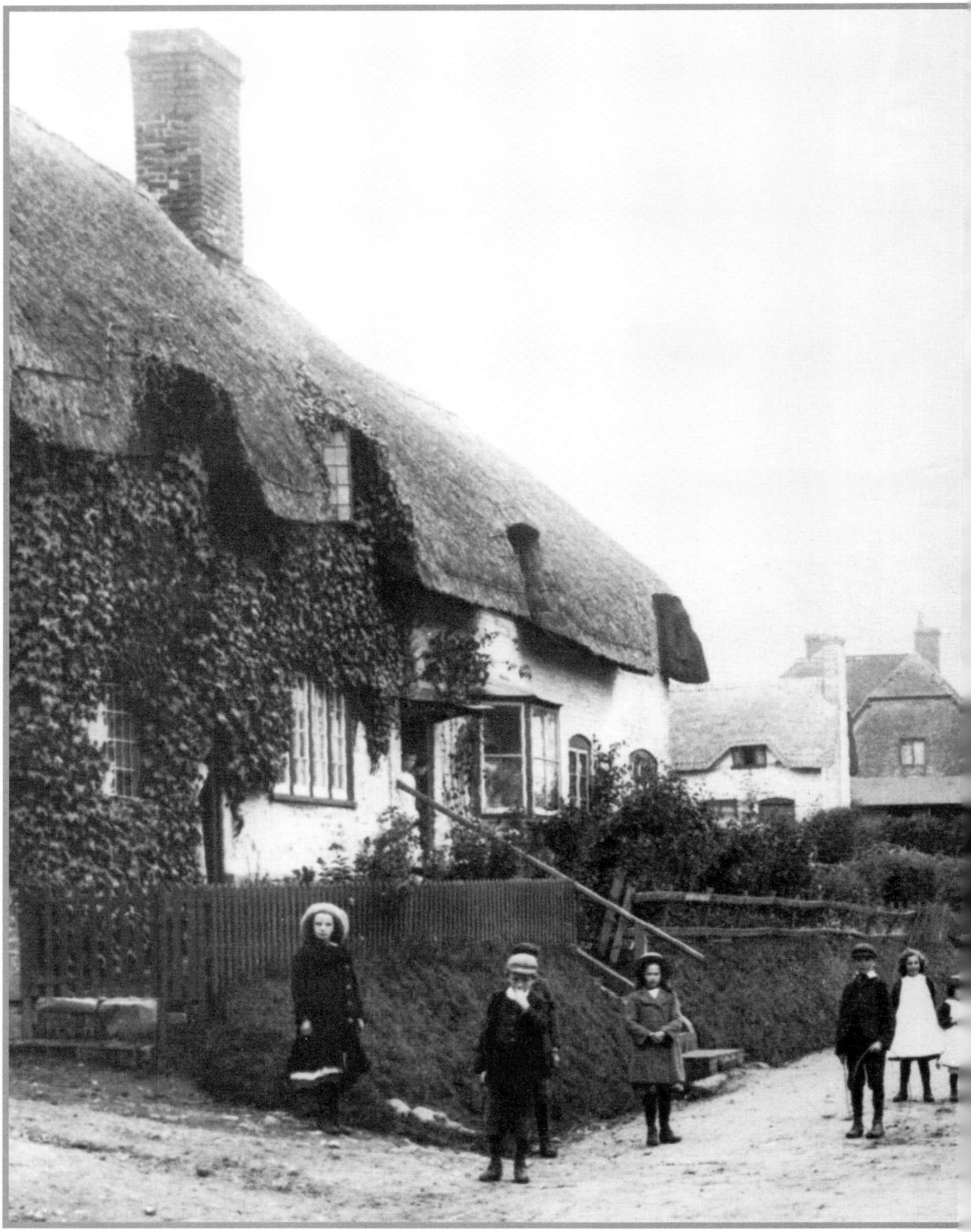

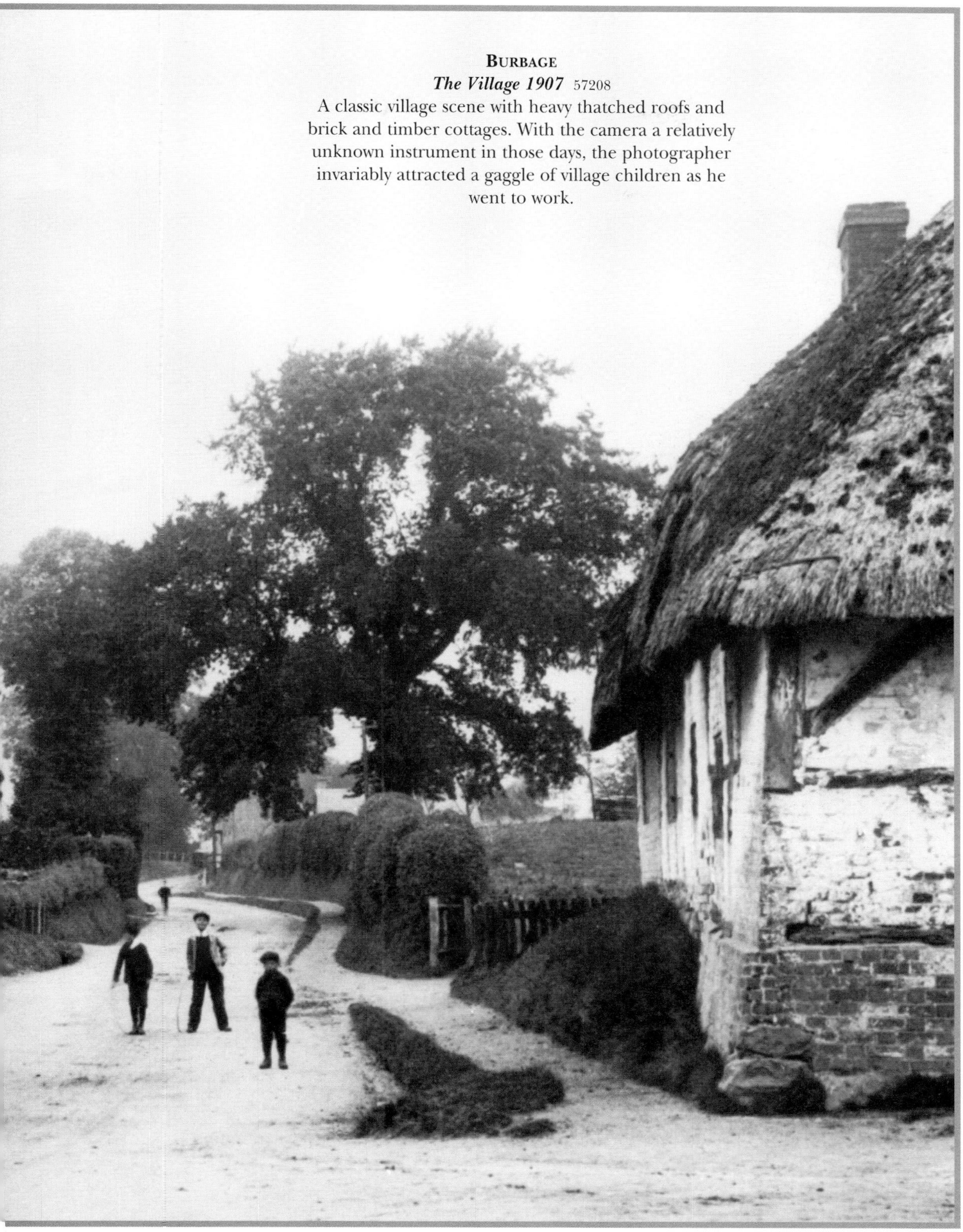

Burbage

The Village 1907 57208

A classic village scene with heavy thatched roofs and brick and timber cottages. With the camera a relatively unknown instrument in those days, the photographer invariably attracted a gaggle of village children as he went to work.

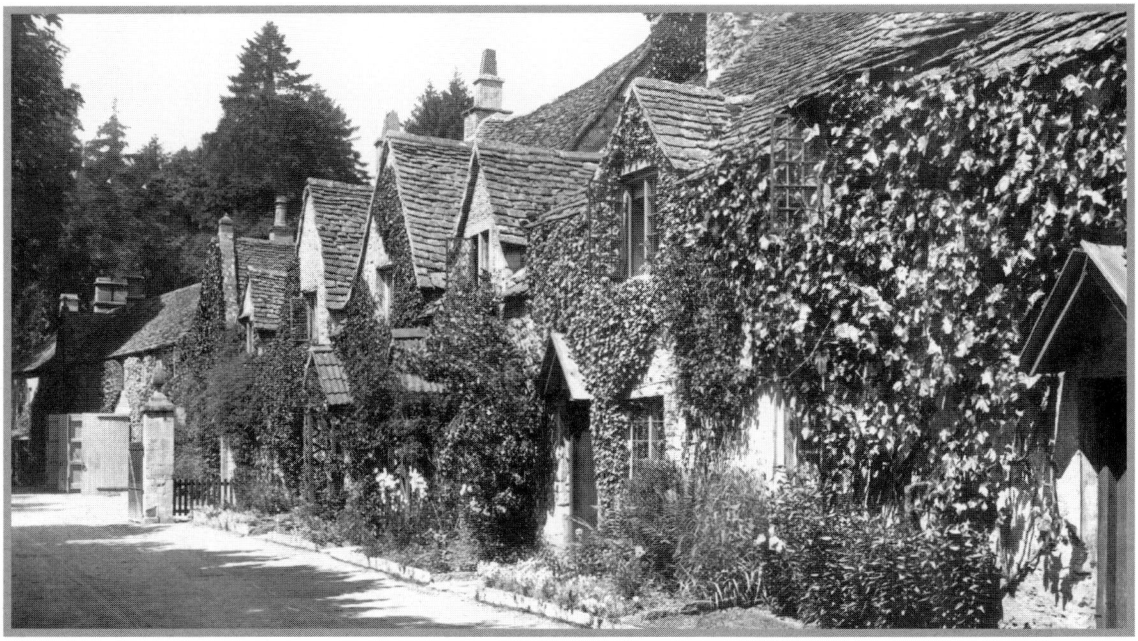

CASTLE COMBE, WEST STREET 1906 53908
Castle Combe was once a centre for cloth weaving but now seems to trade on its picturesque qualities. The village's favourable microclimate encourages the profusion of climbing plants up the walls of the houses, which have the steep pitched stone roofs typical of Cotswold villages.

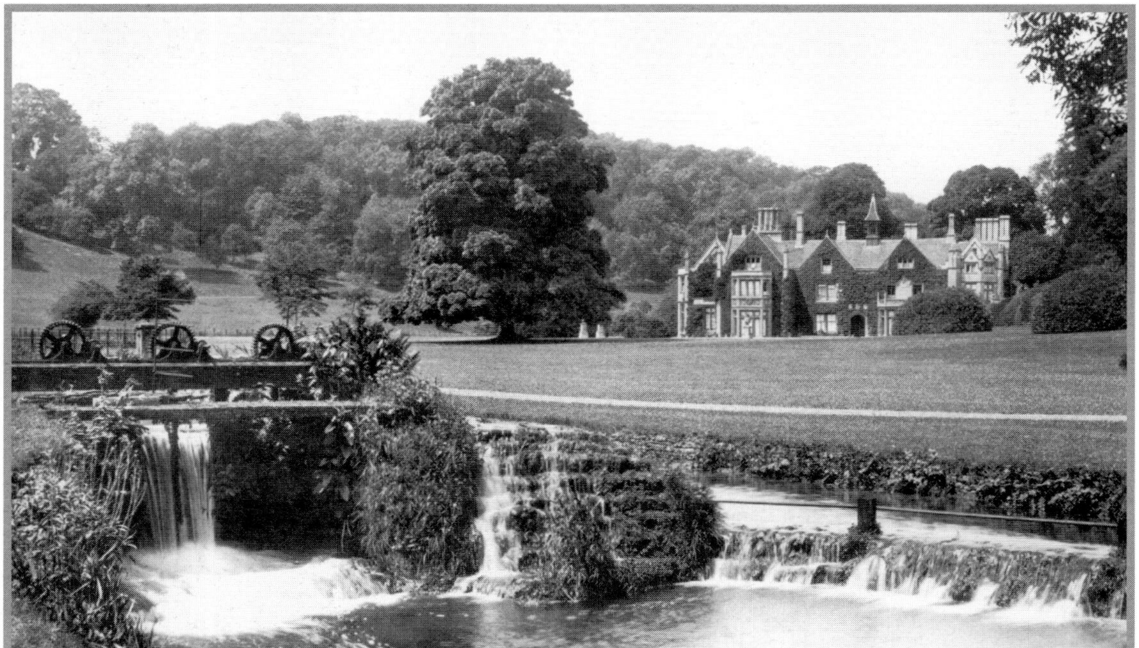

CASTLE COMBE, THE MANOR HOUSE AND WEIR 1907 57838
A little further upstream from the view in the last picture. The Manor House in Castle Combe was built in 1894 and is now a three-star hotel. The sluices have been opened and water tumbles through.

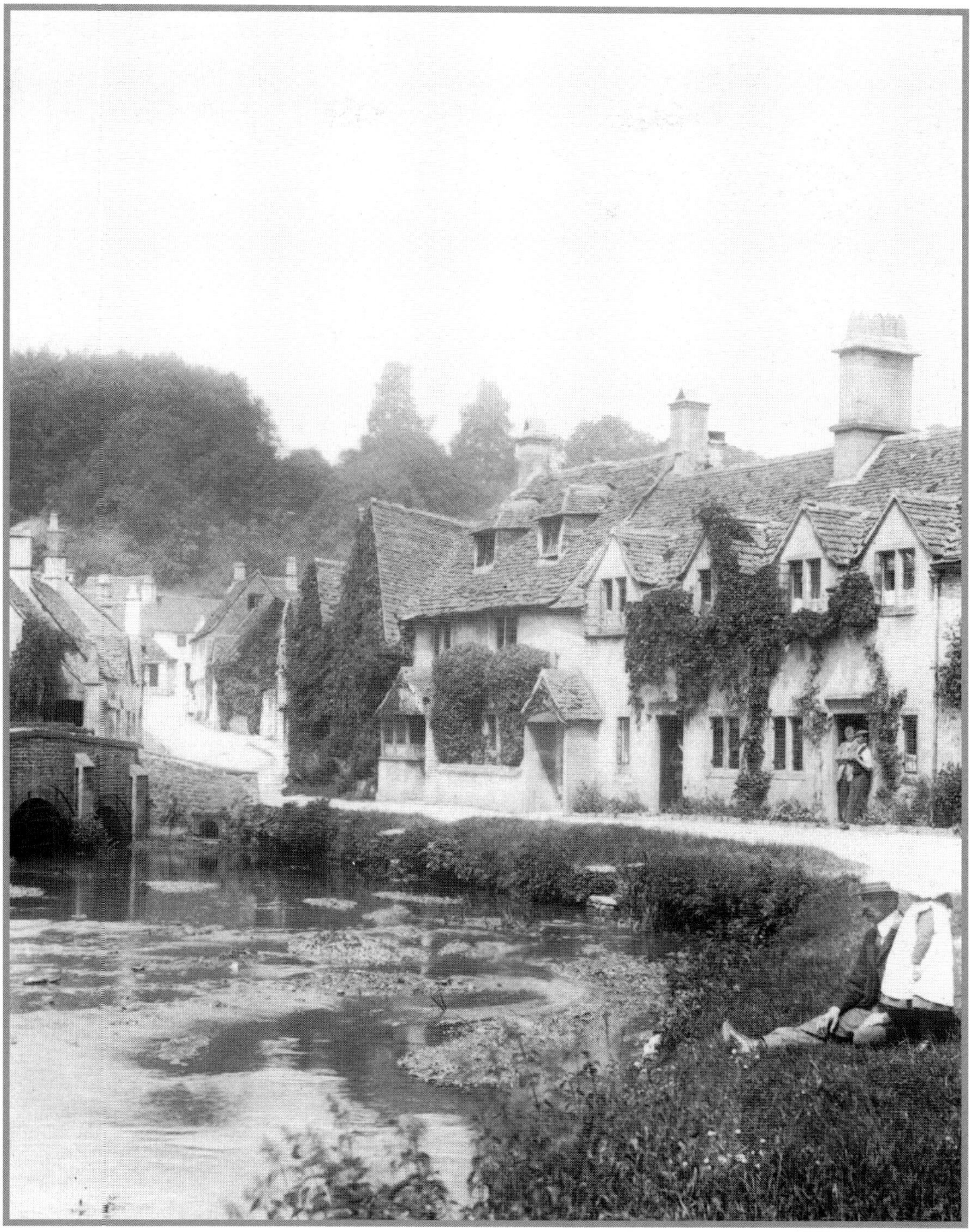

Castle Combe, The Village 1904 51508
Castle Combe must be a strong contender for the 'Prettiest Village in Wiltshire' title. This view gives a good indication of why that should be; the By Brook makes an already attractive scene into something rather special. The steep stone-slated roofs with their many dormers create a pleasing composition.

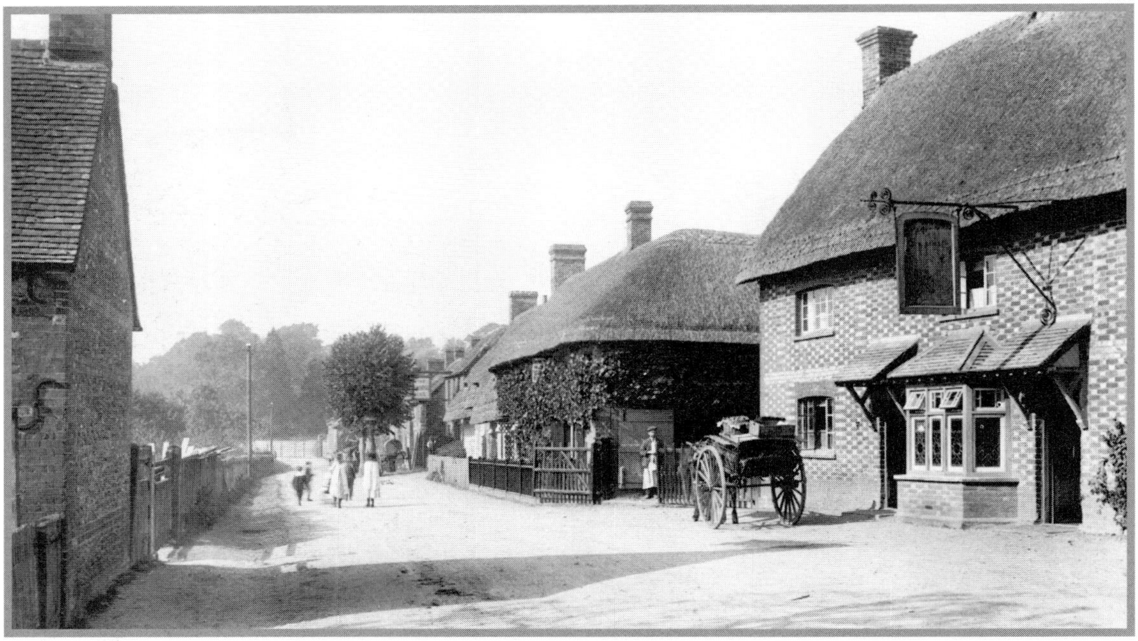

CHILTON FOLIAT, THE VILLAGE 1908 60955
Chilton Foliat is at the eastern extremity of the county, on the river Kennet. Here, a horse waits patiently outside the thatched pub for the return of his driver. The decorative headers on the brick façade of the inn make an interesting chequered pattern.

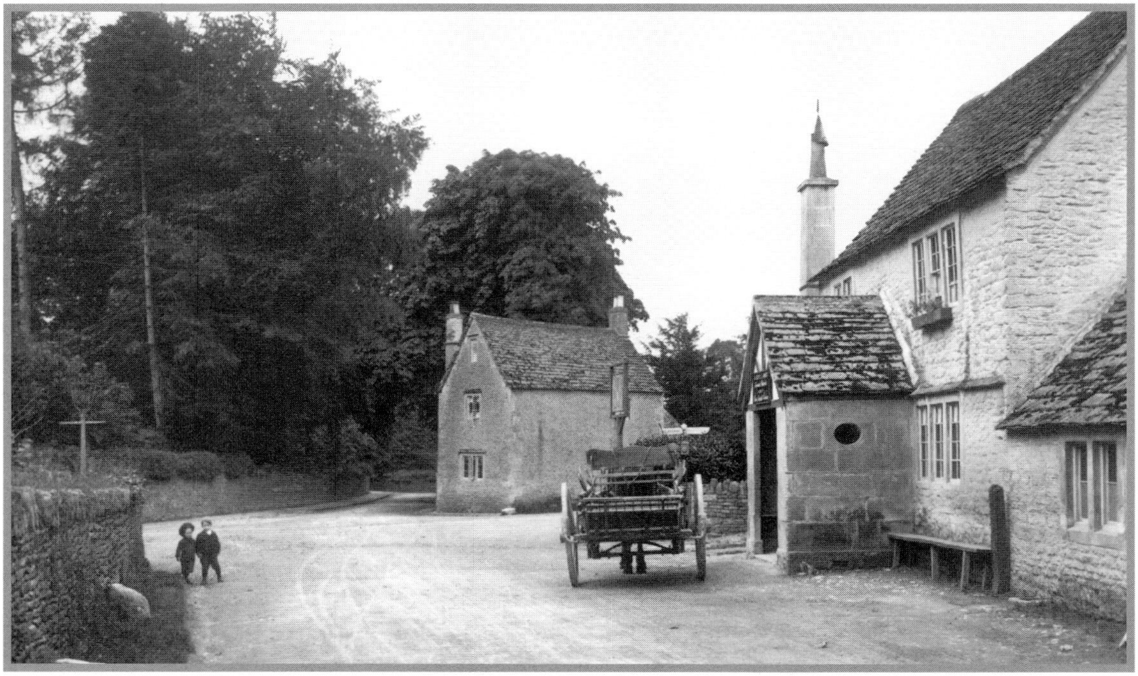

CORSHAM, THE CROSS KEYS INN 1907 57821
The scene depicted in the previous picture is repeated in Corsham. Since this photograph was taken, the town has expanded dramatically. Fortunately, the old part has been granted Conservation Area status.

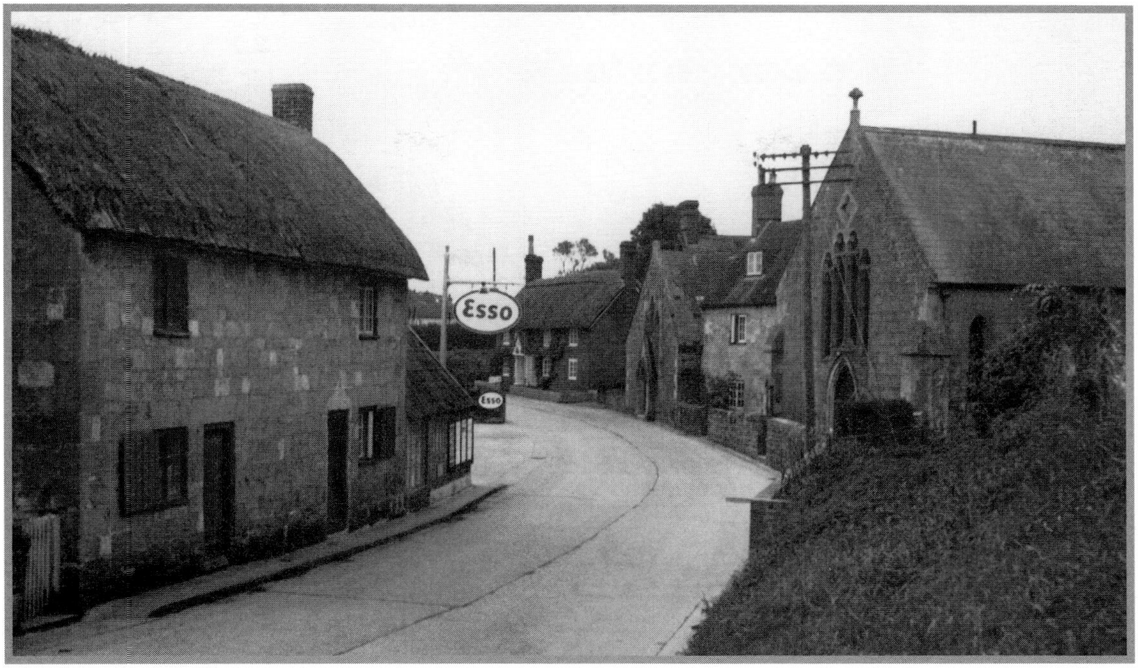

EAST KNOYLE, THE VILLAGE c1955 E163005

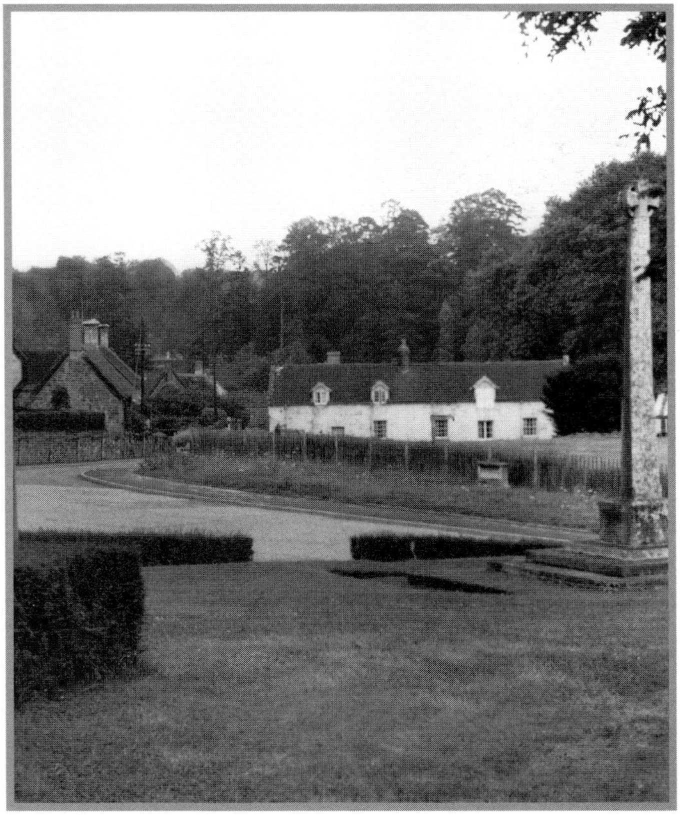

EAST KNOYLE, MEMORIAL CORNER c1955 E163020

EAST KNOYLE
The Village c1955

Doubtless East Knoyle has altered somewhat from the days when Sir Christopher Wren was a boy here. His father was the vicar in the local church. A stone alongside the main road records the fact and notes that Wren was 'Architect, Mathematician, Patriot'.

EAST KNOYLE
Memorial Corner c1955

This whole area is one of great delight, with plenty of trees, a stream and open fields. The sole blight was the main road, the A350, through the centre, but a new by-pass completed a few years ago has helped to restore the calm.

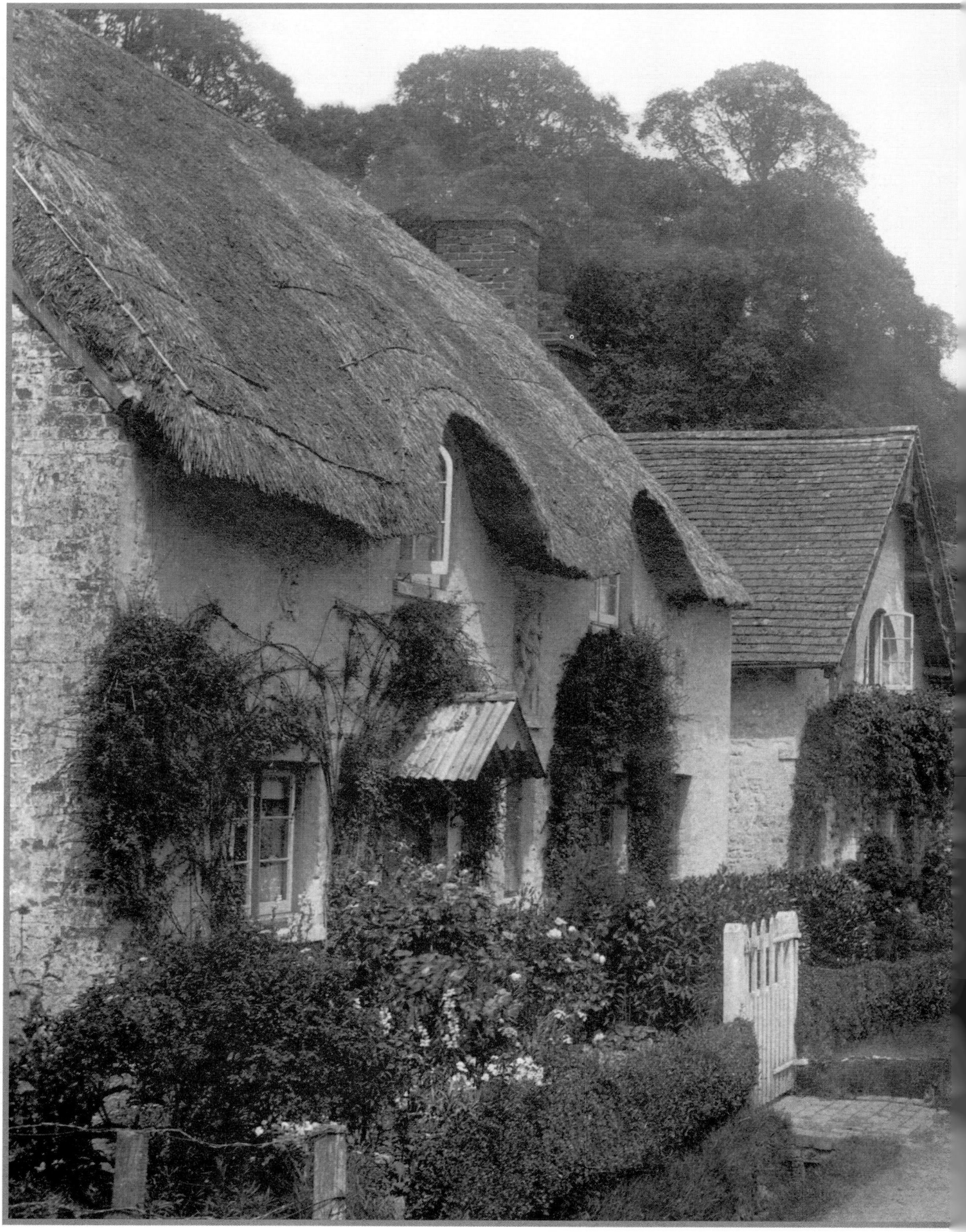

ERLESTOKE

The Village 1900 45360

Erlestoke is on the northern edge of Salisbury Plain and offers views that can still be recognised from this photograph. The gardens are packed with flowers and the neatly clipped hedges and wooden gates create a pleasing harmony.

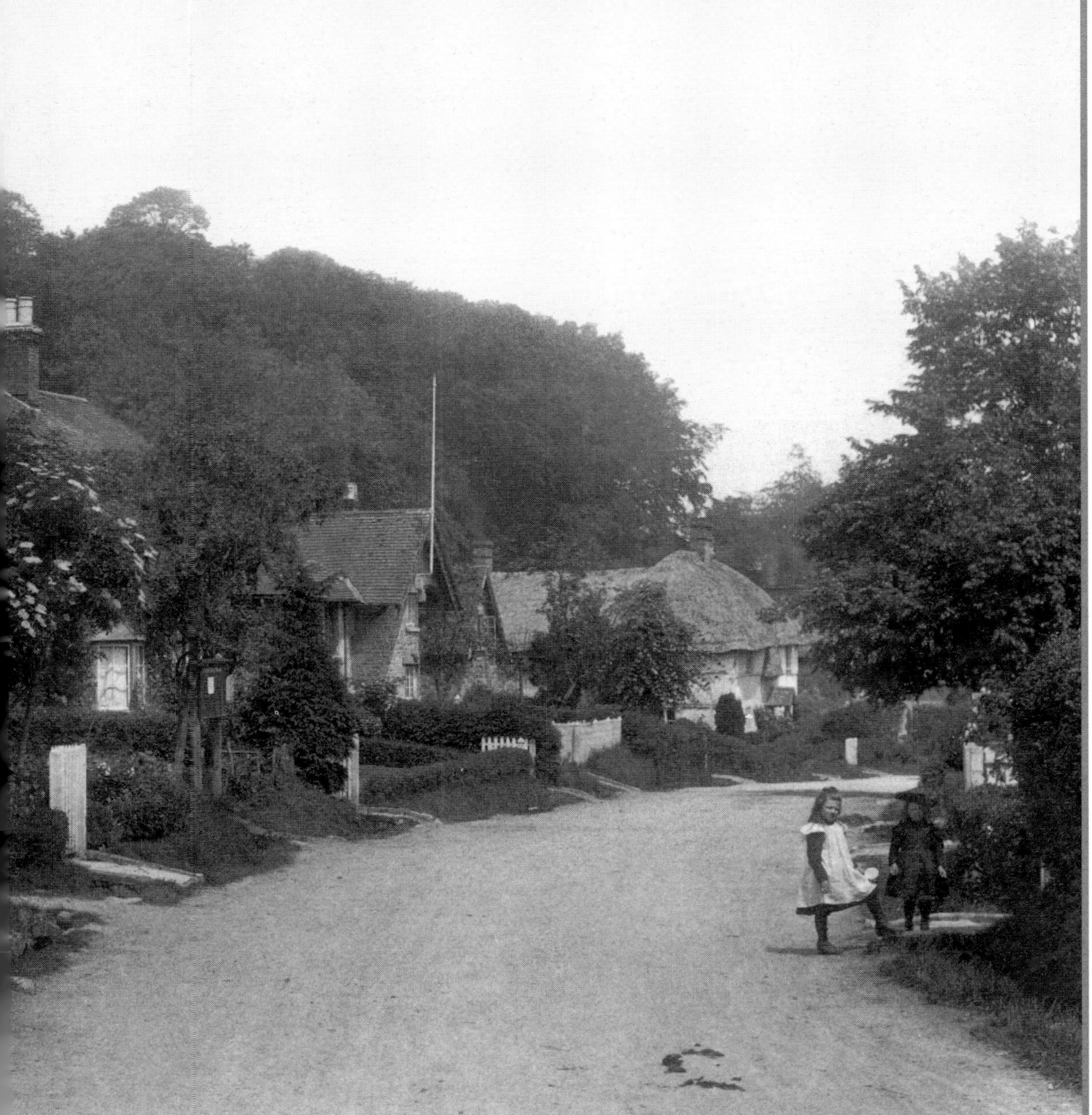

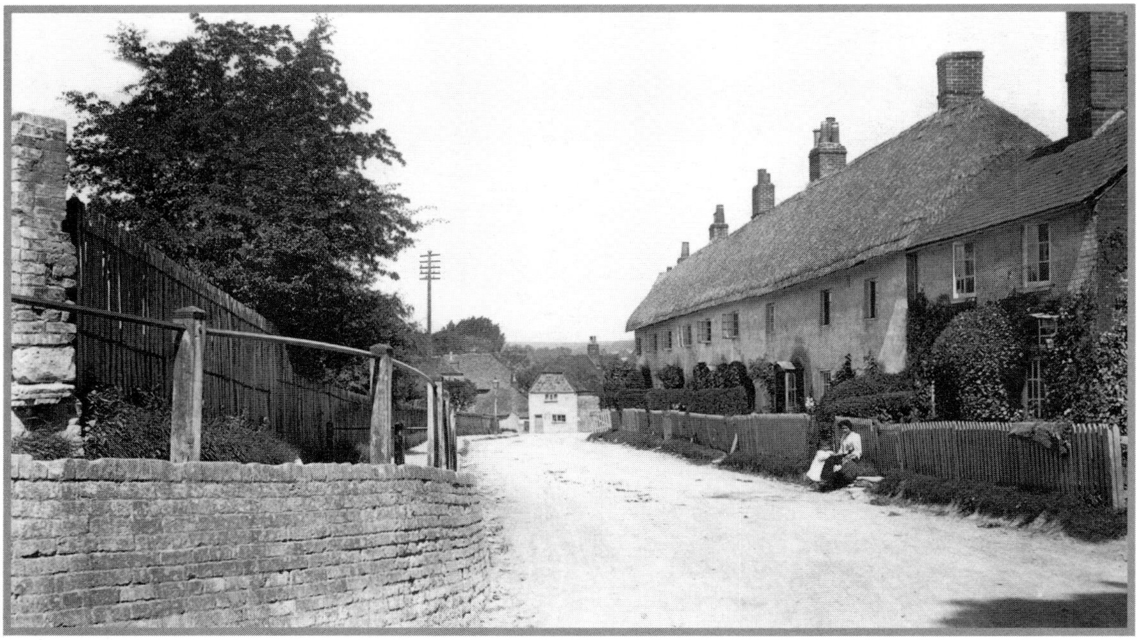

HARNHAM, THE VILLAGE 1906 56377
At this time, Harnham has something of an identity of its own. Harnham Bridge crossed the Hampshire Avon just south of Salisbury between the twin hamlets of East and West Harnham. The former was a parish in its own right. Now it is all part of Salisbury, and the village is disappearing into the city.

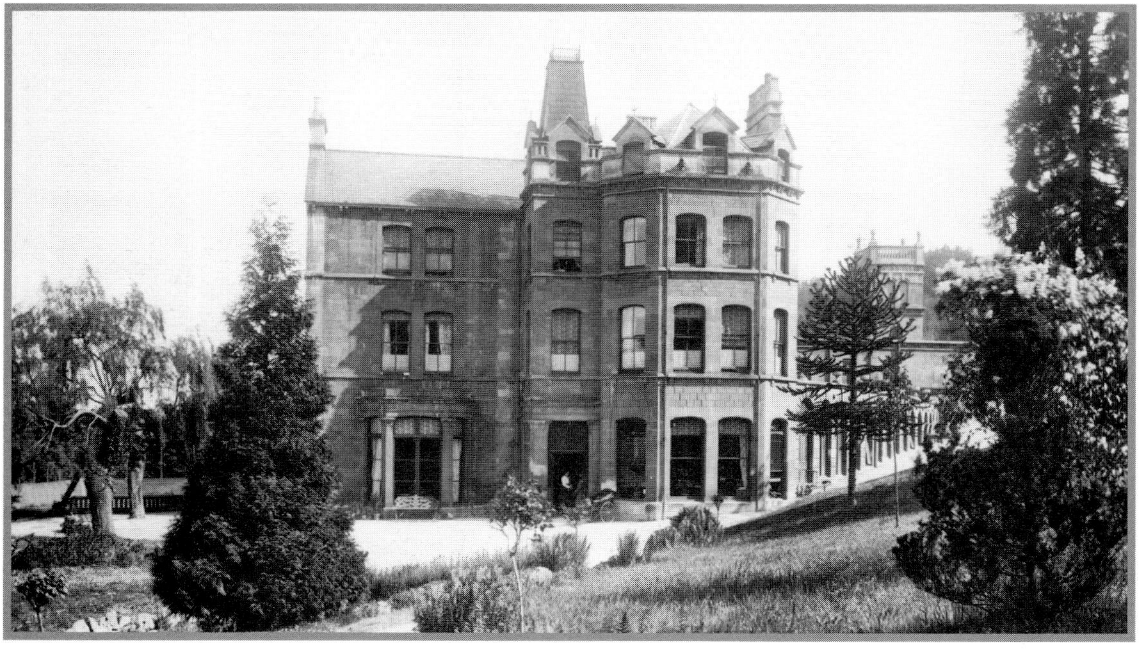

LIMPLEY STOKE, THE HYDRO 1901 46485
Limpley Stoke is tucked in close to the western border of Wiltshire - indeed, the county line runs round the edge of St Mary's churchyard, which is about half a mile away. The impressive old Hydro, where Victorians went to enjoy the benefits of hydropathic cures, is now a hotel.

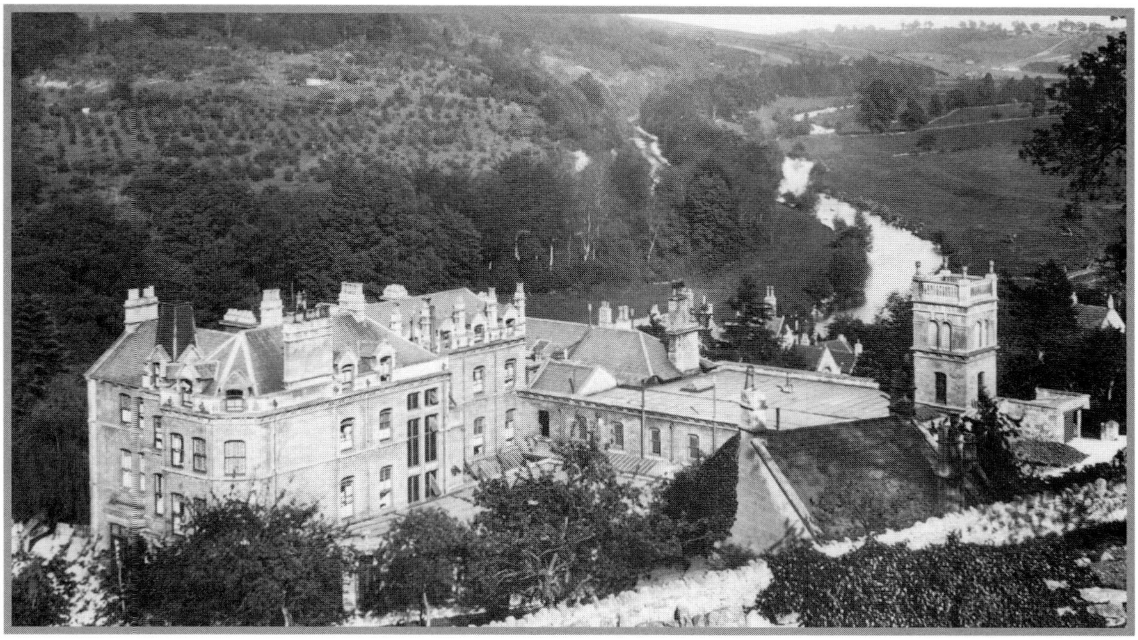

Limpley Stoke, Above the Hydro 1901 46487
Without moving too far, the cameraman then produced another view of Limpley Stoke, this time giving an overview of the hotel whilst still managing to show the extreme beauty of this location in the Avon valley quite close to Bath. In the trees behind the river is the Kennet and Avon Canal.

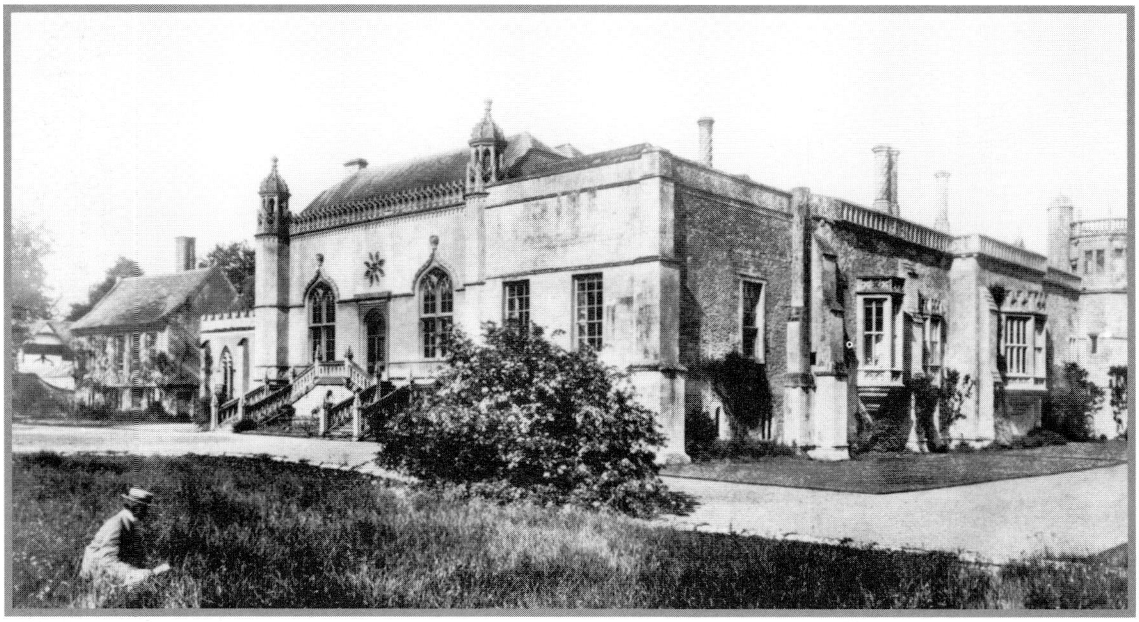

Lacock, The Abbey 1904 51510
Lacock Abbey is one of our national treasures. It was founded as an Augustinian nunnery in 1232 and converted to a private residence after the Reformation. Apart from the fascinating brewhouse and bakery, there is a 16th-century stable courtyard with attractive half timbered gables. The polygonal Sharington's Tower, also dating from the 16th century, is on the right.

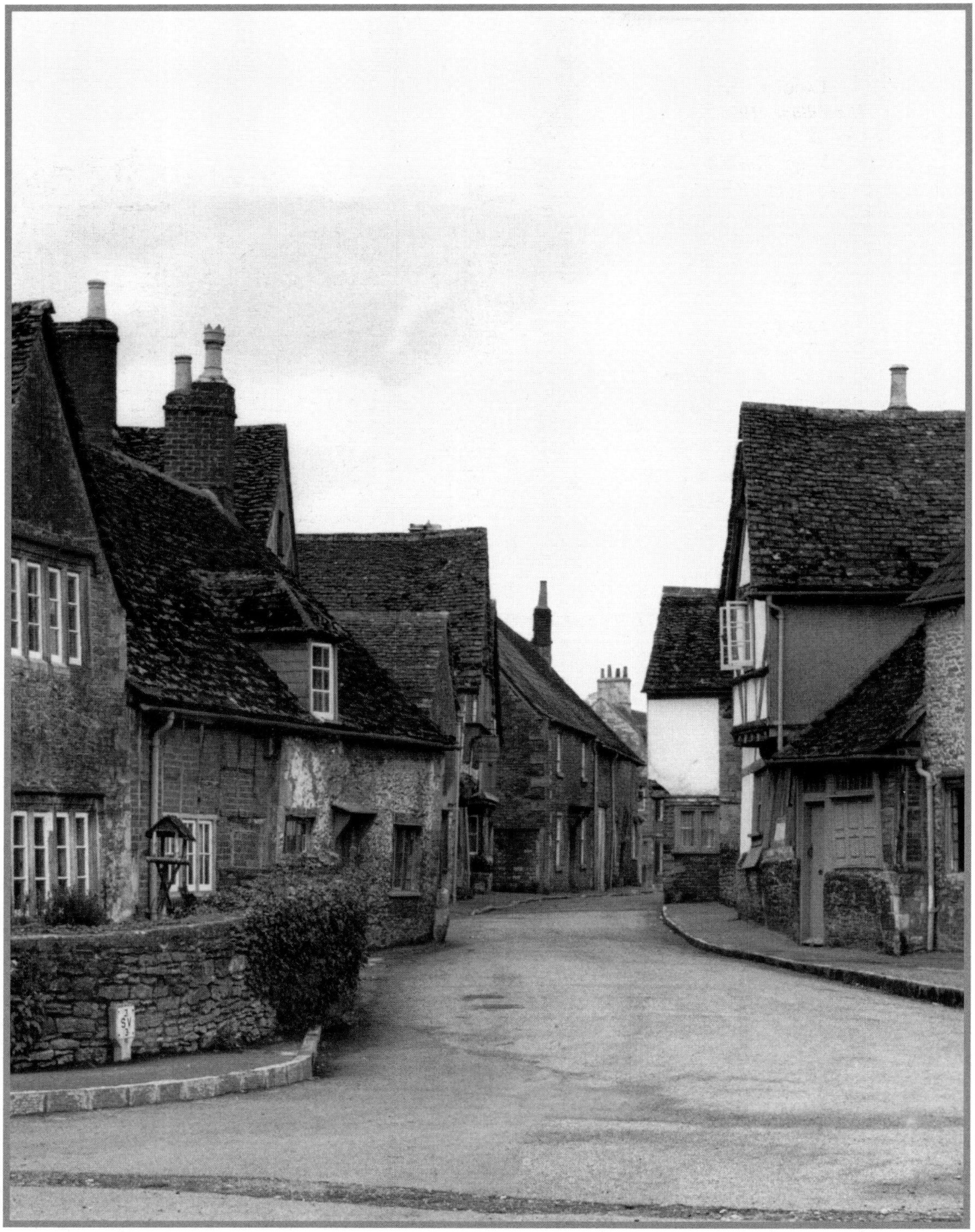

Lacock, The Village c1955 L1014
The unchanging scene at Lacock. The whole village was given to the National Trust in 1944 by descendants of William Fox Talbot. He lived from 1800 to 1877, and in 1832 produced the first modern photographic negative. Without his work, we would perhaps not be enjoying this book.

Lacock
The Village c1955
For an estate village, the houses are considered very large. This is believed to be because they were built to accommodate looms. It was a wealthy wool village for many years.

Lacock
High Street c1955
One thing that is clear from this view of Lacock is the delightful amalgam of building styles. Half-timbered and stone houses blend well together. Note also the lack of television aerials (forbidden by the National Trust).

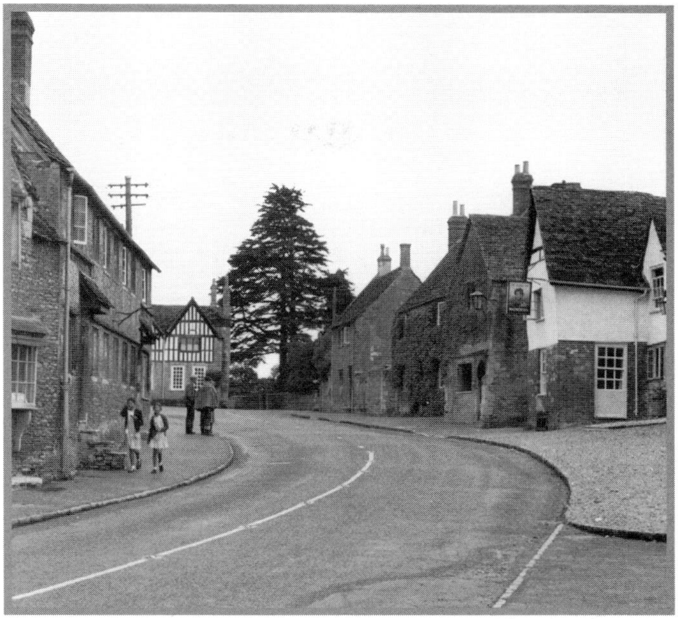

Lacock, The Village c1955 L1013

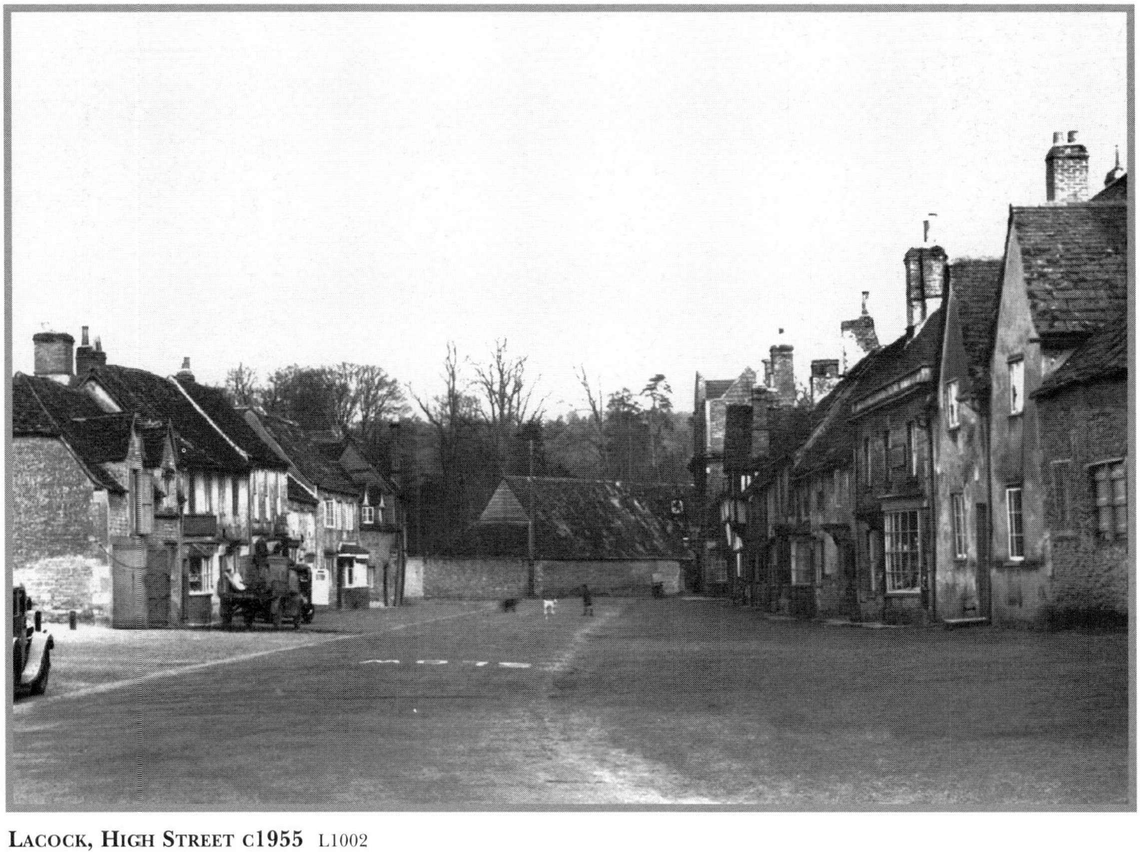

Lacock, High Street c1955 L1002

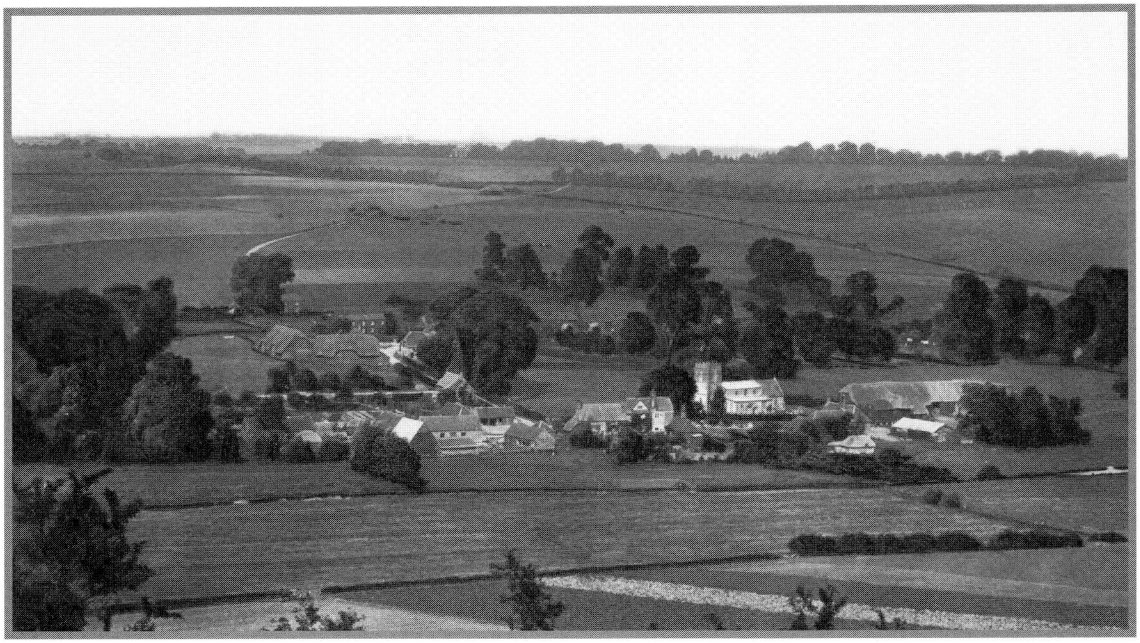

MILDENHALL, THE VILLAGE 1906 57191
Sitting in the delightful Kennet valley a couple of miles east of Marlborough is Mildenhall - known locally as 'Minal'. The church - right of centre - is a treasure, with box pews, multi-deck pulpit and a Jacobean moulded plaster ceiling. Its shell is mainly 12th century.

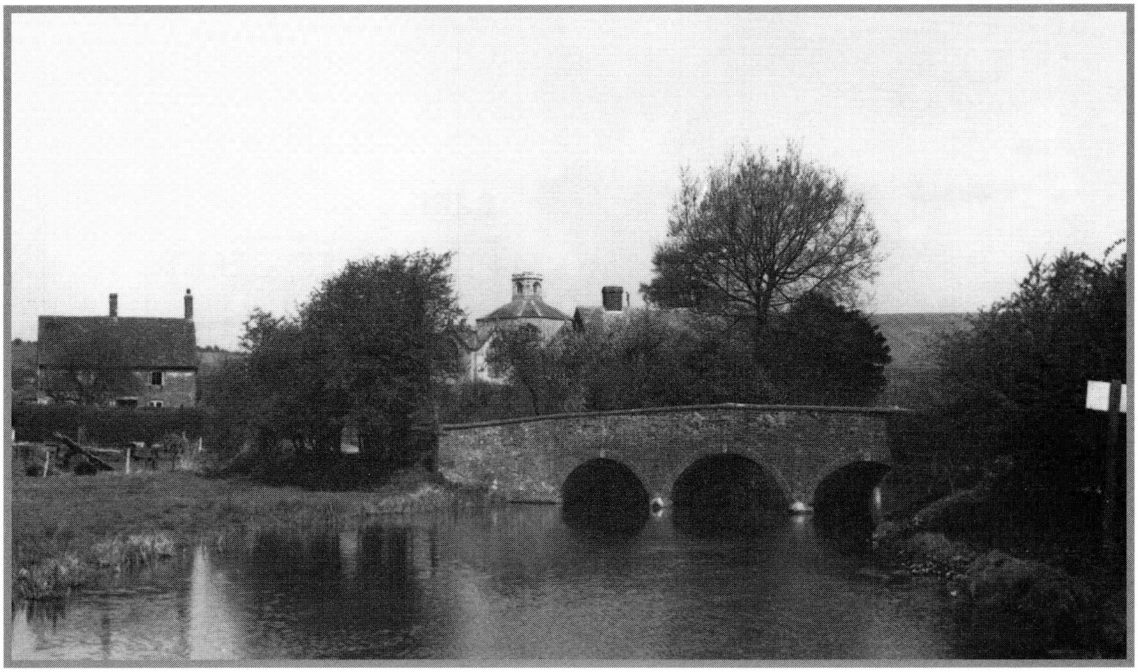

MILDENHALL, THE OLD BRIDGE c1955 M326001
The old stone bridge straddles the river Kennet, fringed by meadows and trees. The village is in a Conservation area, with plenty of brick-built thatched houses in its centre.

MILDENHALL
The River c1955
A final view of the delightful river Kennet. The river rises near Marlborough Down and flows for 44 miles before joining the Thames at Reading. These unpretentious houses enjoy fine riverside views.

PEWSEY
General View 1929
Pewsey is a small town in the middle of the Vale that bears its name, noted for its white horse cut into the downland at Milk Hill. The whole area is classified as an Area of Outstanding Natural Beauty.

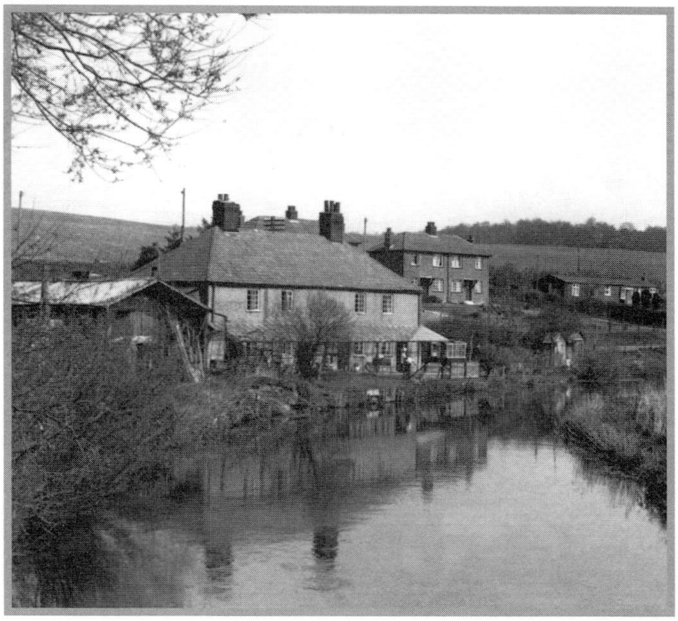

MILDENHALL, THE RIVER c1955 M326002

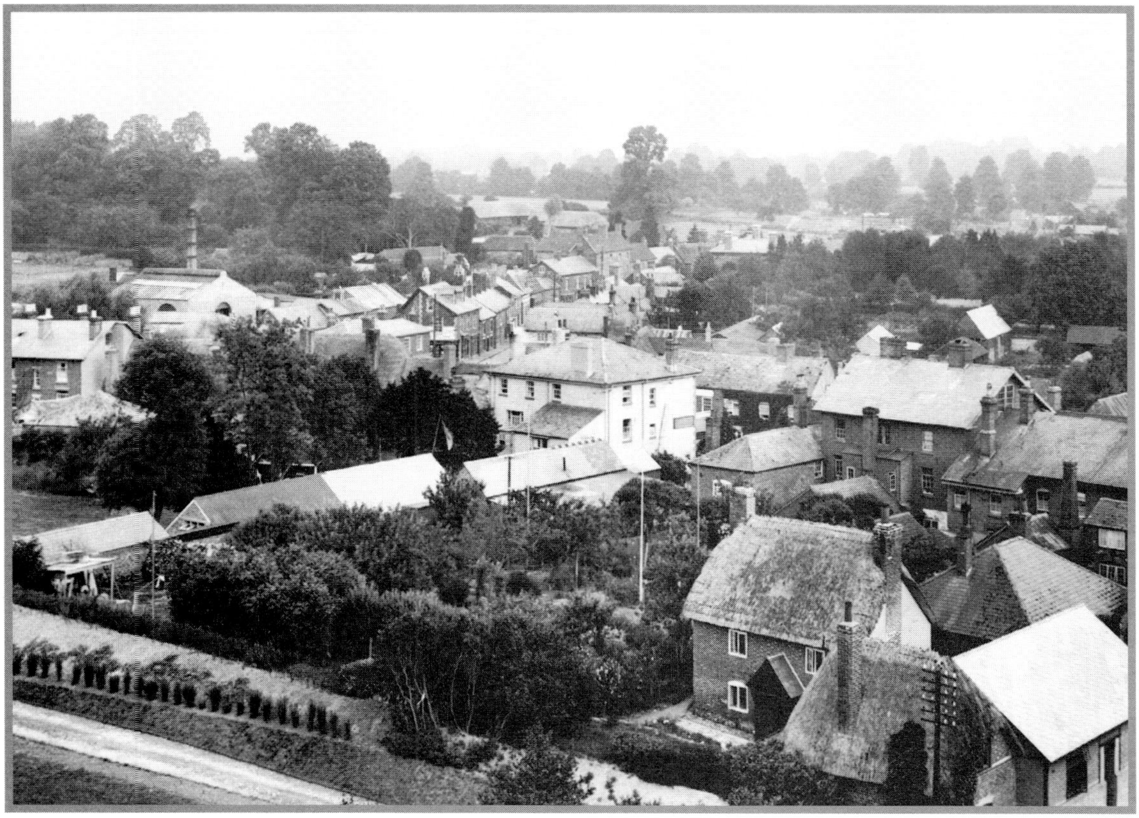

PEWSEY, GENERAL VIEW 1929 82304

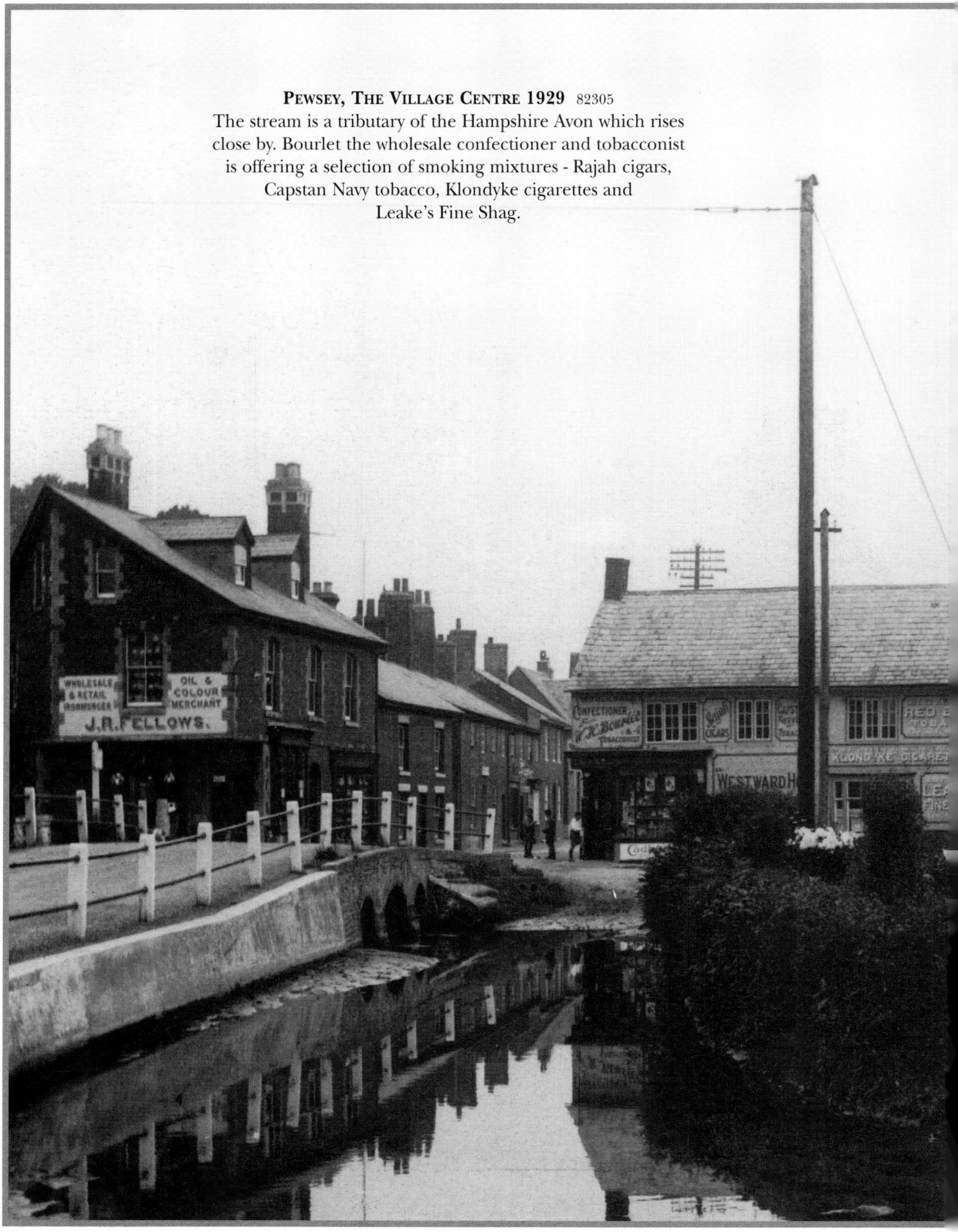

PEWSEY, THE VILLAGE CENTRE 1929 82305
The stream is a tributary of the Hampshire Avon which rises close by. Bourlet the wholesale confectioner and tobacconist is offering a selection of smoking mixtures - Rajah cigars, Capstan Navy tobacco, Klondyke cigarettes and Leake's Fine Shag.

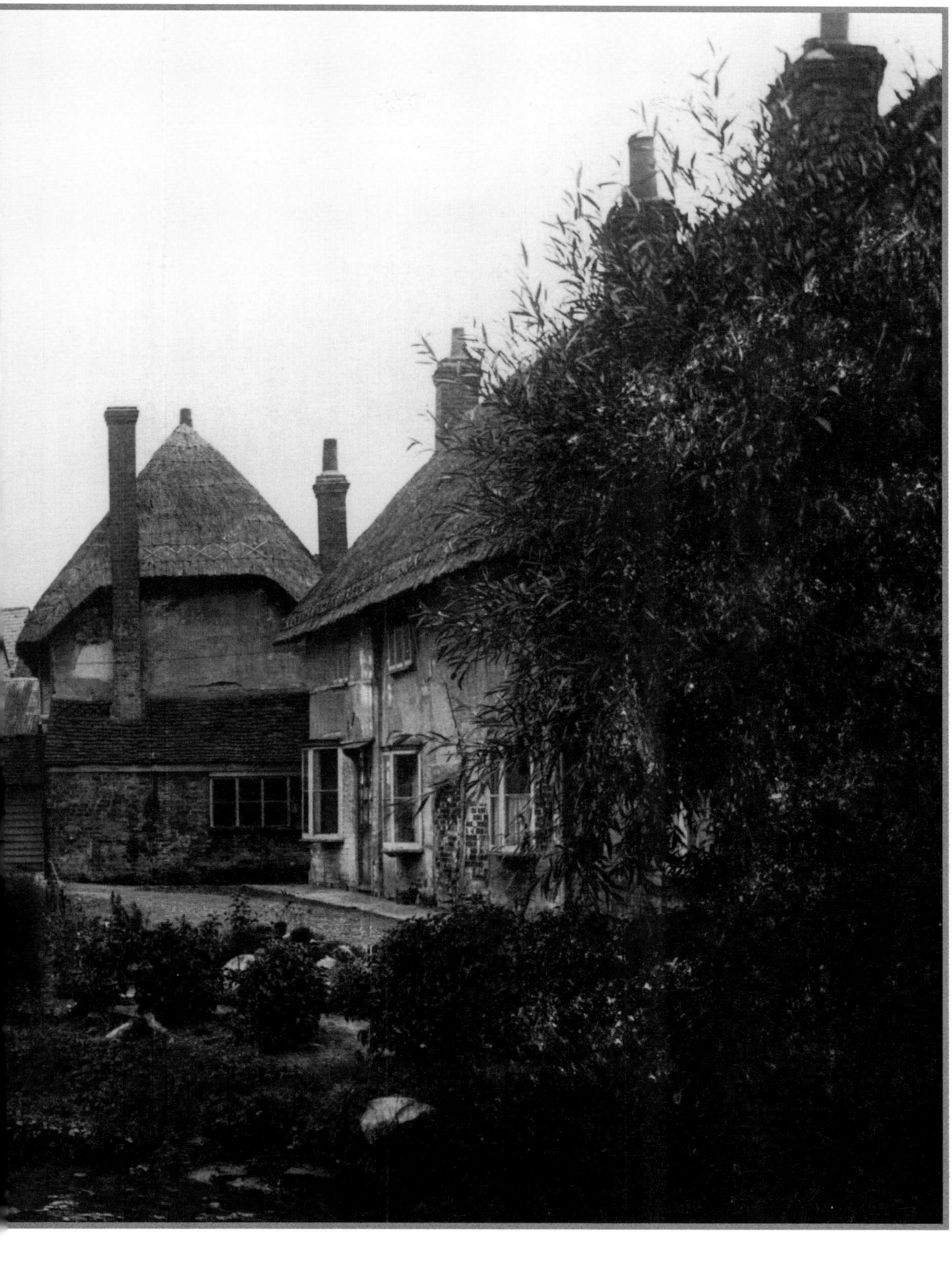

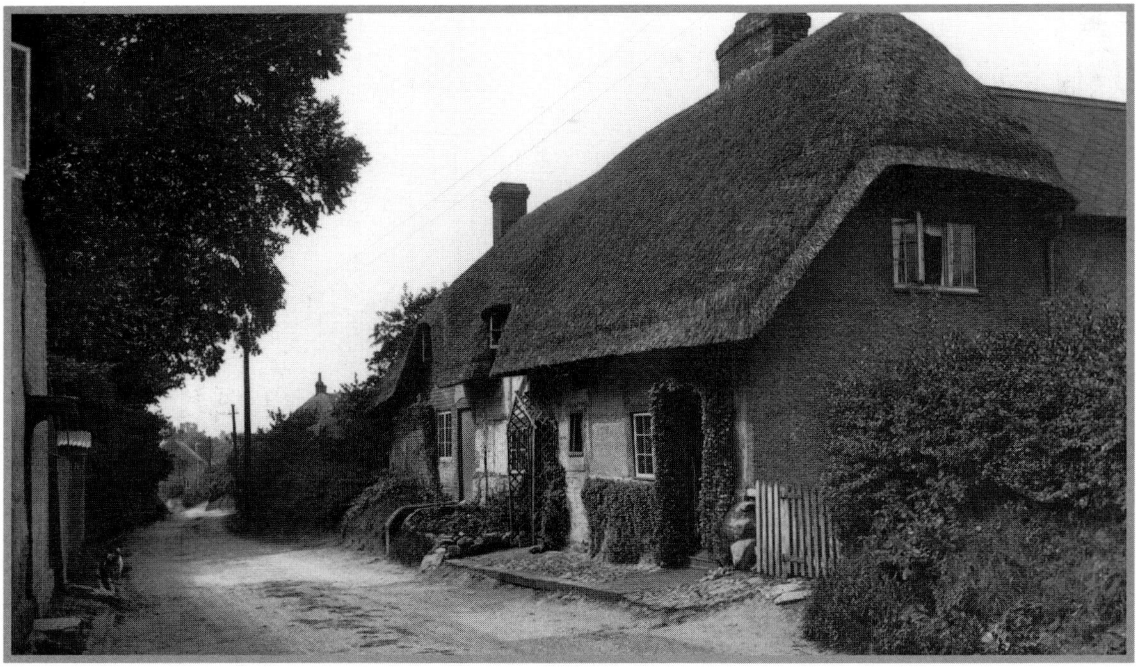

PEWSEY, SOUTHCOTT ROAD 1929 82315
At one time Pewsey had many venerable houses such as this one. It is a sad fact that most have now disappeared, but some survive on the edge of the town centre. Note the rustic porch and traditional picket fence.

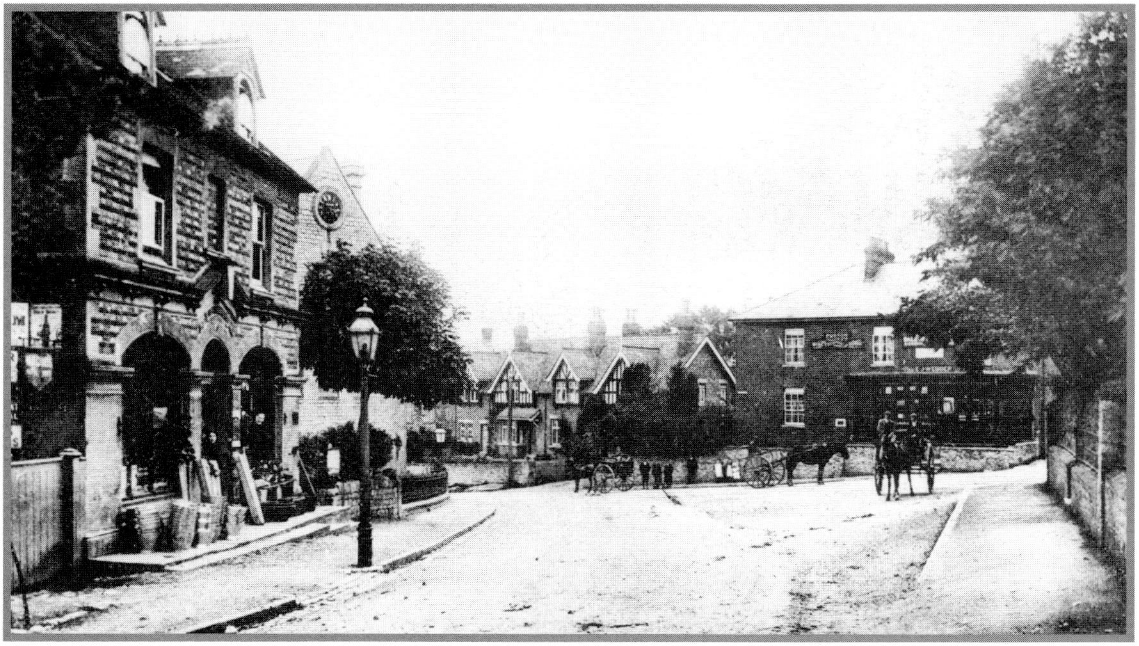

PURTON, LOWER SQUARE 1910 P138001
Purton was a small settlement to the west of Swindon. With the arrival of the railway age in Swindon it started to grow, and many of the buildings you can see in this photograph are clearly Victorian. The village had a large brick works, and its products helped to build Swindon and many other towns and villages.

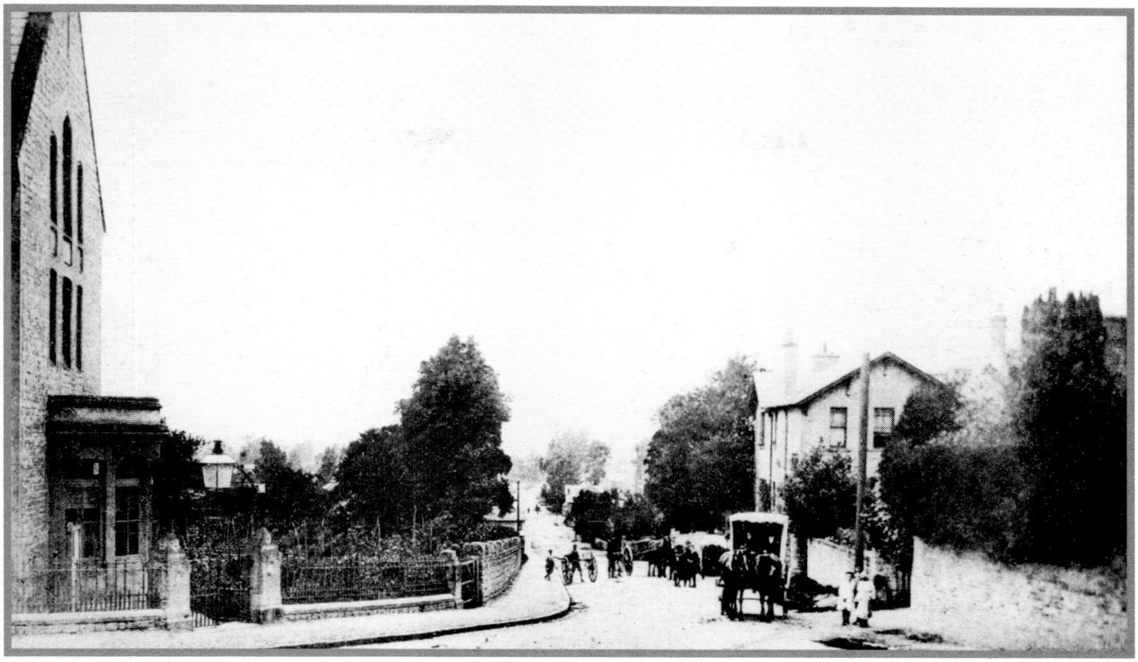

Purton, The Hill 1910 P138003

A busy scene, despite the absence of motor traffic. Village carters and carriers have paused to give the horses a brief rest. St Mary's church is in the older part of the village, close to Purton House.

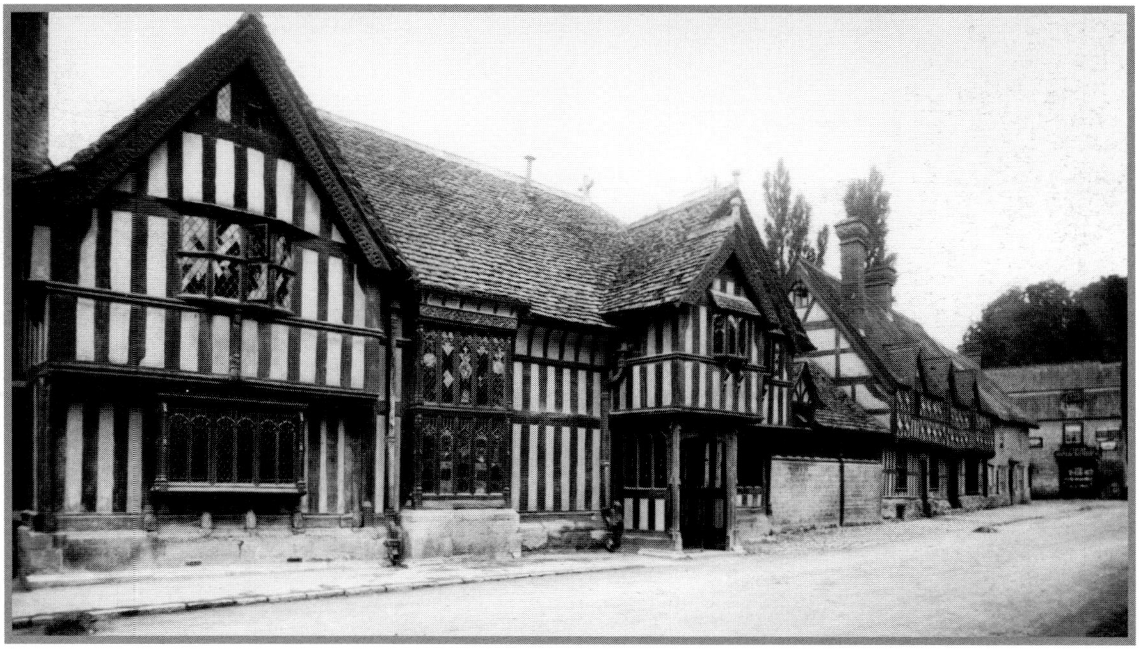

Potterne, Church House 1898 42323

A small village just south of Devizes, Potterne still has some famous and wonderfully ancient buildings. It was once a manor of the Bishops of Salisbury. This is the late 15th-century timber-framed Porch House, pictured about 20 years after its last restoration.

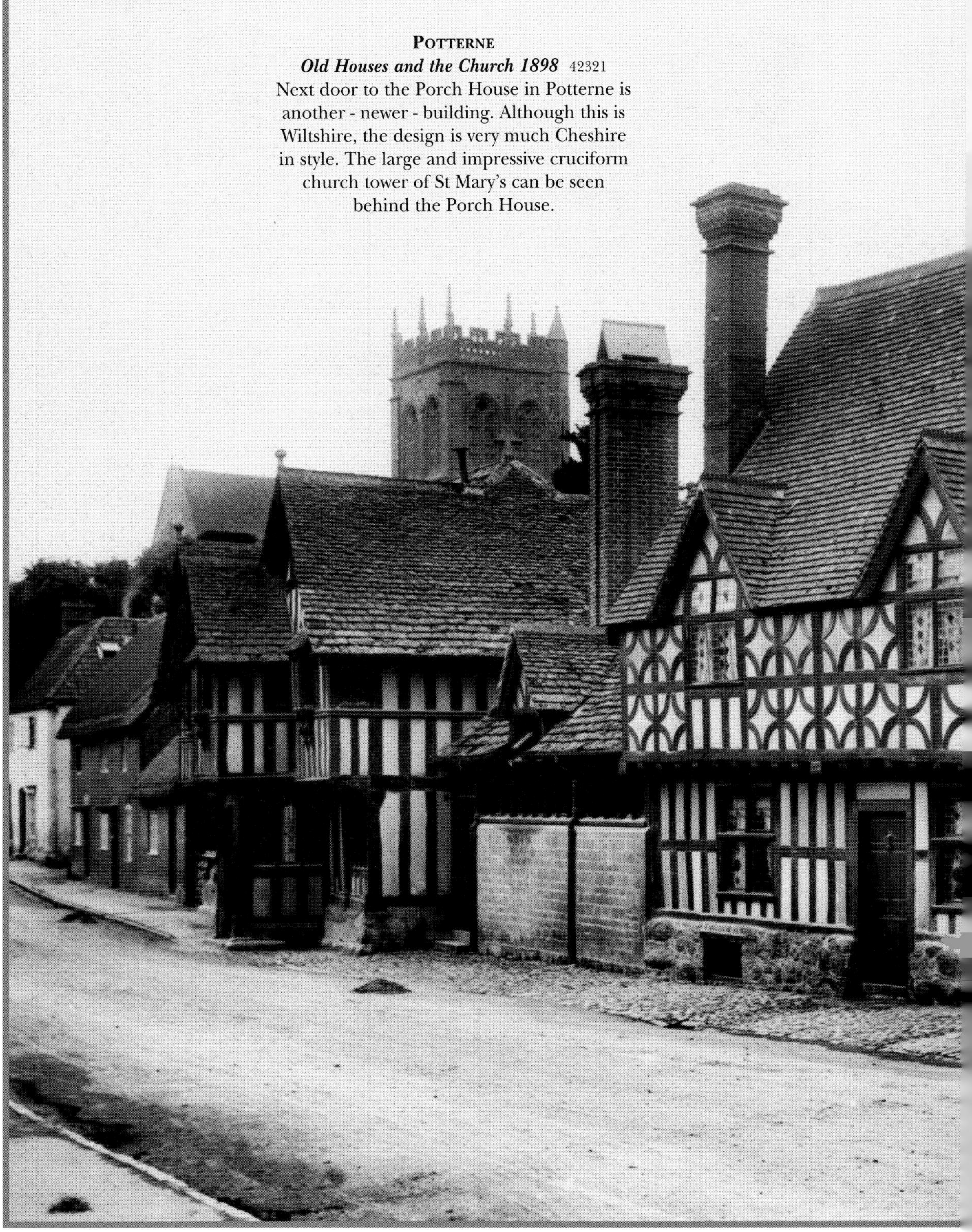

POTTERNE

Old Houses and the Church 1898 42321

Next door to the Porch House in Potterne is another - newer - building. Although this is Wiltshire, the design is very much Cheshire in style. The large and impressive cruciform church tower of St Mary's can be seen behind the Porch House.

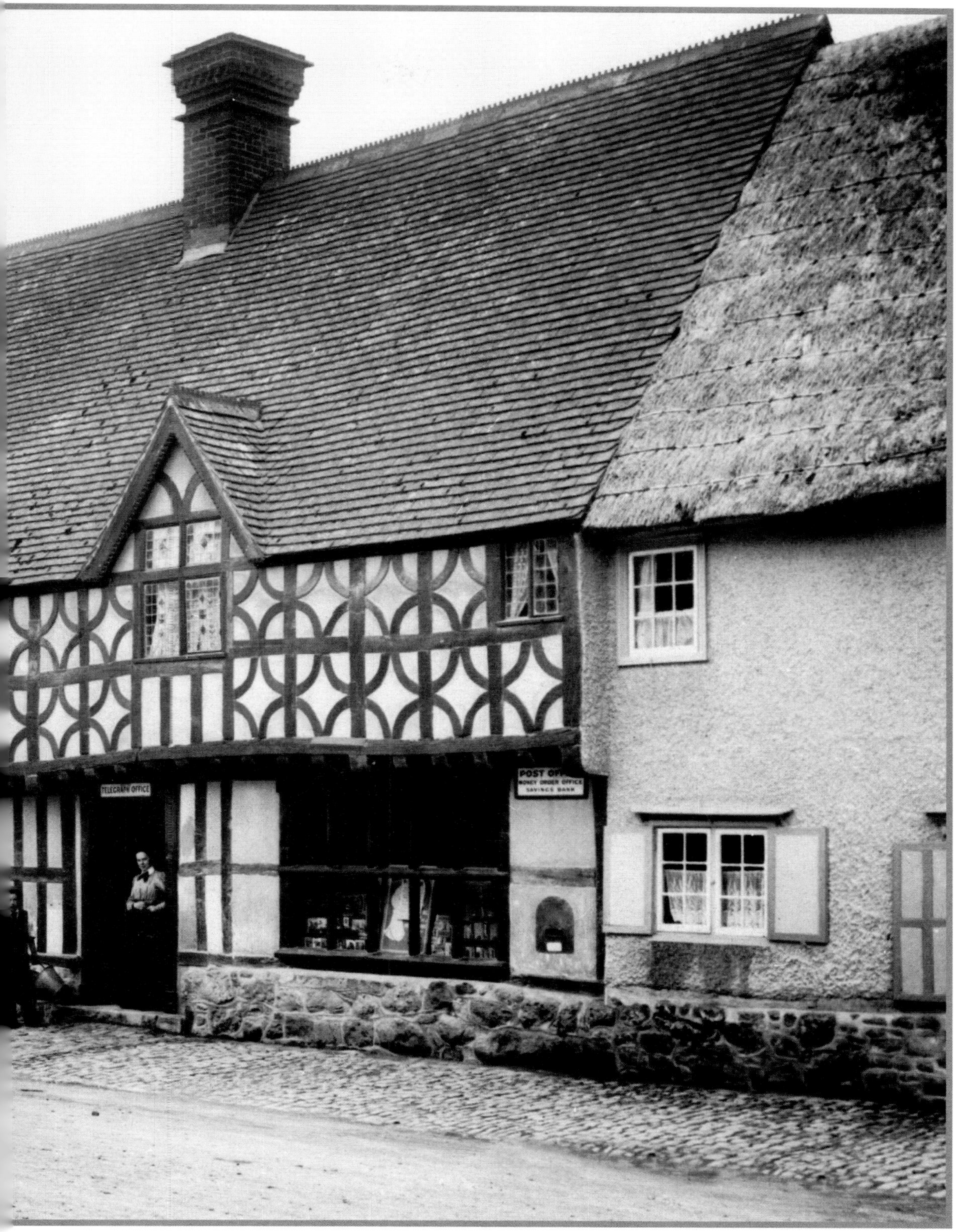
TELEGRAPH OFFICE
POST OFF
MONEY ORDER OFFICE
SAVINGS BANK

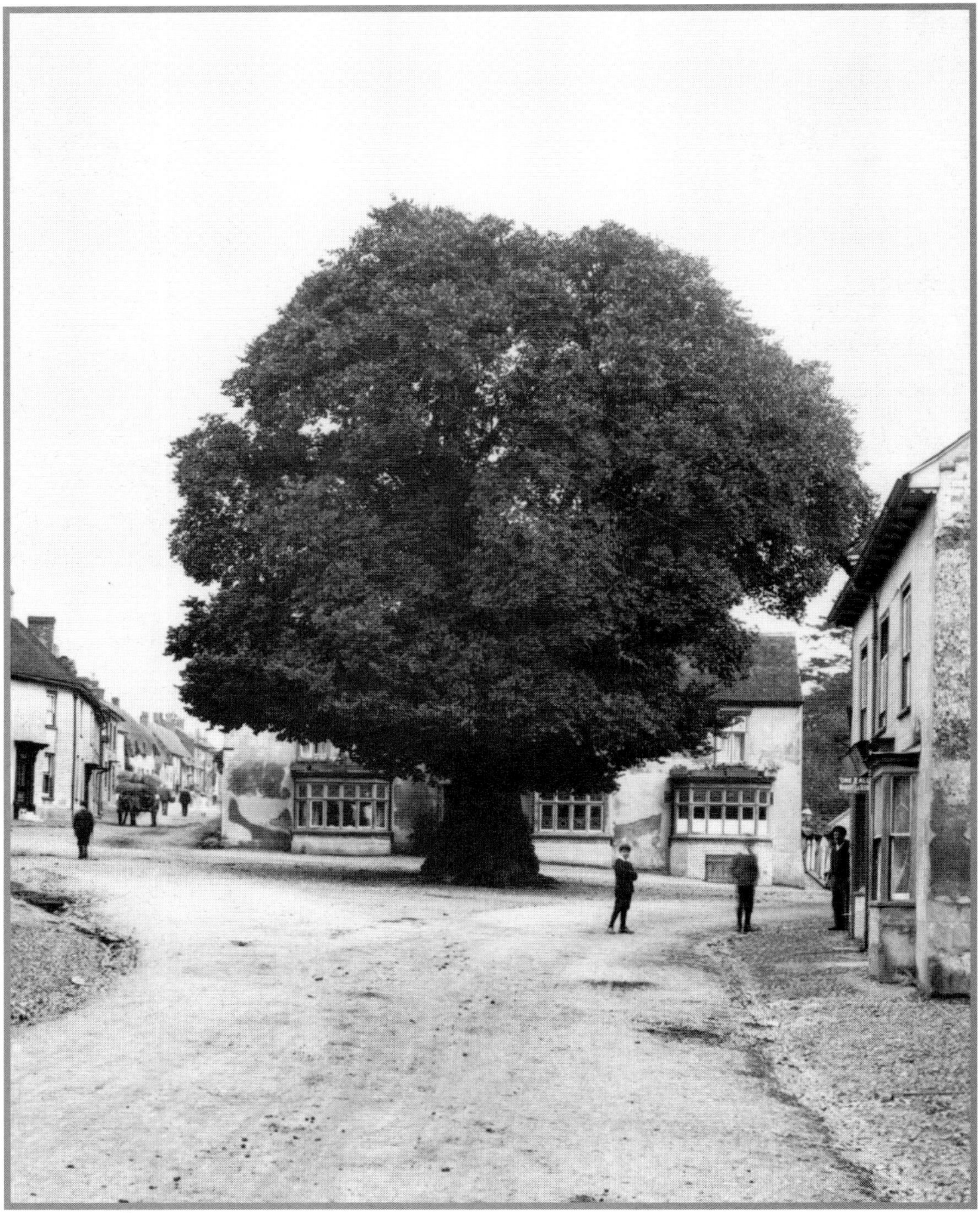

RAMSBURY, HIGH STREET 1906 57195
The old elm tree stands in the village square. It was felled in the 1980s after it became dangerous and replaced with an oak tree in 1986. The Bell Inn is behind the tree. Ramsbury was unique for a village of this size in that it had its own building society which was formed in 1846 (the elm was used as its emblem) and ceased trading only recently.

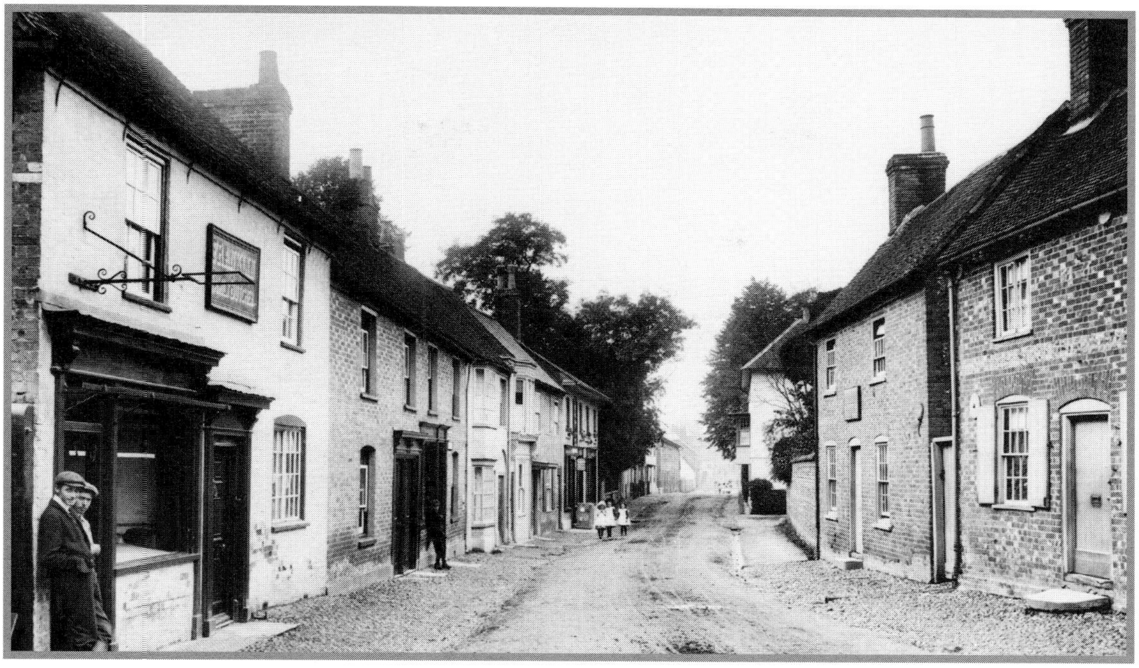

Ramsbury, High Street 1906 57196
This view is almost unchanged today. The names on the shops are different, some of the trees have gone, the road has been resurfaced and fashions have changed, but not much else. The narrow street is fringed with cobbles.

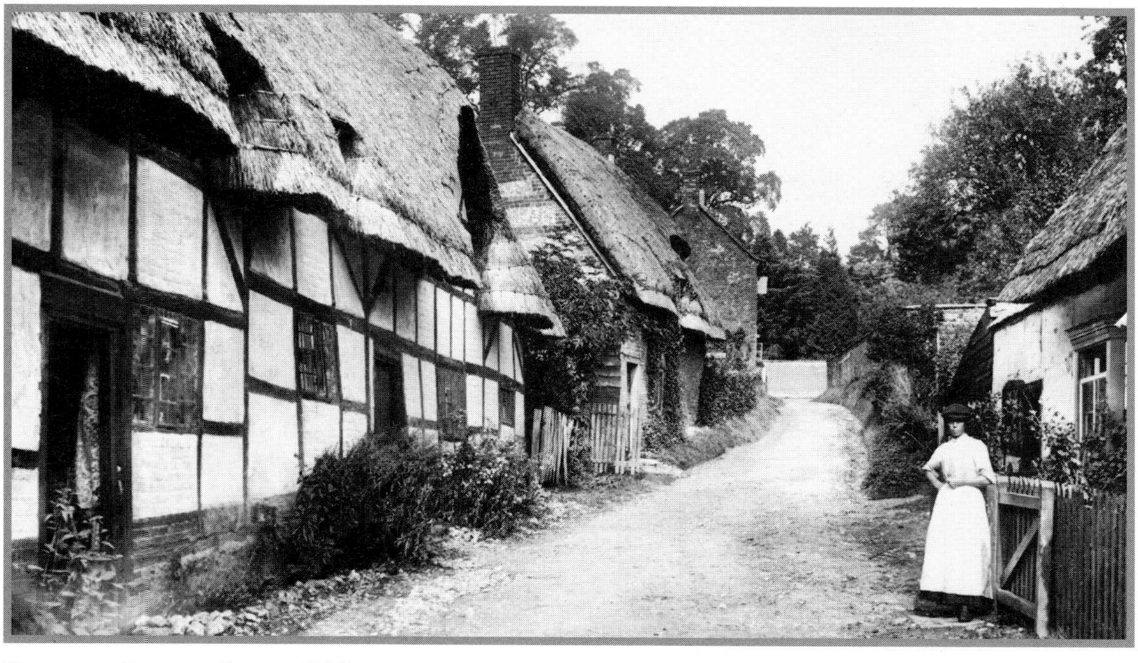

Ramsbury, Burdett Street 1906 57200
Even less has changed in this scene in the old part of what is a very old small town, which had its own Bishop at the beginning of the 10th century. Note the small windows, dictated by the timber framing and thatched roofs of the cottages.

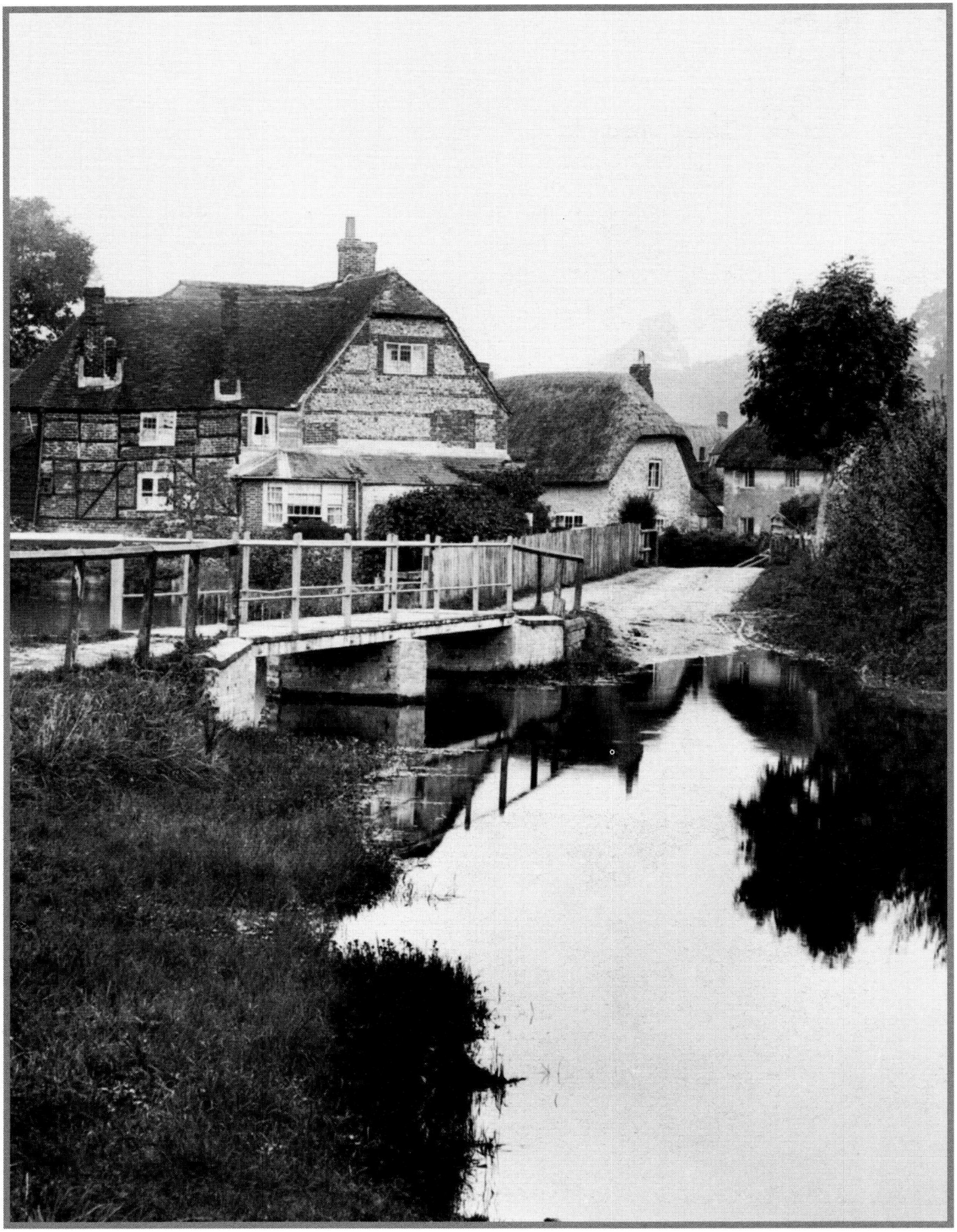

RAMSBURY, EDWARDS MILL 1907 57202
A peaceful and tranquil scene alongside the river Kennet. The irregular roofs of the mill suggest that the building has been added to over the centuries.

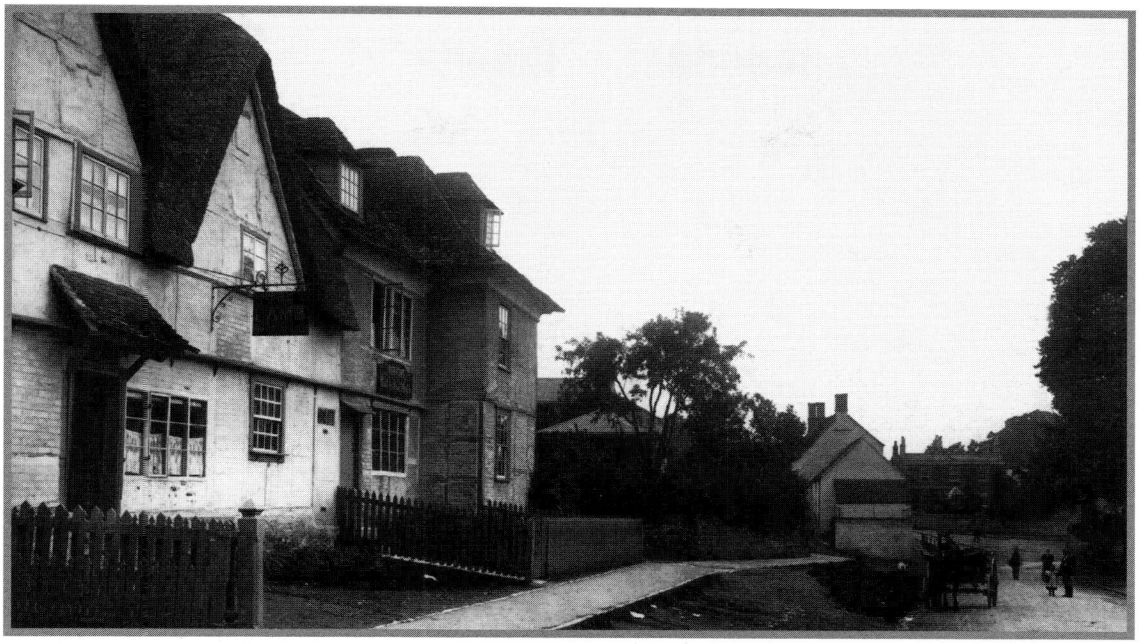

ROWDE, THE VILLAGE 1899 44850

Today the main road (the A342) is thronged with traffic travelling between Devizes and Chippenham. The Lamb (with the sign) has closed but the George and Dragon just beyond is still going, although its entrance and car park are to the rear.

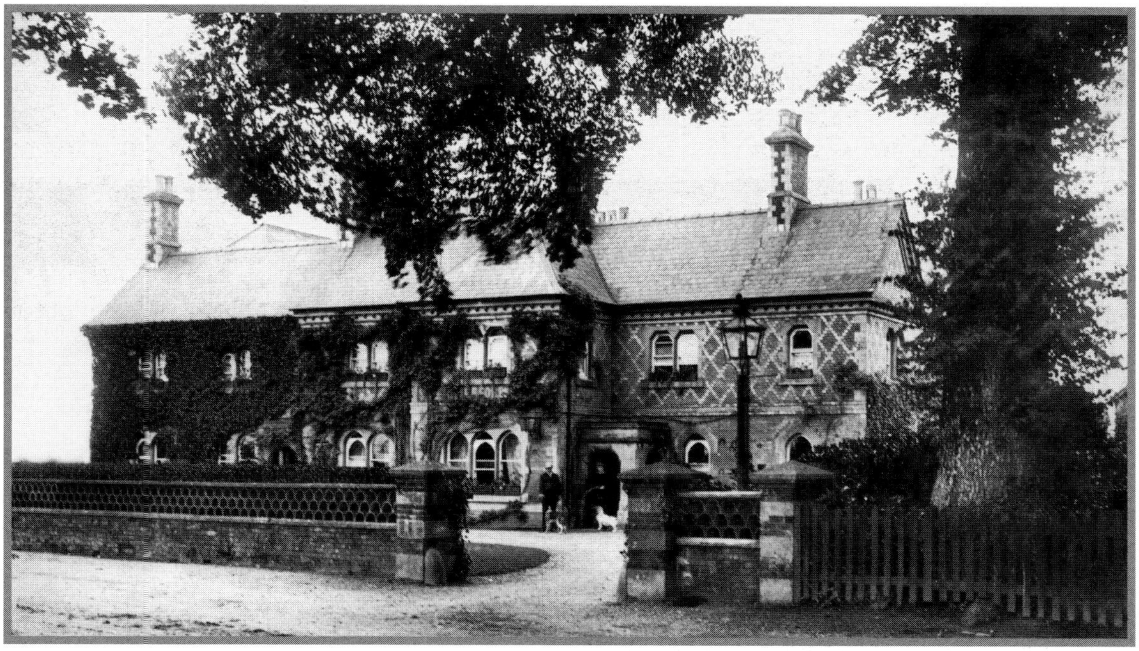

SAVERNAKE, SAVERNAKE FOREST HOTEL 1907 57216

This famous Edwardian county hotel was built on the edge of Savernake Forest, where the Great Western Railway and the Kennet and Avon Canal enter the Vale of Pewsey. Now, more than 90 years after this picture was taken, this fine building, which is no longer a hotel, seems to be located in the middle of nowhere.

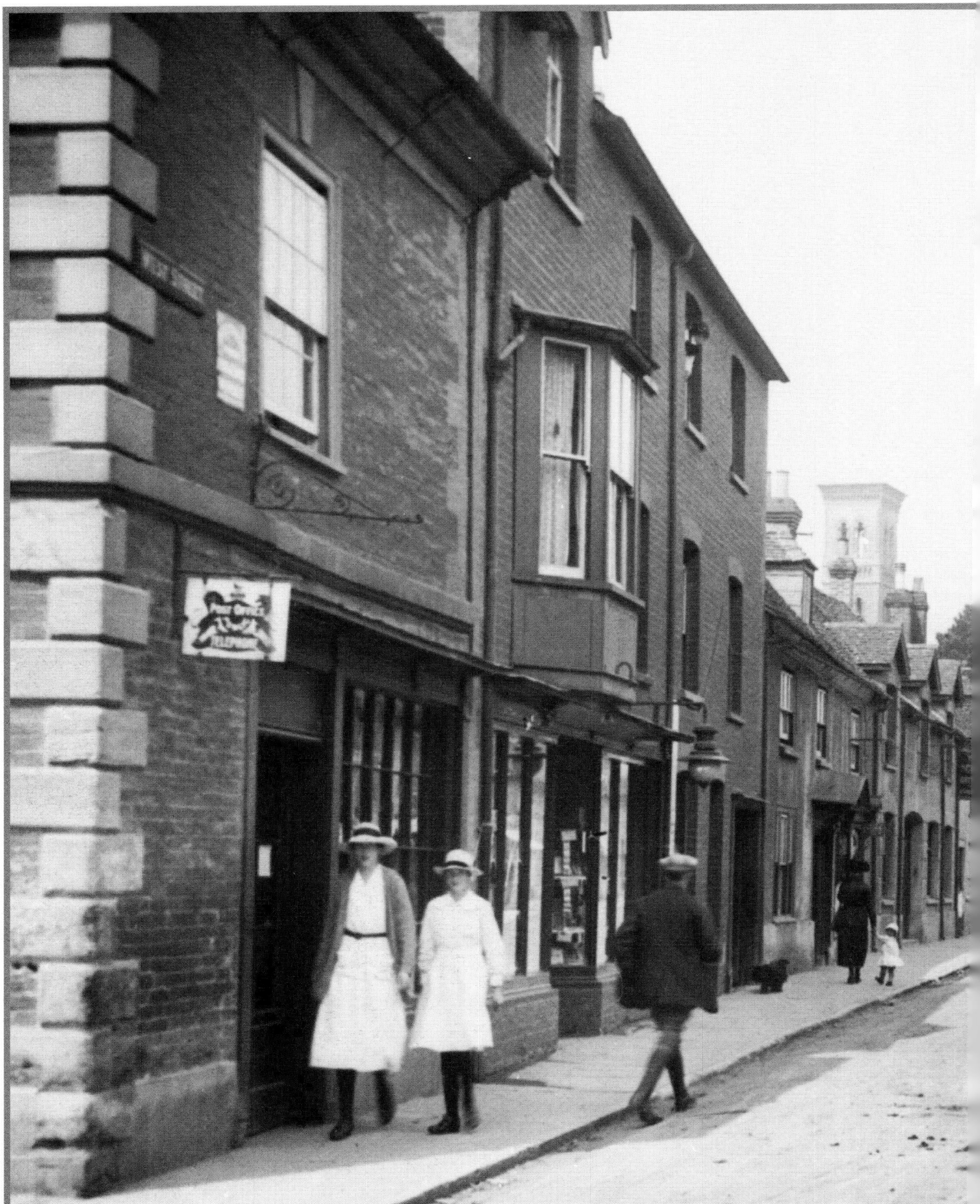

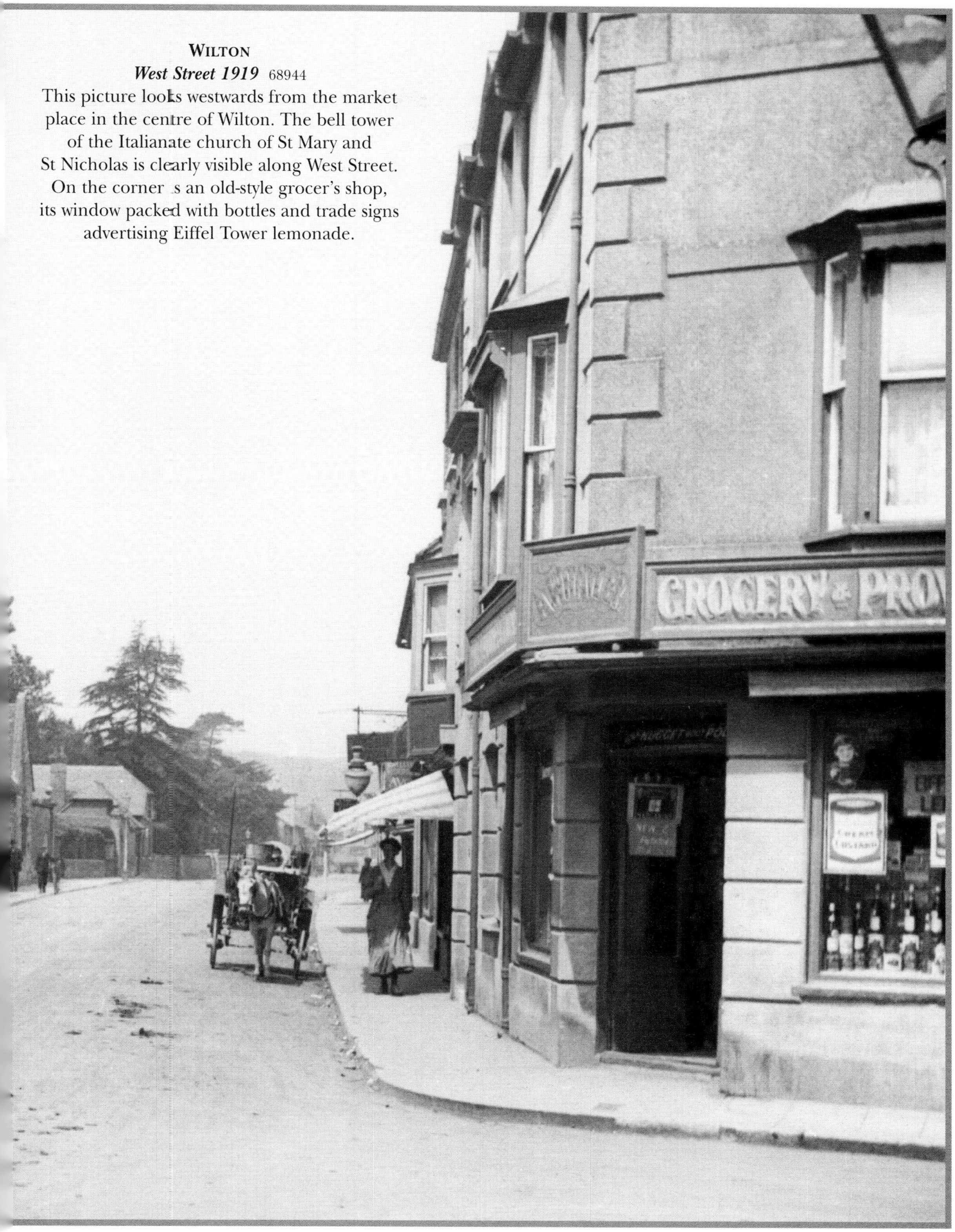

Wilton

West Street 1919 68944

This picture looks westwards from the market place in the centre of Wilton. The bell tower of the Italianate church of St Mary and St Nicholas is clearly visible along West Street. On the corner is an old-style grocer's shop, its window packed with bottles and trade signs advertising Eiffel Tower lemonade.

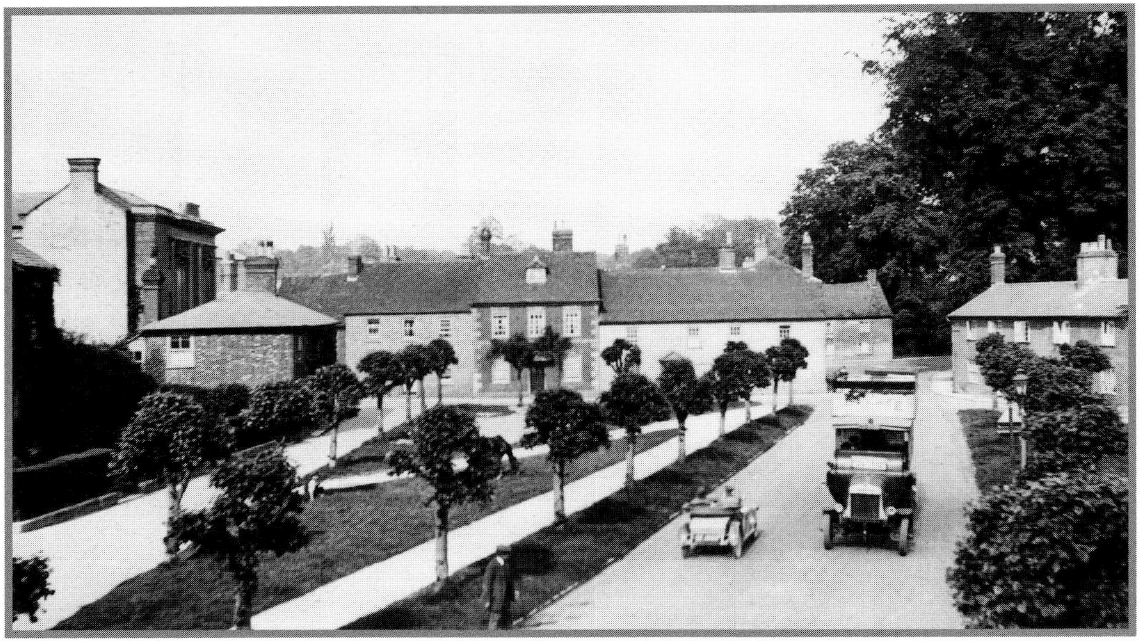

WILTON, KINGSBURY SQUARE 1919 68943
Wilton, once the capital of Wessex, was the most important town in early medieval Wiltshire. This is Kingsbury Square, on the A30, with St Edith's church on the left. The neatly-pollarded trees give the square a sedate air. An open-topped bus is coming from Salisbury.

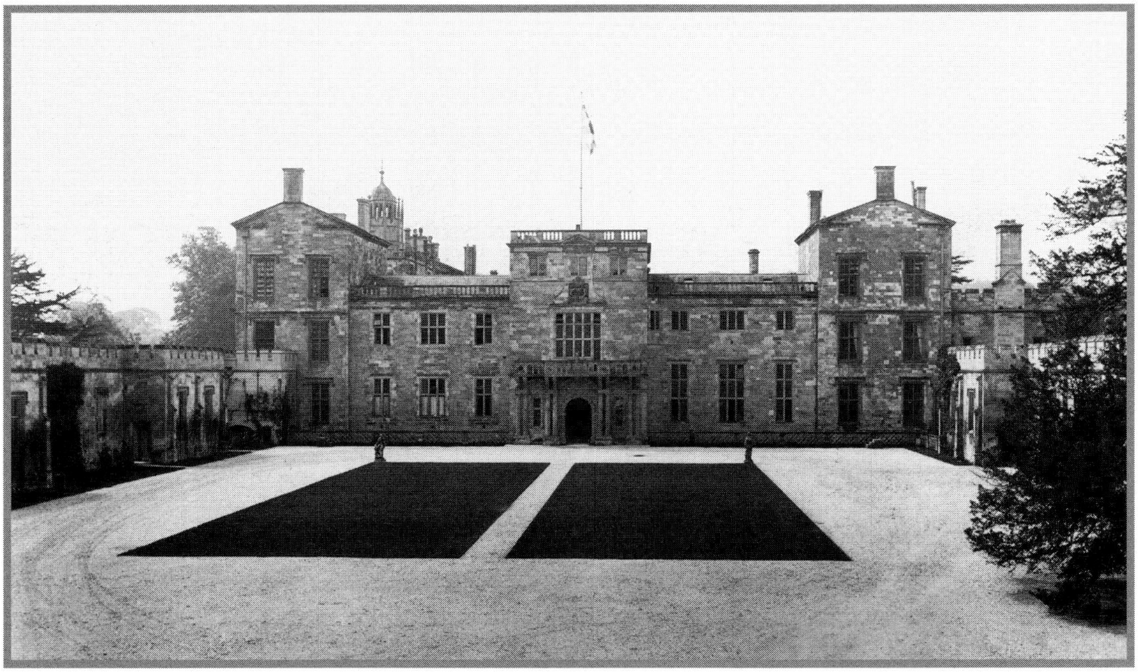

WILTON, WILTON HOUSE, FRONT ENTRANCE 1919 68931
The forecourt at the north front of the elegant Wilton House. The house was built for the first Earl of Pembroke when he was granted the old nunnery estate after its dissolution 1544. His descendants have lived here ever since.

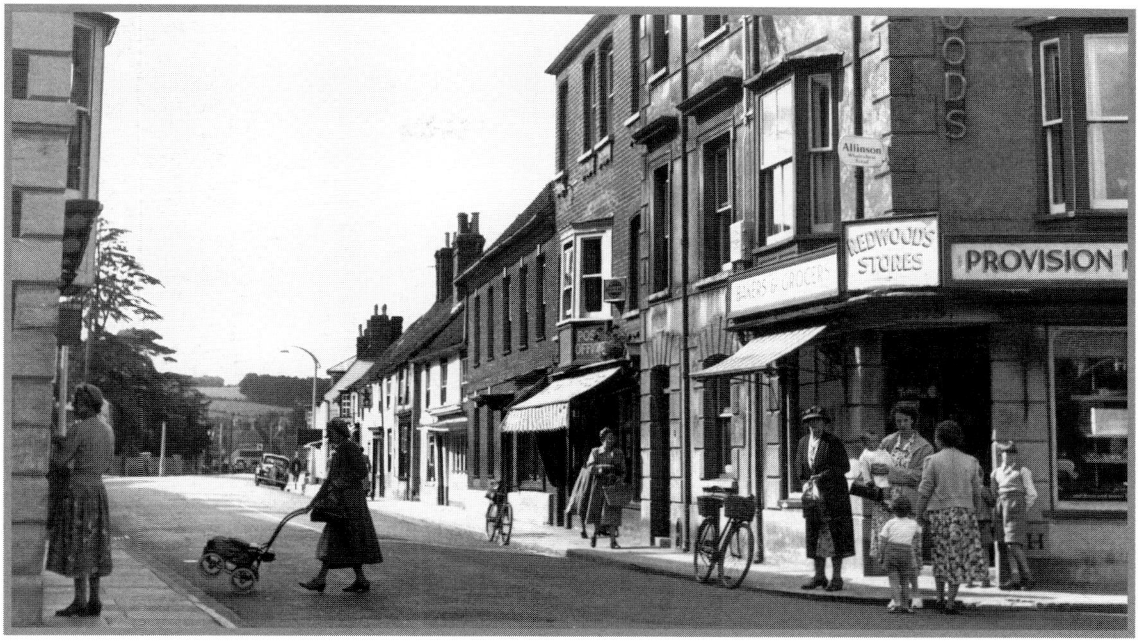

Wilton, West Street c1955 W166027

By 1955 the horse and cart have made way for the car, the street lamps have appeared, but the shops and everything else have changed very little in West Street. The street is a pleasing mixture of Georgian and Victorian houses and shops.

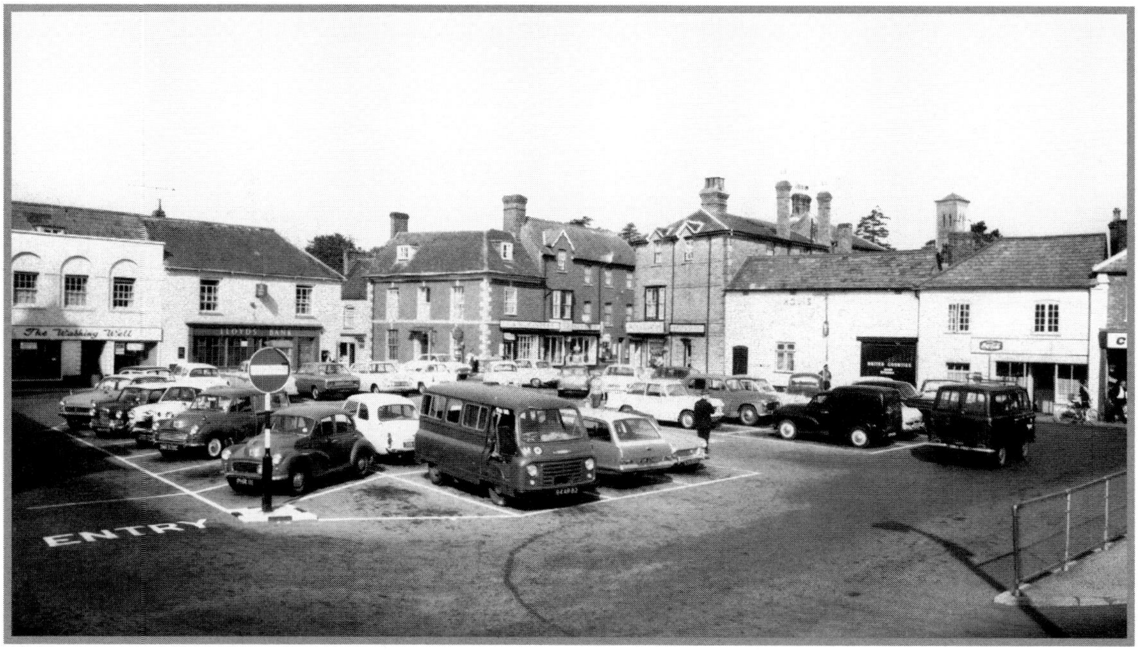

Wilton, The Market Square c1965 W166066

The vehicles in the car park are typical of the period, and the van in the centre probably came from RAF Chilmark nearby. Since the photograph was taken most of the shops in the picture - and the RAF base - have gone.

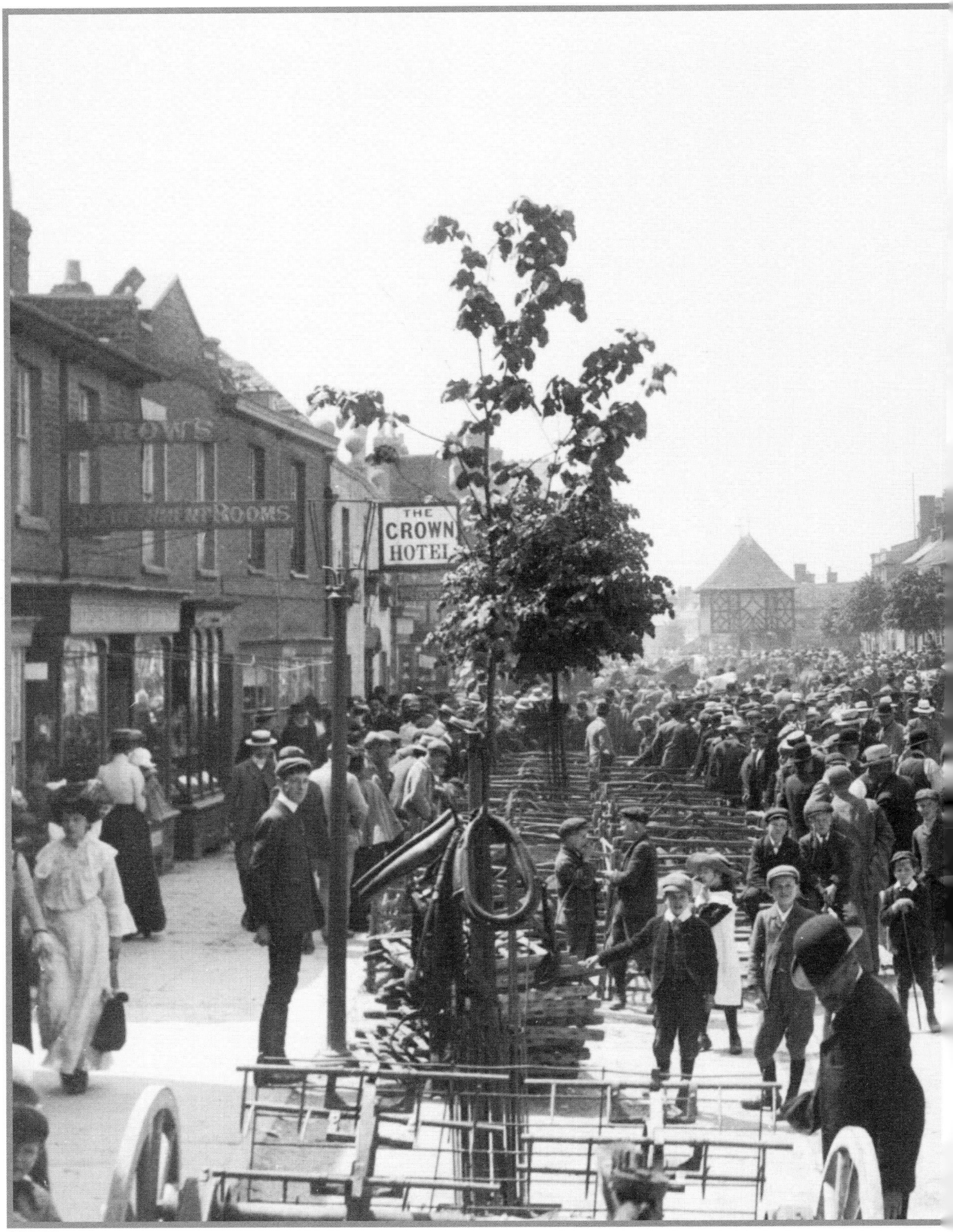
THE
CROWN
HOTEL

Wootton Bassett

High Street 1906 W171007

At the time of this photograph it was possible to hold a cattle market in the High Street of Wootton Bassett. This view is looking south towards the old Town Hall, the central building in the distance. The broad street is thronged with farmers and their families. On the left are the animal pens, and on the right farmer's horses are tied up outside the inn.

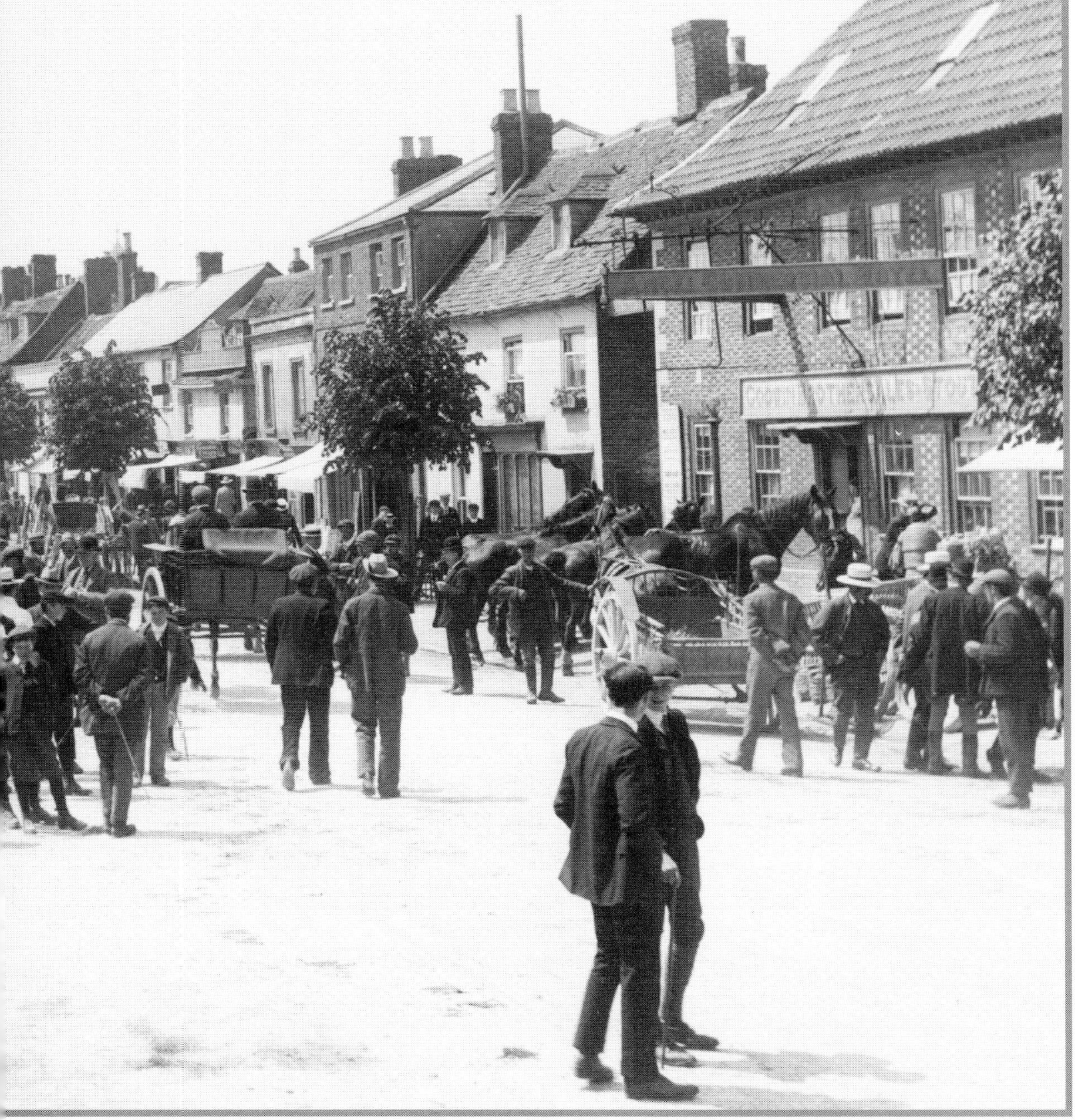

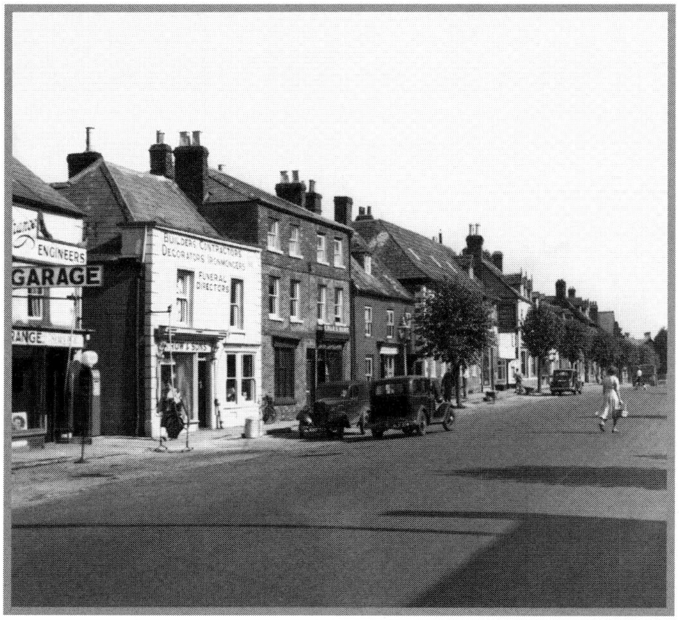

WOOTTON BASSETT, HIGH STREET c1955 W171010

WOOTTON BASSETT
High Street c1955
The cattle pens, horses and farmers of the previous photograph are replaced by cars and vans: but as yet, traffic levels are light. Note the interesting combination of trades carried on next door to the garage - in country districts builders often acted as undertakers, since they employed joiners.

WOOTTON BASSETT
High Street c1965
A clearer view of the decorative-timbered Town Hall. Built in 1700, it was restored in 1889 and served for some time as a library. The parked vehicles are greater in number than in the last photograph, taken 10 years earlier.

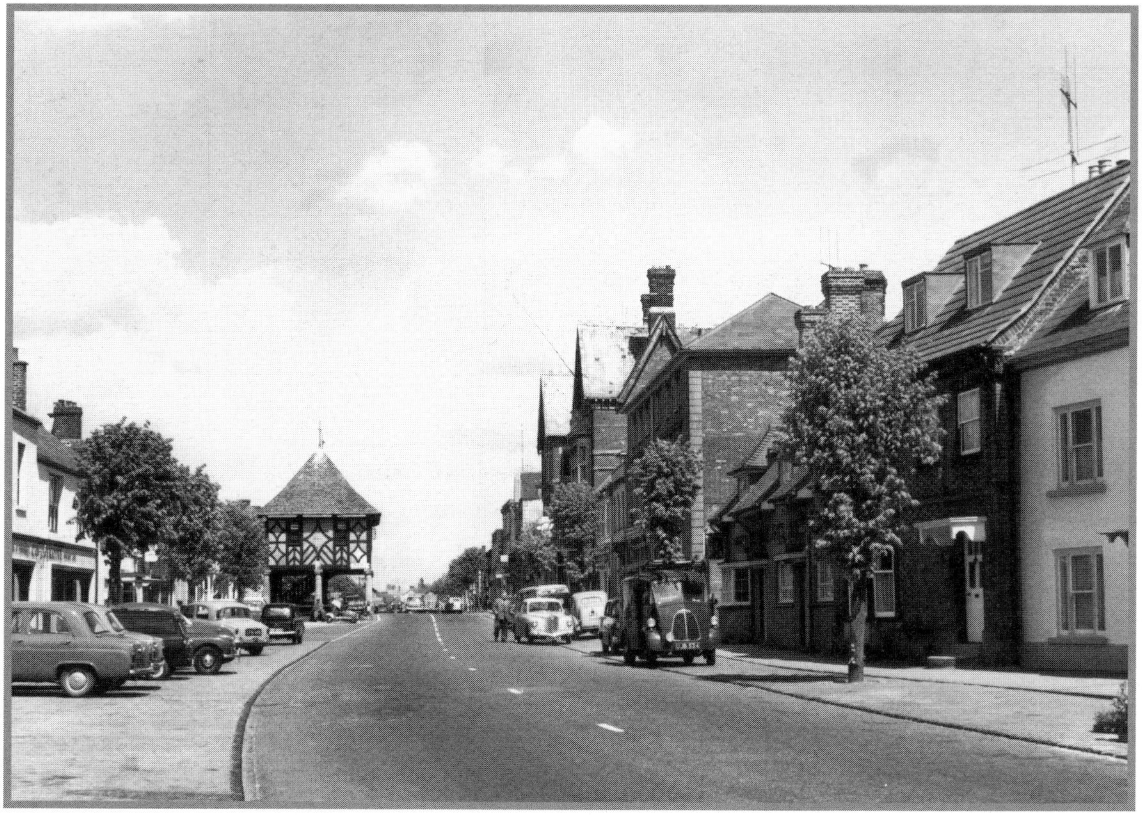

WOOTTON BASSETT, HIGH STREET c1965 W171039

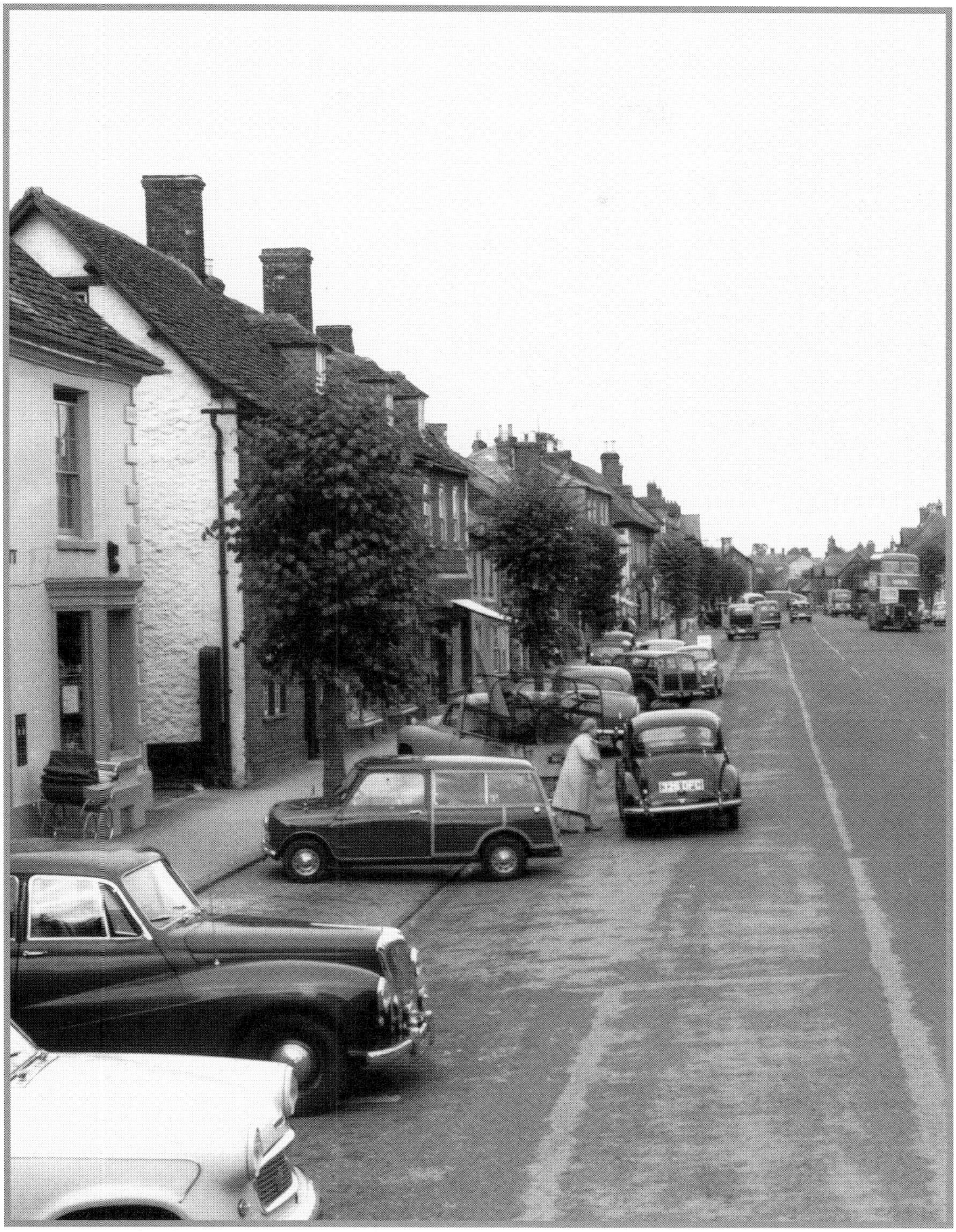

WOOTTON BASSETT, HIGH STREET c1965 W171032

Another five years on, and the High Street is distinctly busier. Otherwise, life seems to be pretty much unchanged in this pleasant small town, now largely a dormitory for Swindon. The street is fringed with pollarded trees.

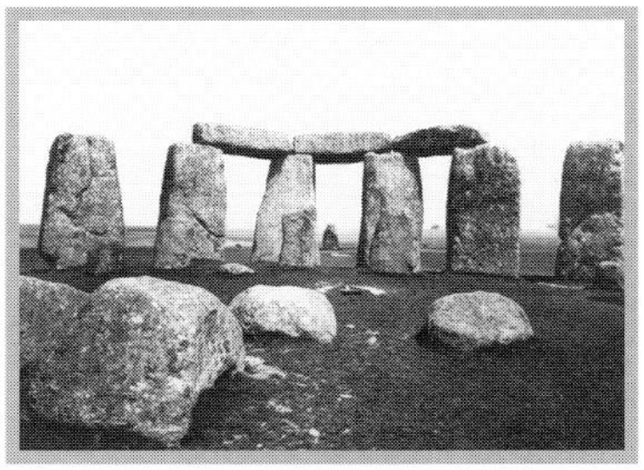

The Ancient Monuments

WILTSHIRE has been a centre for religious activity for thousands of years. Three main centres of such activity dominate belief and landscape: Avebury Stone Circle, Stonehenge and Salisbury Cathedral. When work started on Salisbury Cathedral in 1220AD, Stonehenge lay in ruins: when Stonehenge was finally completed in 1700BC, Avebury had long since been discarded. Sequentially they fall in order, symbols of man's changing spiritual needs.

The county is the richest in Britain for archaeological sites. From the new stone age - the Neolithic era - to the Bronze and Iron ages, early man has left his indelible mark on the landscape. Earlier Palaeolithic artifacts have been found, but it is around 4000BC that Neolithic peoples began to clear the forest, fire pottery, hunt and bury their dead in magnificent chambered long barrows. The most impressive of these is the West Kennet Long Barrow near Avebury, whose excavated chambers are well worth a visit. Then, as it is now for walkers, travel and communication was on the high chalkland paths. The most impressive of these is the Ridgeway, which today stretches from Overton Hill to Ivinghoe Beacon in Buckinghamshire. It would be a mistake to believe that people lived in isolated closeted groups in Neolithic times: the evidence is that in fact trade and commerce took people long distances - for instance, axe heads from the Lake District were exchanged for flint scrapers and pottery from Wiltshire. Little is known concerning the origins of the Neolithic people, but the monuments they have left behind continue to stimulate and excite our curiosity.

The combination of copper and tin brought in the period known as the Bronze Age. Archaeologists tend to agree that there was an invasion of Britain from the continent by people bringing with them their new technology. Whatever the truth may be, the Beaker Folk, as they are known, shaped the Wiltshire landscape. The rich downlands provided farming for barley and some wheat. Organised communities sprung up that demanded leadership and organisation in order to build large monuments like Stonehenge, other stone circles and the numerous burial mounds known generally as round barrows. Trading flourished, with amber from the Baltic and even gold from Ireland. Here, in Wiltshire, was the flowering of the Bronze Age; Stonehenge, roughly as we know it today, was completed about 1700BC, and a walk within its environs among the hundred or so round barrows, ancient prehistoric paths and various religious circles, will tell its own story.

About 500BC Britain was invaded by people from Europe who brought with them mastery in iron work; this period is know as the Iron Age. Seemingly more warlike than the prosperous people of the Bronze Age era, they built large hill forts throughout the county. There are many of them in Wiltshire, but perhaps the most famous is Old Sarum, since it became the city of Salisbury in Norman times, with its own cathedral and castle ramparts - until the 13th century, when the city moved to its present location and Old Sarum gradually fell in to ruin. These Iron Age inhabitants were more warlike than previous invaders, and we know from Julius Caesar's writings that they drove chariots and painted their faces with colours made from the woad plant. Their power, however, was shortlived. When the Romans invaded Britain the fortified hill forts fell, though not without fierce resistance from the Iron Age tribes.

The invasion of Britain by the Romans in 43AD ends the pre-historic period. They introduced the written word, laws, a paid army, heated villas and a belief in pagan Gods, all of which transformed Britain from intellectual stagnation to new conceptual horizons. This is not to underestimate the achievements of the British peoples. It was they who shaped the Wiltshire landscape and made their mark upon it. We can only marvel at their impressive monuments, empathise with their motives and preserve their lasting legacy.

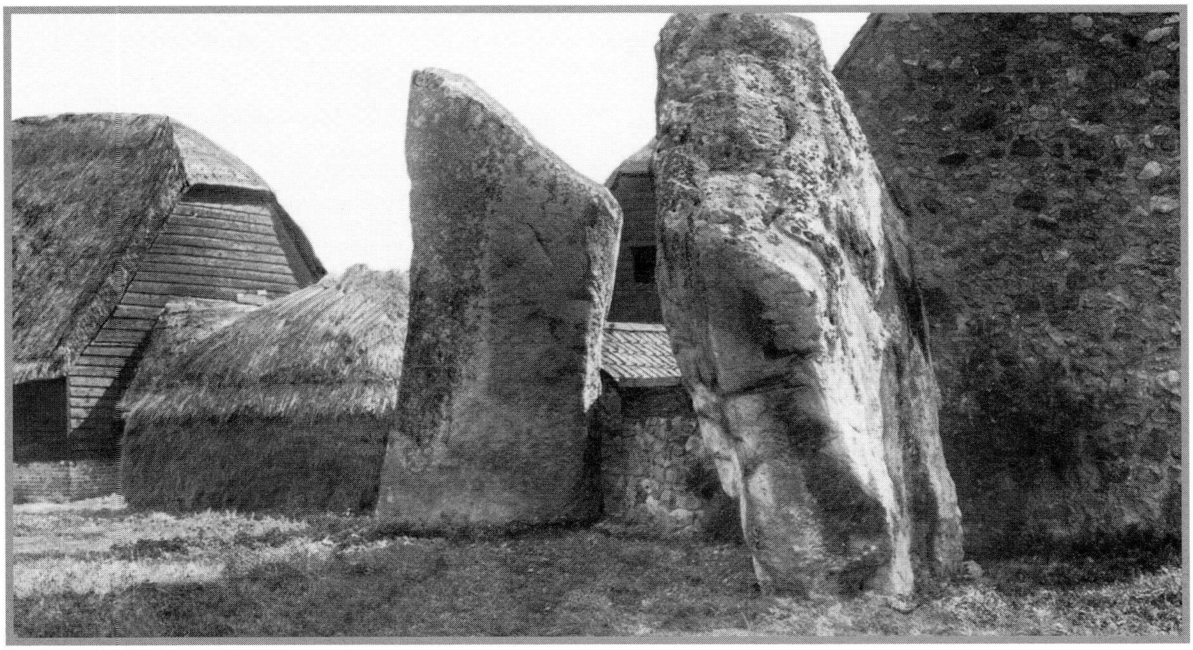

AVEBURY, DRUID STONES 1899 44860
The farm buildings pictured were demolished in the 1930s to present the two sarsen sandstones as they were originally erected some 4,500 years ago in the Neolithic age. These two form part of the Cove, which was possibly a shrine, in the northern inner circle of the Avebury henge.

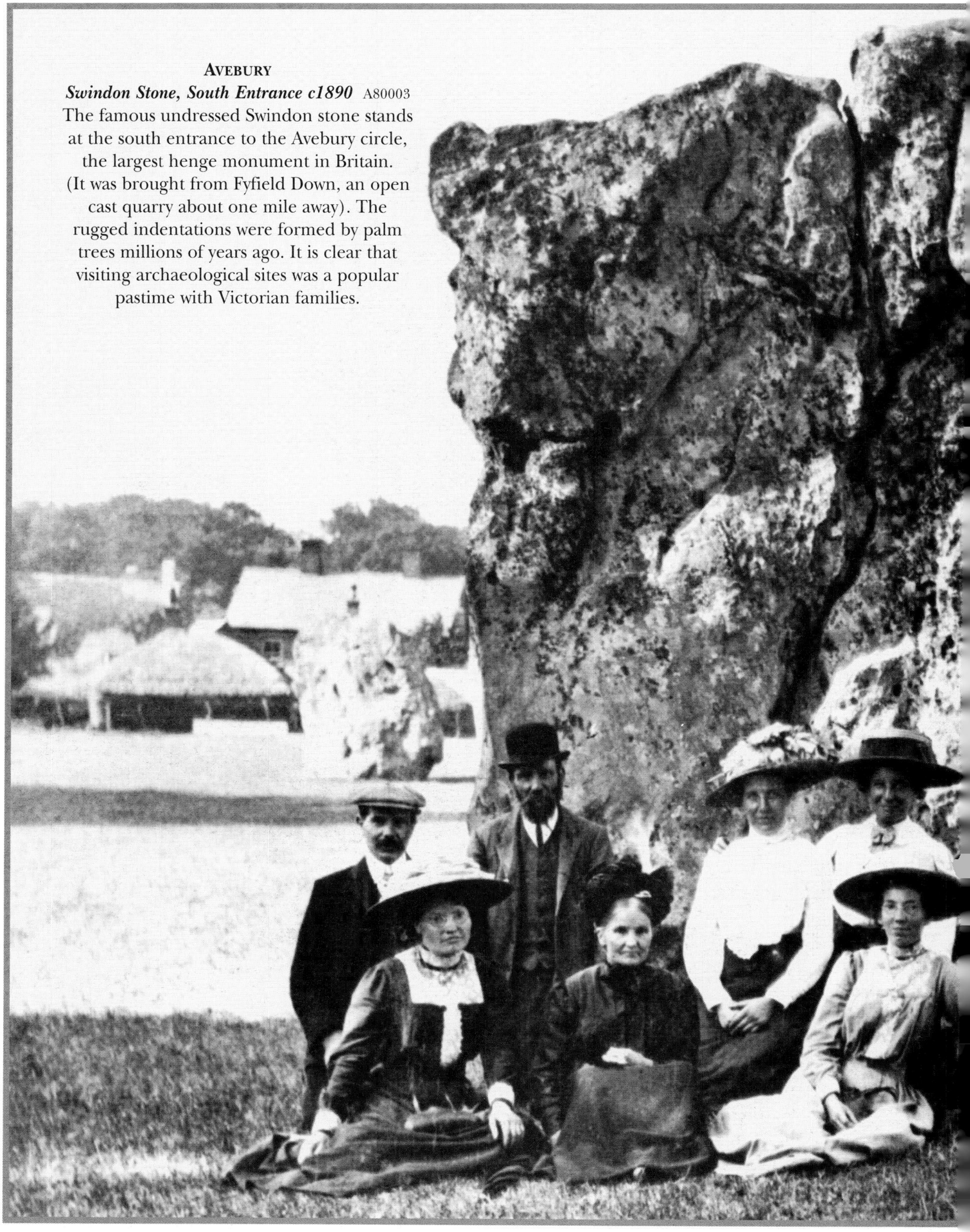

AVEBURY

Swindon Stone, South Entrance c1890 A80003

The famous undressed Swindon stone stands at the south entrance to the Avebury circle, the largest henge monument in Britain. (It was brought from Fyfield Down, an open cast quarry about one mile away). The rugged indentations were formed by palm trees millions of years ago. It is clear that visiting archaeological sites was a popular pastime with Victorian families.

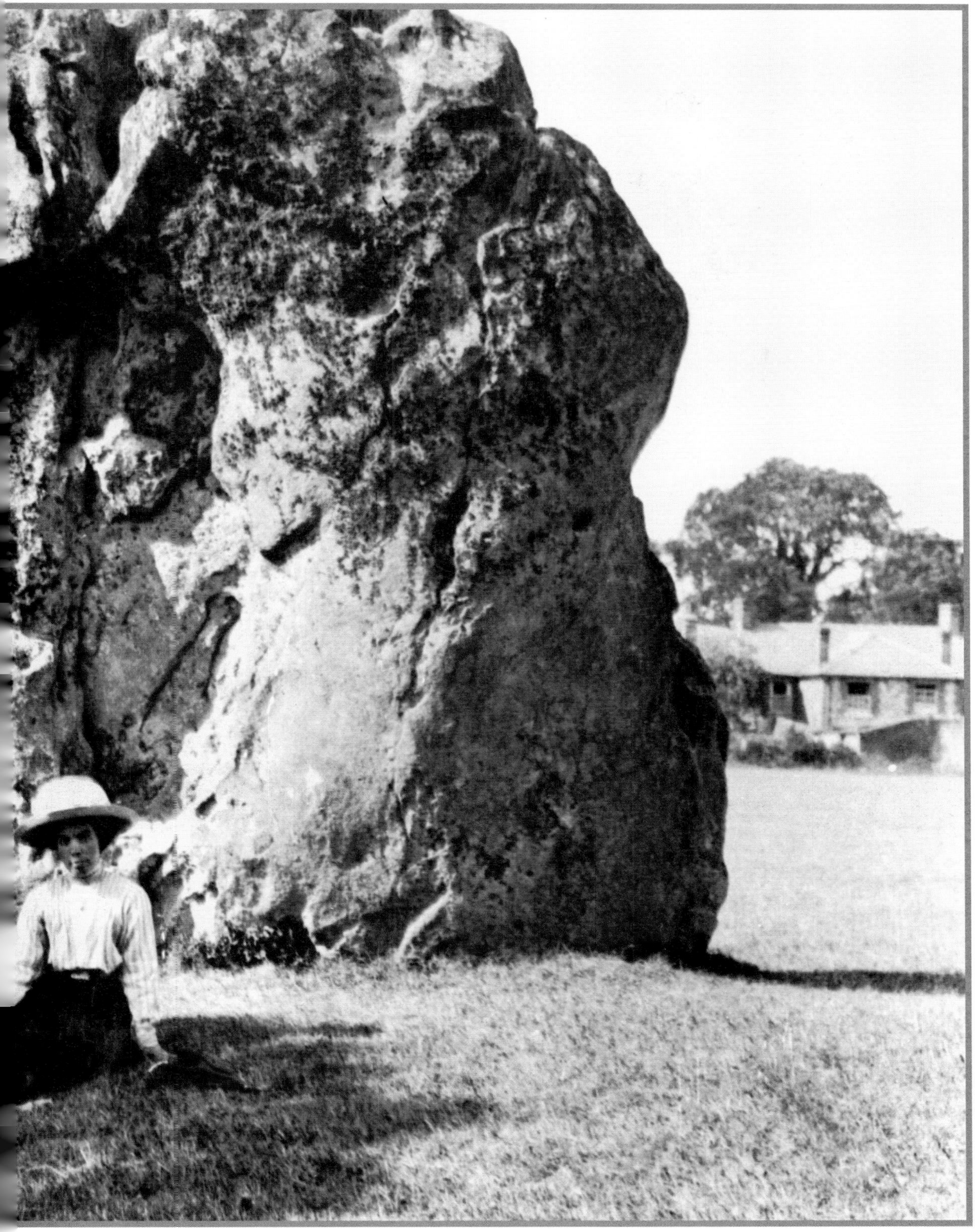

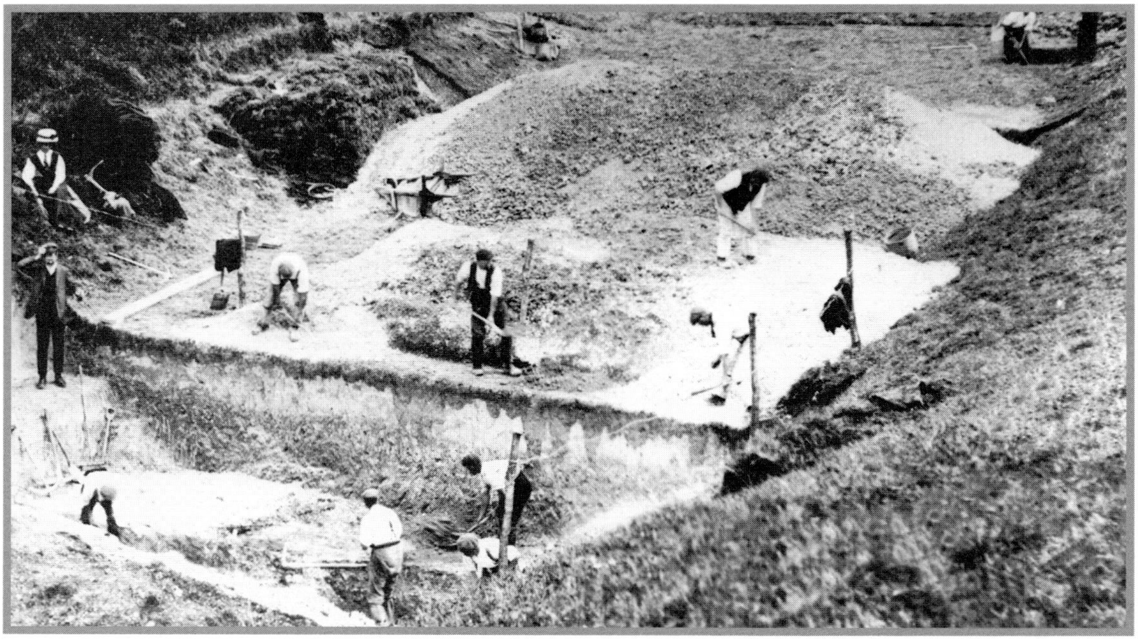

AVEBURY, AVEBURY CIRCLE c1920 A80001
This is almost certainly the excavation of the great ditch carried out by H St George Gray in 1922, when he established that Avebury was built in the Neolithic age. Flint tools, pottery fragments, human and animal bones and deer antlers (used as picks) were found.

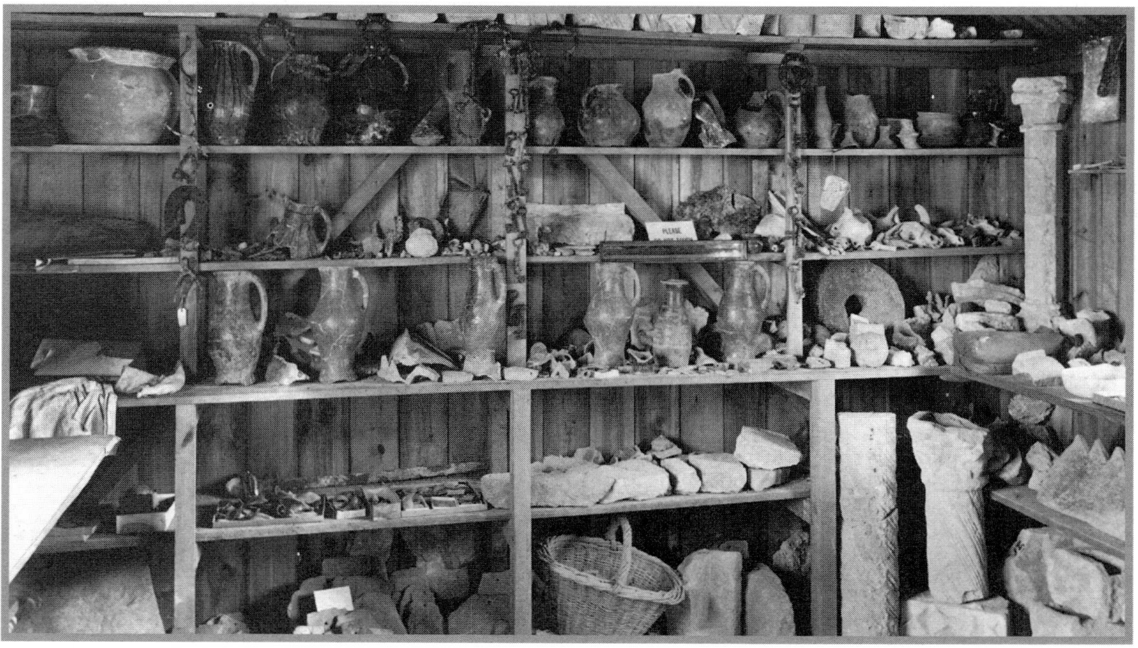

OLD SARUM, OBJECTS DISCOVERED DURING EXCAVATIONS 1913 65303
Old Sarum, an Iron Age fort, a junction for four Roman roads, a cathedral town and the original Salisbury, reveals its past with this display of excavated artefacts. Medieval vases, iron keys, Norman stonework and animal bones summarise the story of its troubled and relatively short-lived past.

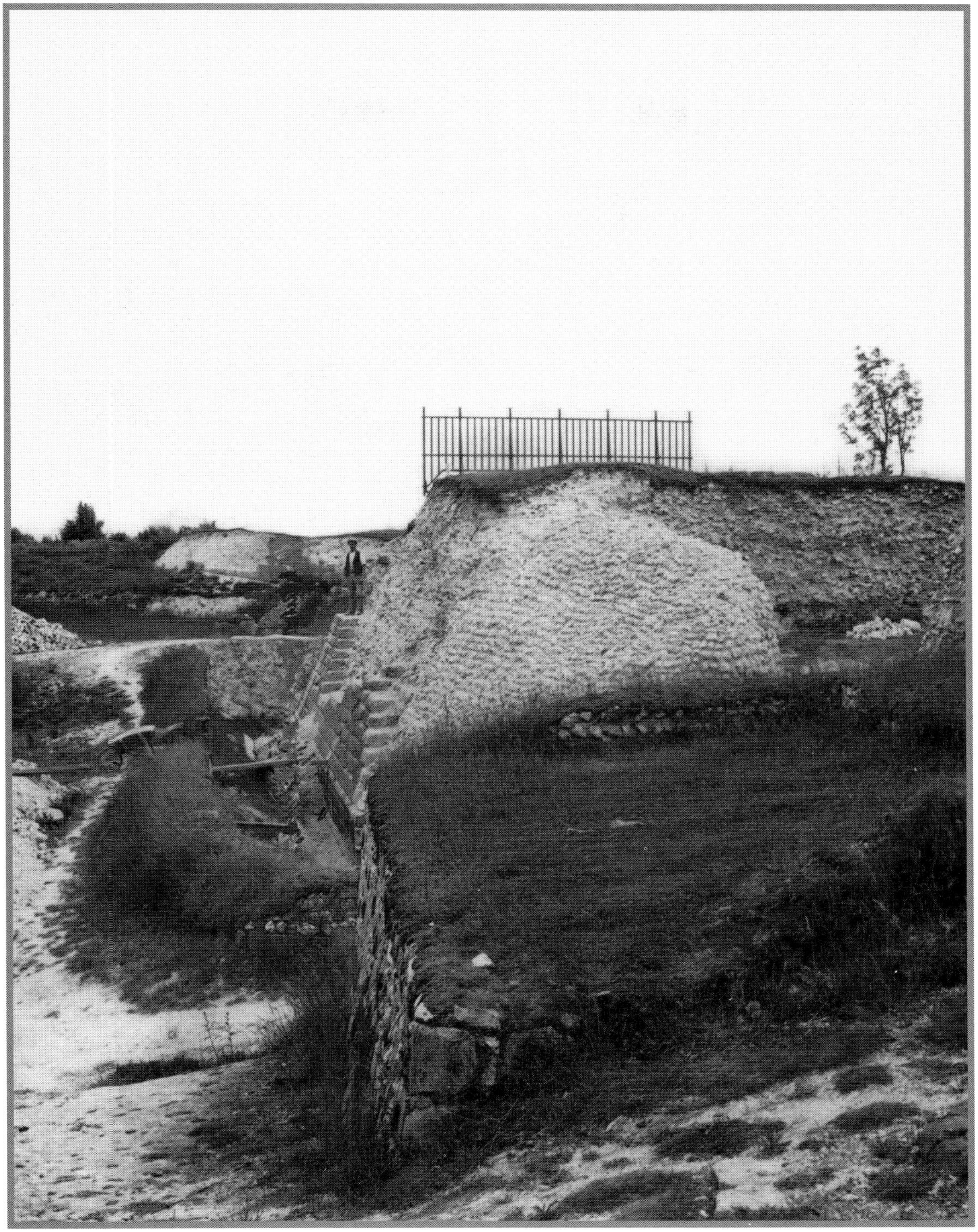

Old Sarum, 1913 65302
The banks of the original Iron Age fort can still be seen in this photograph. The Normans built a cathedral within it which was abandoned in the 13th century. Until the 1832 Reform Act this site, a 'rotten borough', returned two members of Parliament.

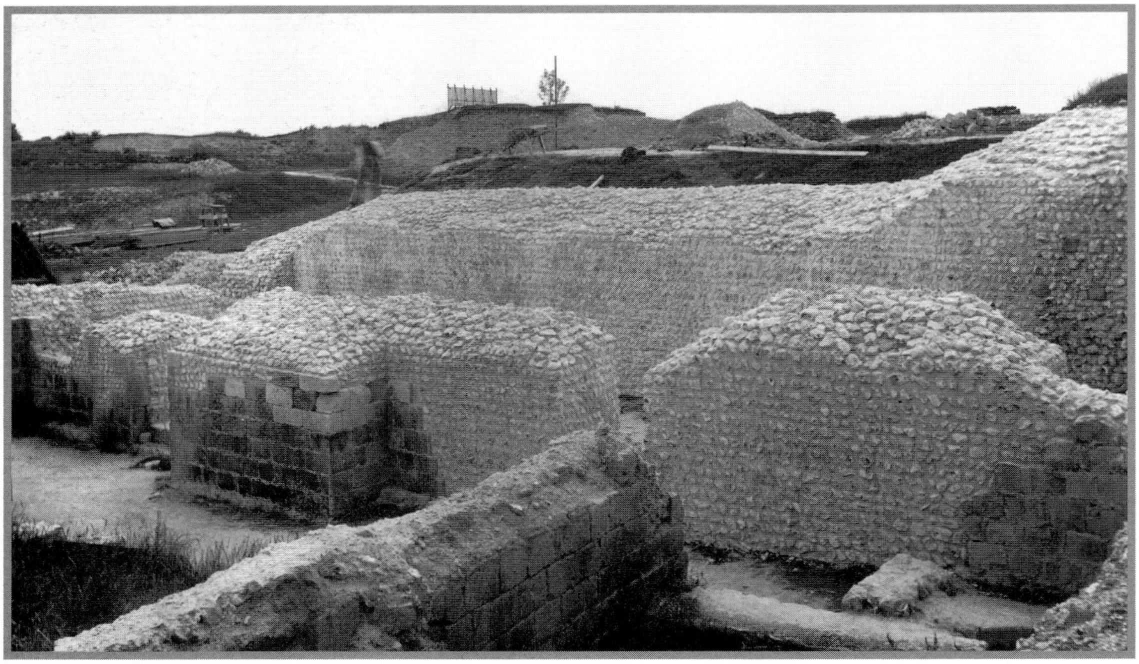

OLD SARUM, GARDEROBE PITS AND THE FOUNDATIONS OF THE GREAT TOWER 1913 65300
The Garderobe Pits - medieval toilets - are shown on the foreground, along with stone and flint walling. Flint walls were normally supported on firm stone foundations owing to their brittle and uneven structure.

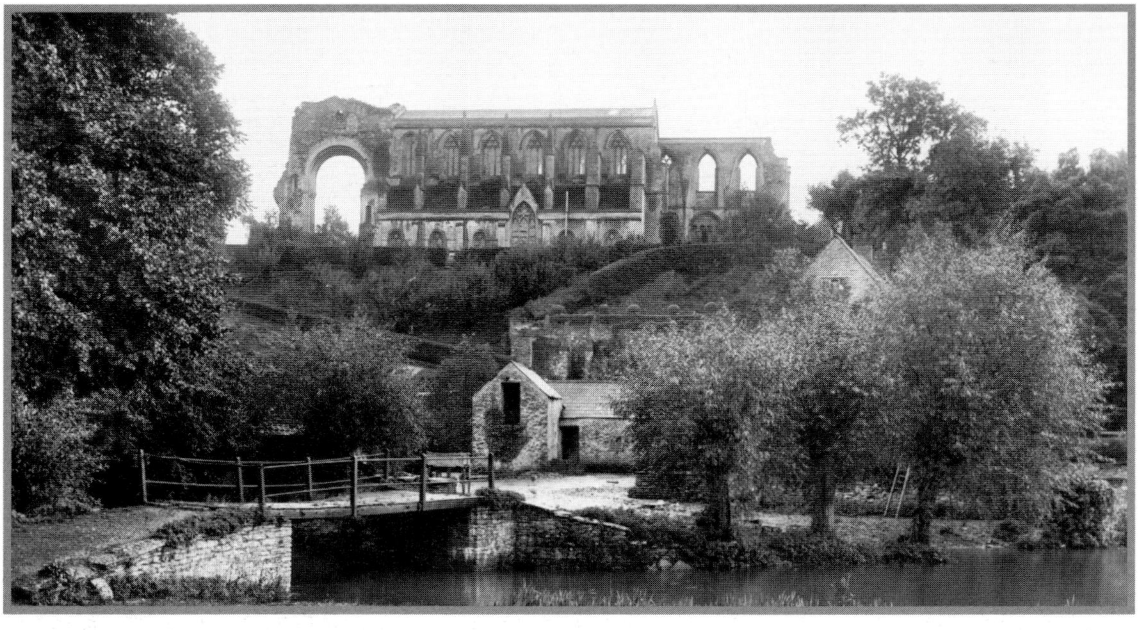

MALMESBURY, THE ABBEY 1924 76149
The impressive and imposing ruins of Malmesbury Abbey look down on the river Avon 60 feet below. Destroyed in 1539 by Henry VIII, it is said to have had a Gothic spire higher than that of Salisbury Cathedral and, according to a medieval manuscript, a flying monk called Elmer who flew from the tower for a furlong before falling to the ground, and surviving!

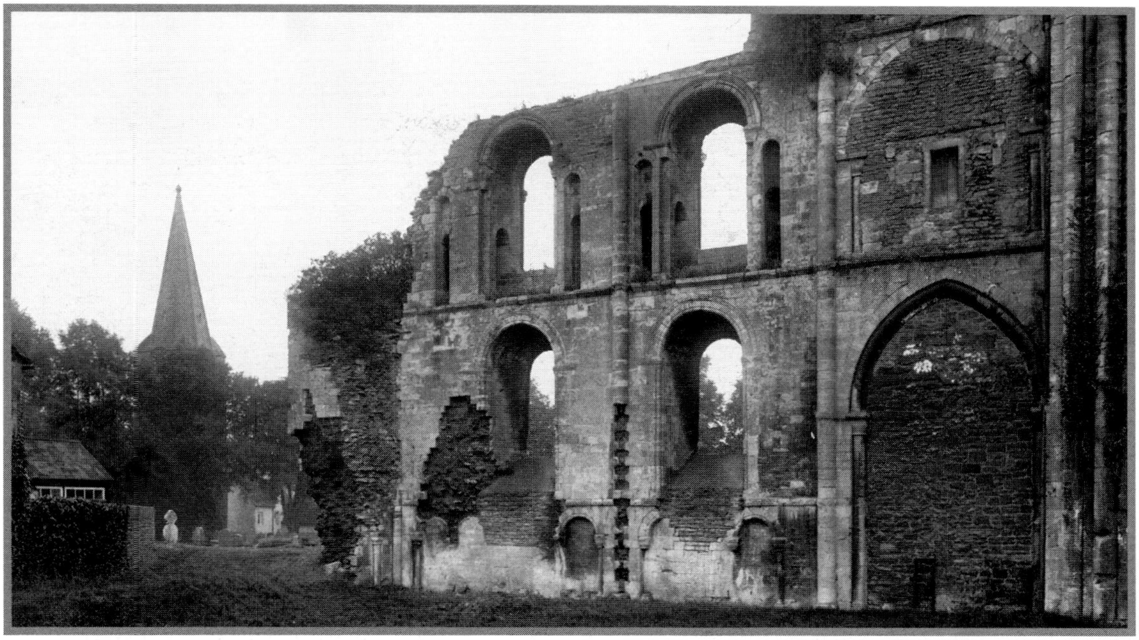

MALMESBURY, THE ABBEY RUINS 1924 76156
Early Norman arches can still be viewed in this picture. The abbey possessed a magnificent library full of early medieval writings which in the 12th century was presided over by the historian William of Malmesbury. Few manuscripts survived the Dissolution.

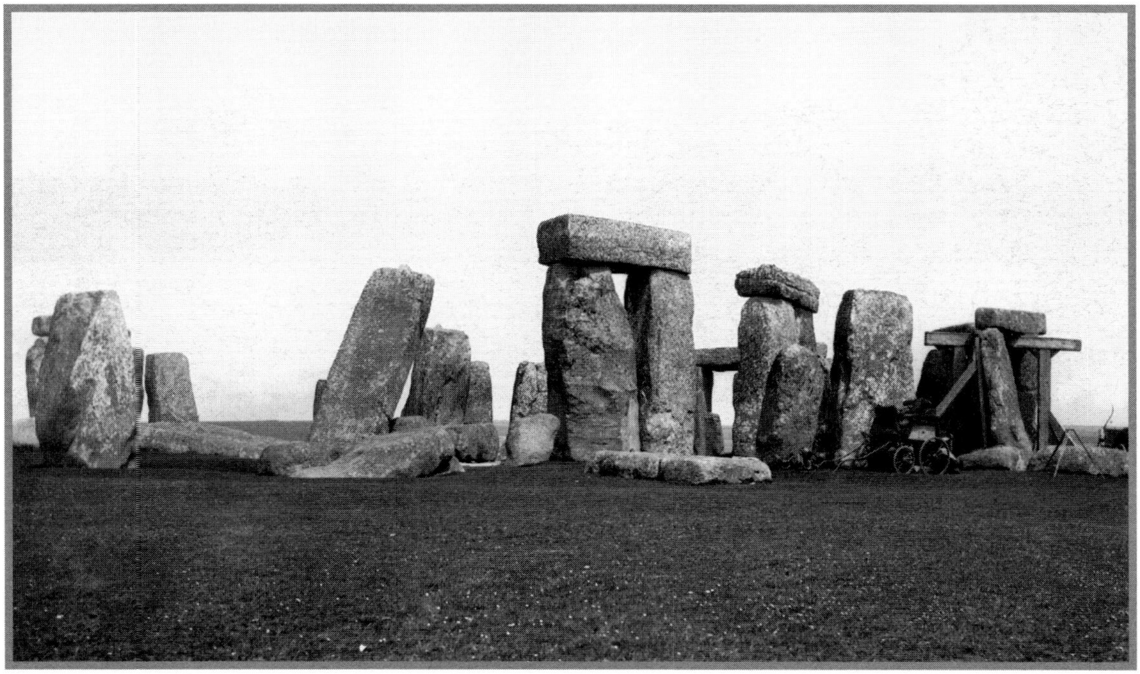

STONEHENGE, 1887 19797
A cluttered Stonehenge before gradual restoration took place in the early part of this century. There is a camera tripod in the right foreground, and note the temporary support given to the stones on the right of the picture.

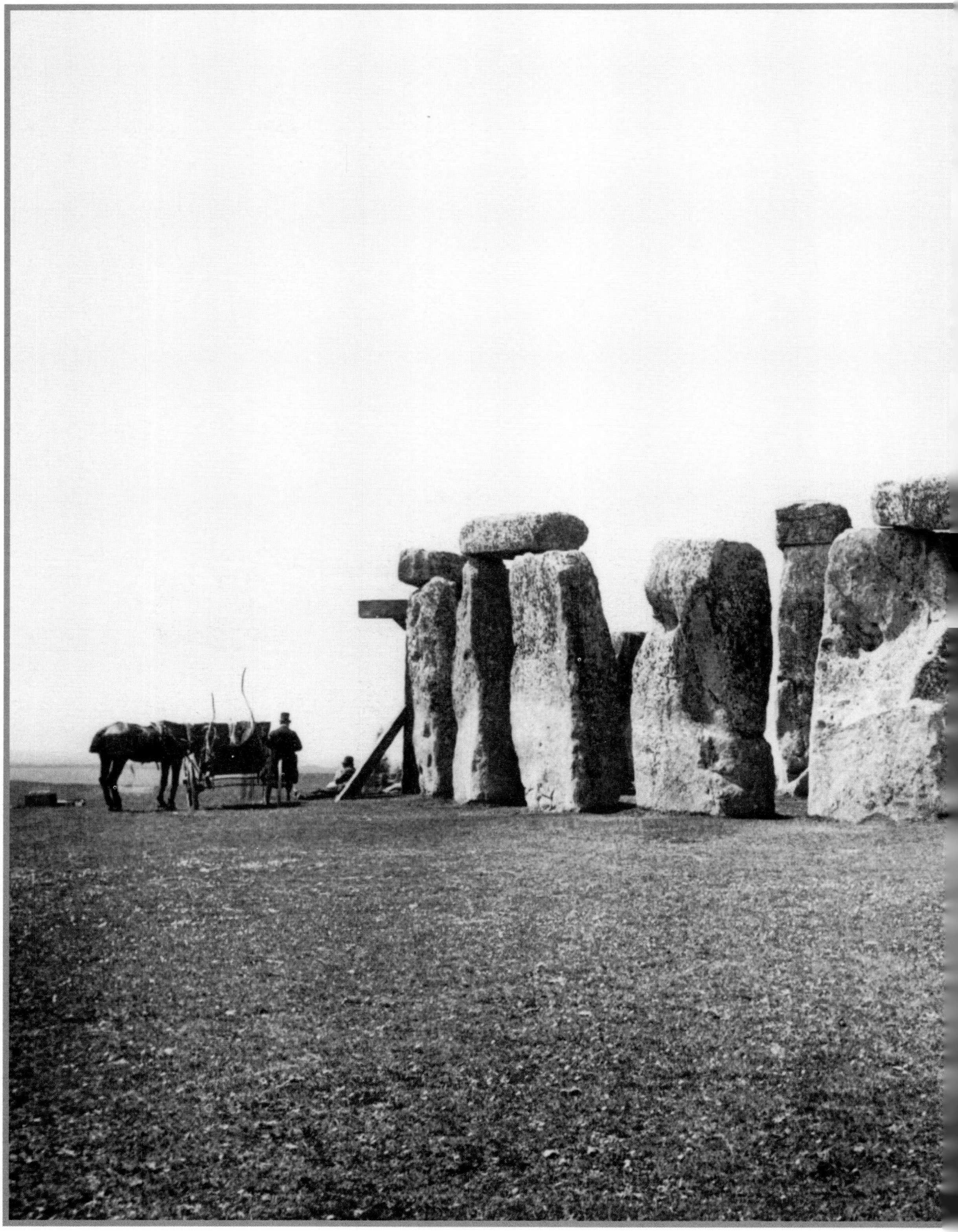

STONEHENGE
1887 19796
This view of Stonehenge shows its circular shape and the precise engineering needed to raise the 30 ton sarsen sandstones and cap them over their tenons whilst maintaining a perfect horizontal. It is still not known for certain how the lintels were raised.

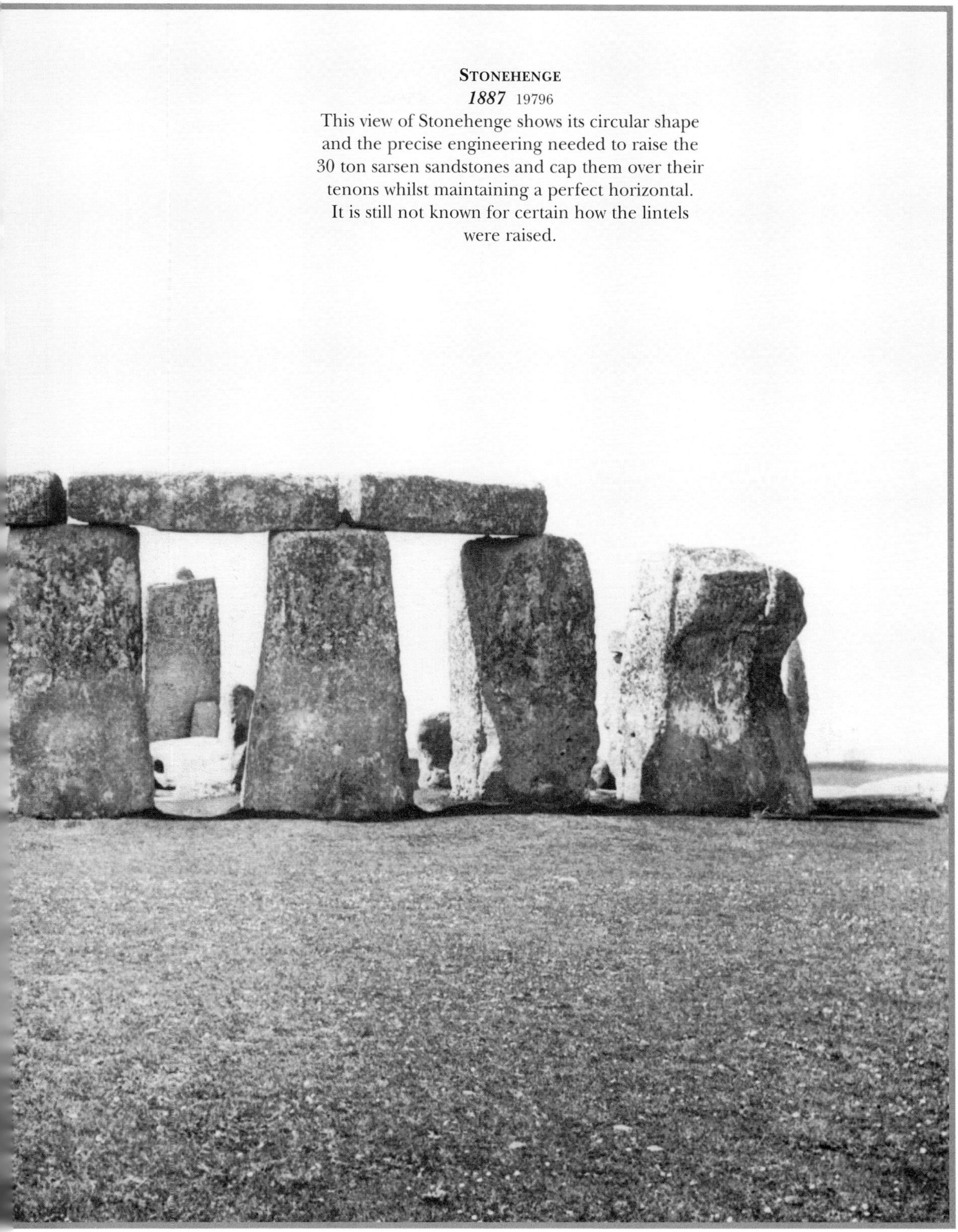

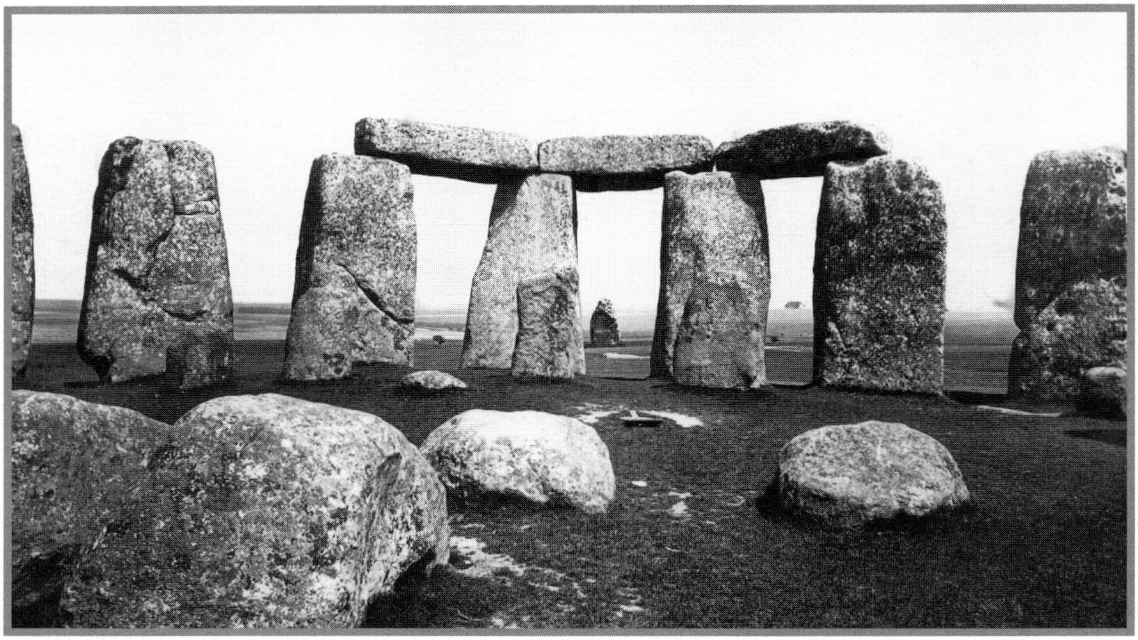

STONEHENGE, FROM THE ALTAR STONE 1887 19799
The Heelstone can be viewed through the middle of the three remaining arches where for 3,700 years the summer solstice can be observed. The sun rises directly above the stone on June 21st, the longest day of the year. There is no historical connection between Stonehenge and Druidism.

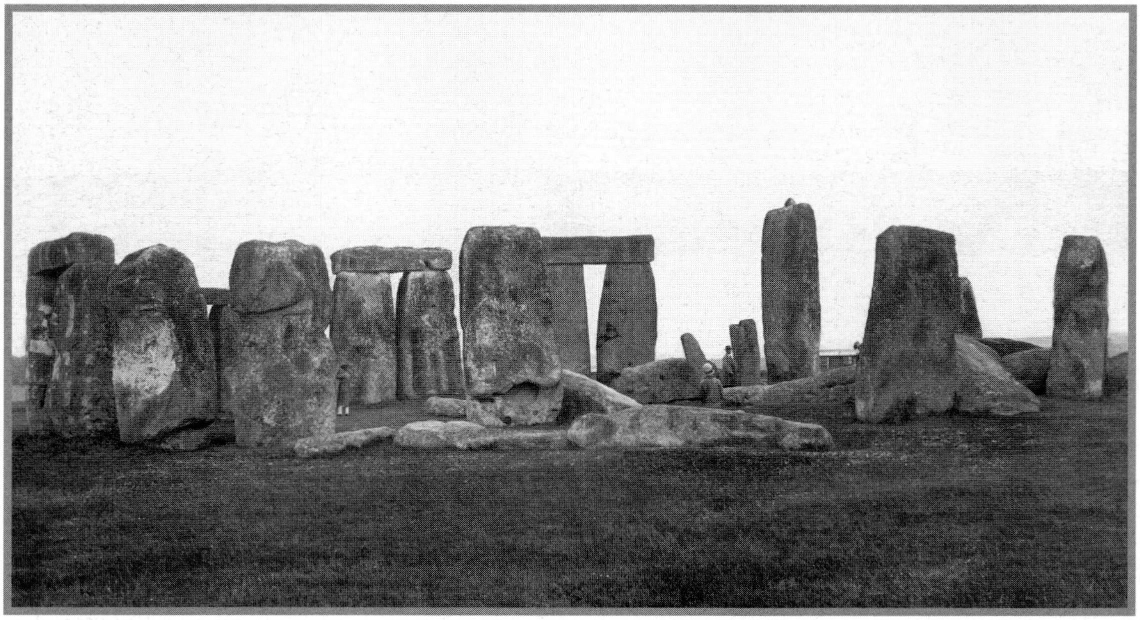

STONEHENGE, 1928 80943
Stonehenge is the most famous stone circle in Europe. Its building, and constant rebuilding, went on for a thousand years until completion about 1700BC. The large dressed stones, weighing some 40 tons, were brought from the Marlborough Downs 20 miles to the north. Only the smaller stones, inside the circle, came from the Prescelly Mountains in Wales.

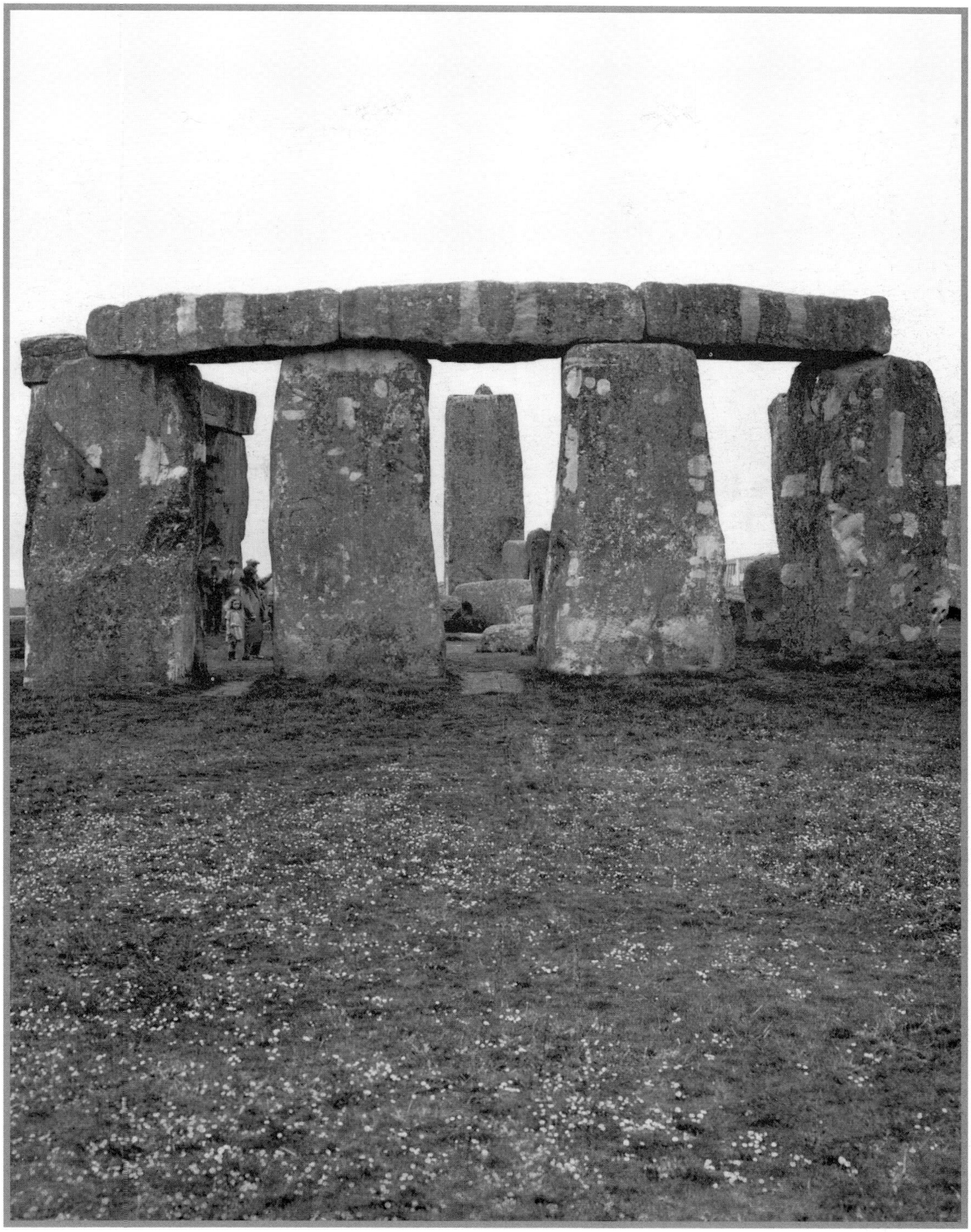

STONEHENGE, 1928 80953
Looking south from the ceremonial entrance to the stones, this view frames the largest stone still standing, which displays the first known tenon in Britain. Note the dressed lintels in the foreground and the accuracy of their horizontal planes.

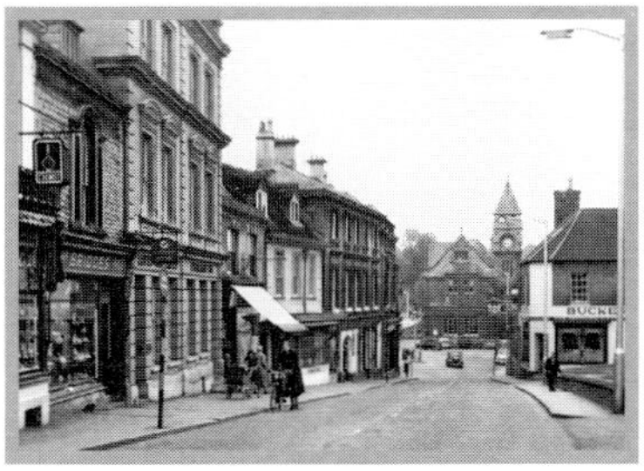

The Towns

WILTSHIRE is not overburdened with large towns and cities, which is probably why it is such a pleasant county. The largest settlement is Swindon, with a population well in excess of 200,000. The town has had three distinct development phases. Before the arrival of the railways, Swindon was an agricultural community. Then the Great Western Railway arrived. The decision to establish its main locomotive works here, at the junction of several railways, brought about a huge explosion in the population. A New Town was created, including a model village of some three hundred houses for its new employees. These were built with stone excavated from Box Tunnel, and the buildings are now designated a Conservation Area. Later, the contraction of the railway network brought savage cuts, culminating in the closure of the works in the 1980s. But Swindon is nothing if not resilient. Today, the electronics industry is a large employer and the town is growing fast again. Being close to the motorway network, Swindon offers an ideal location for distribution companies.

The only city in Wiltshire is Salisbury. This beautiful place, lying alongside the banks of the river Avon, has inspired poets and painters over the centuries. The cathedral itself is magnificent. With the Bishop's Palace, the Cathedral School, Taylors Almshouses and the dozens of other fine buildings in the Close, Salisbury is all but irresistible.

Similar claims can be made for some of the county's smaller towns. Devizes, perched on the top of a hill, has a huge market square and boasts many venerable properties within its small boundaries. Bradford-on-Avon is a warren of narrow lanes and old buildings, enough to justify an extended stay in the area. Marlborough, with its wide main street, and Chippenham, with its narrow pedestrianised centre, are utterly different in character, but delightful.

This diversity is one of the attractions of Wiltshire. You can travel from tiny hamlet to large market town in quick succession and find each just as enjoyable, for the majestic architecture of the towns is replicated on a more modest scale in the villages.

Wool was the catalyst for much of Wiltshire's historical wealth, and funded its great buildings; there is still much sheep farming today, but huge monetary returns are now largely a thing of the past. Brewing, food production and motor car manufacture are also to be found. In Calne in 1770, a Mr Harris started curing bacon. His name was to become famous for a whole range of pig products. The name 'Wiltshire Ham' carries connotations of taste and flavour even today. Wiltshire pork sausages are equally well known.

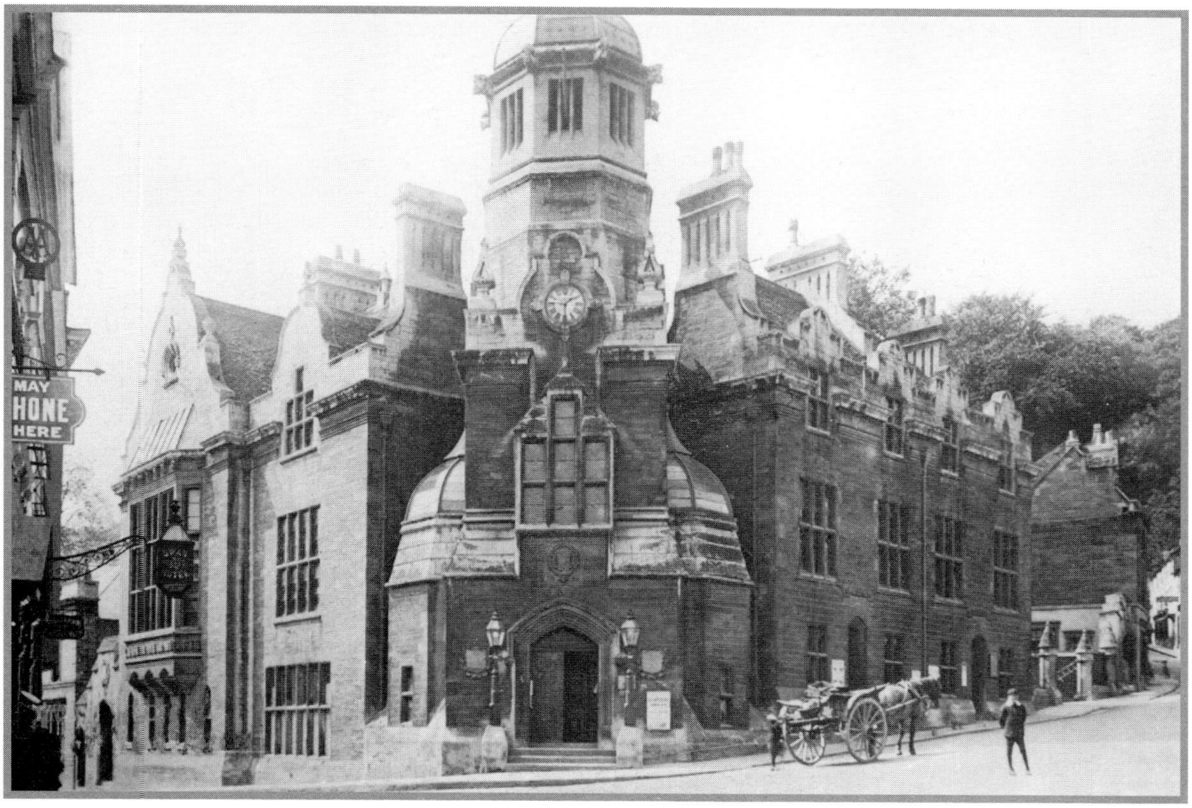

BRADFORD-ON-AVON, THE TOWN HALL 1914 66624
Bradford-on-Avon has changed little in the last century. There has been no by-pass, no rash of new developments. In fact, the town is instantly recognisable from early photographs, such as this one of the huge Jacobean Style Town Hall. Its ornate style contrasts with the plainer stone houses that are more characteristic of the town.

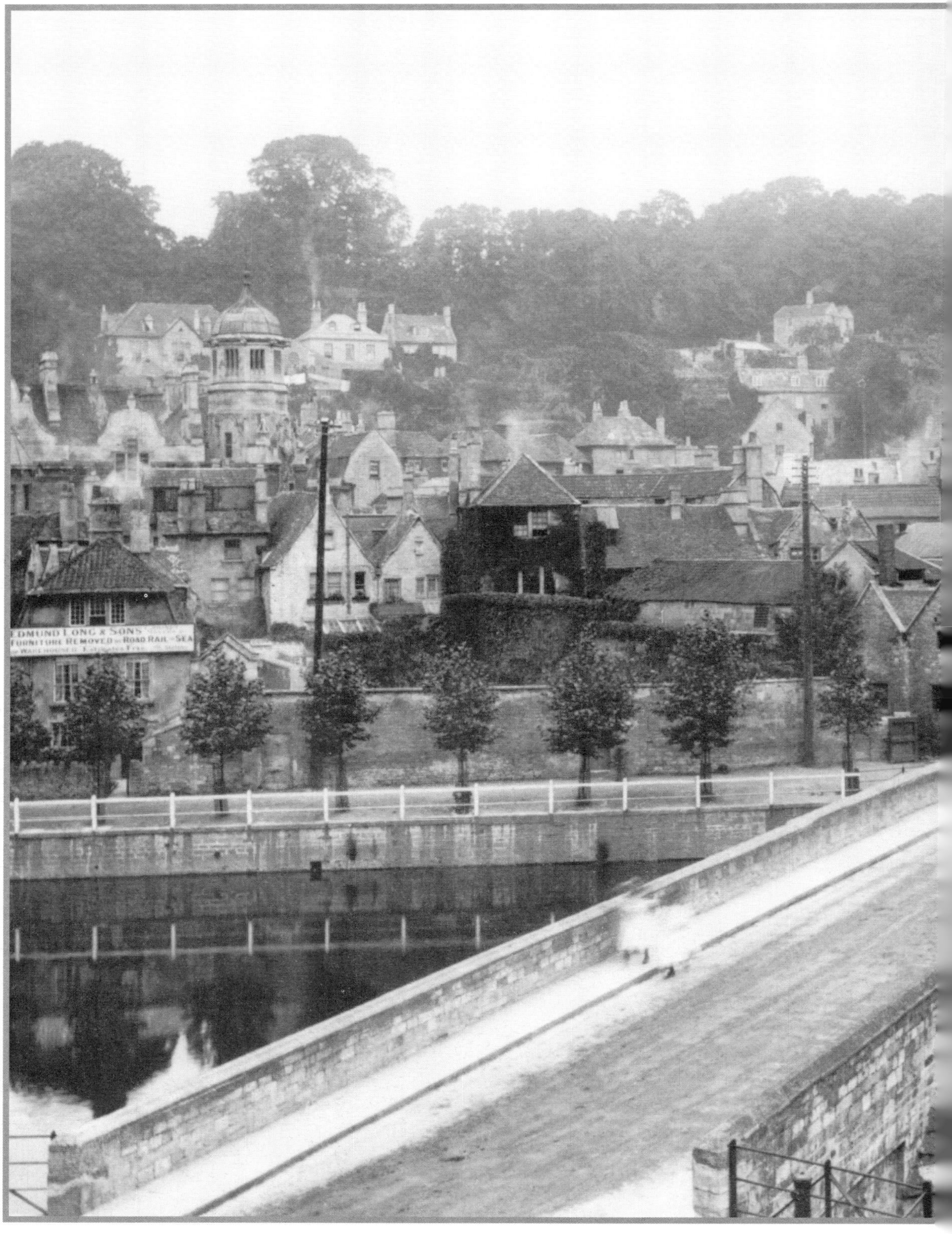
EDMUND LONG & SONS
FURNITURE REMOVED BY ROAD RAIL OR SEA

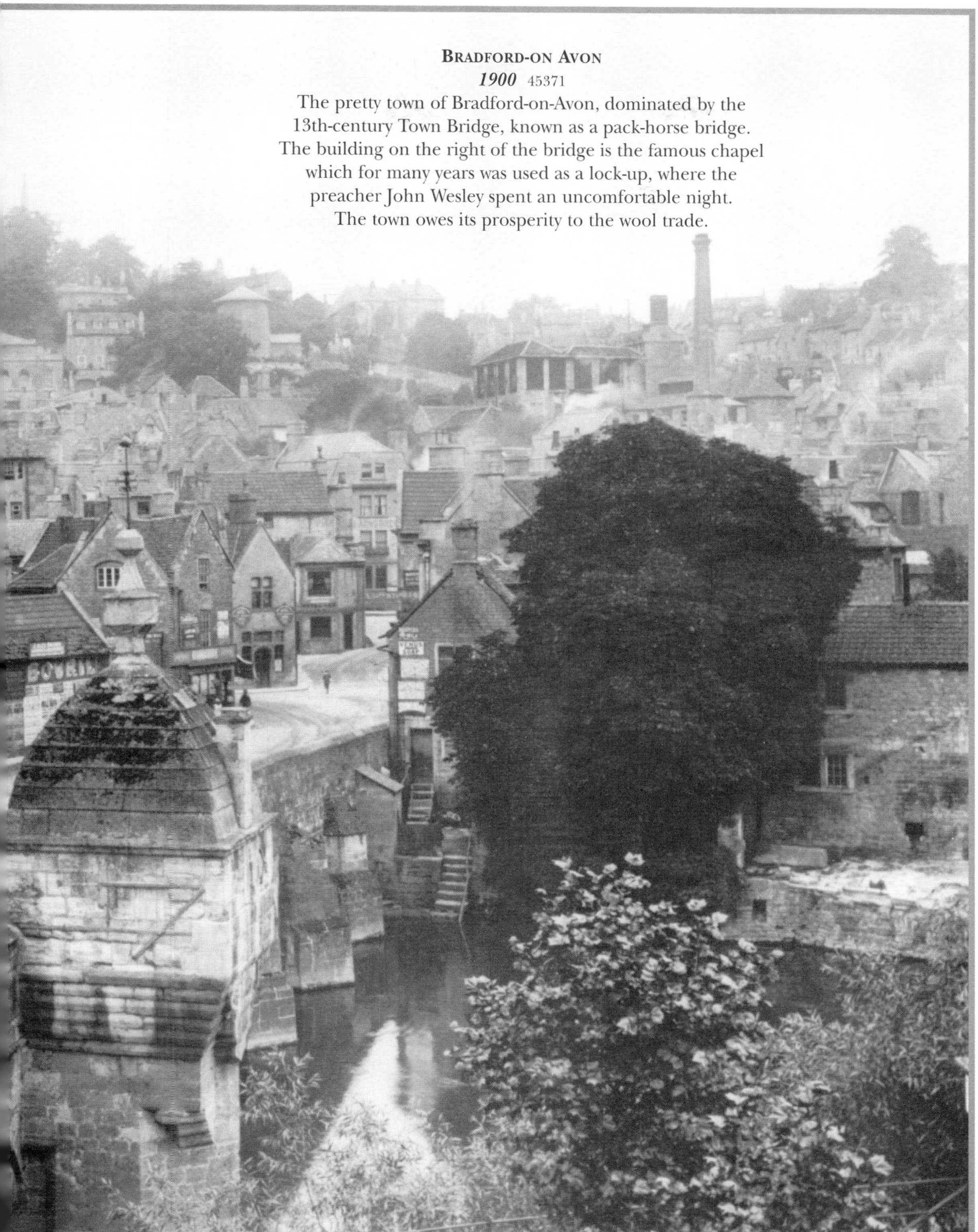

Bradford-on Avon
1900 45371
The pretty town of Bradford-on-Avon, dominated by the 13th-century Town Bridge, known as a pack-horse bridge. The building on the right of the bridge is the famous chapel which for many years was used as a lock-up, where the preacher John Wesley spent an uncomfortable night. The town owes its prosperity to the wool trade.

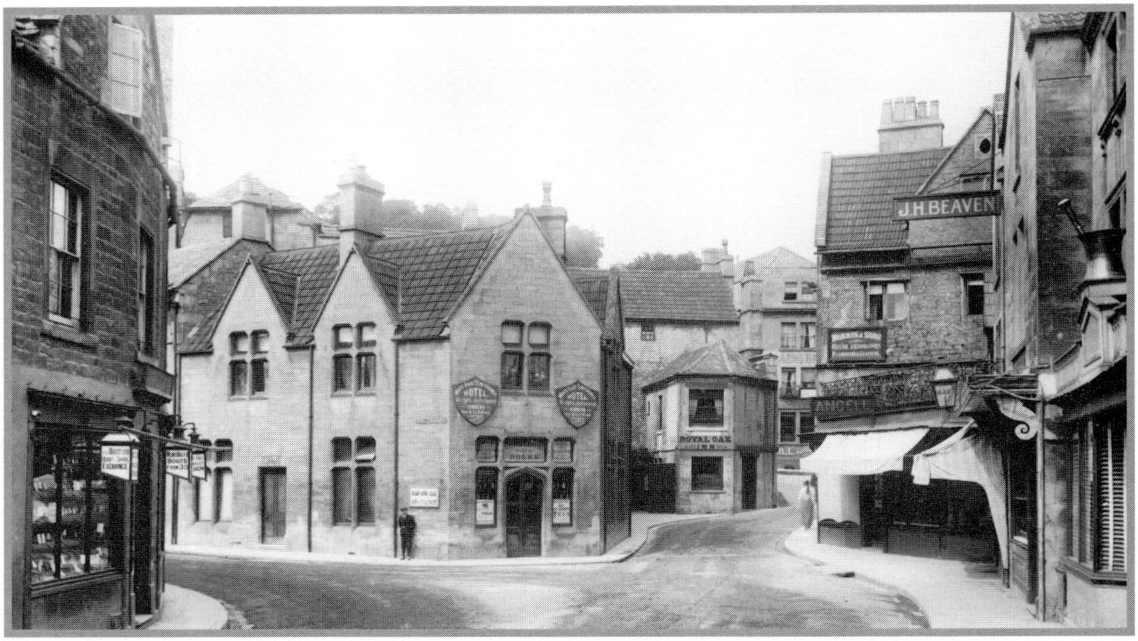

BRADFORD-ON-AVON, MARKET STREET 1900 45377

Most of the town's finest buildings are Georgian - the woollen mills and the merchants' houses. Bath stone was used for many of the buildings. This junction of the narrow streets creates a serious bottleneck for modern traffic. Note the decorative lamps outside the shop on the left.

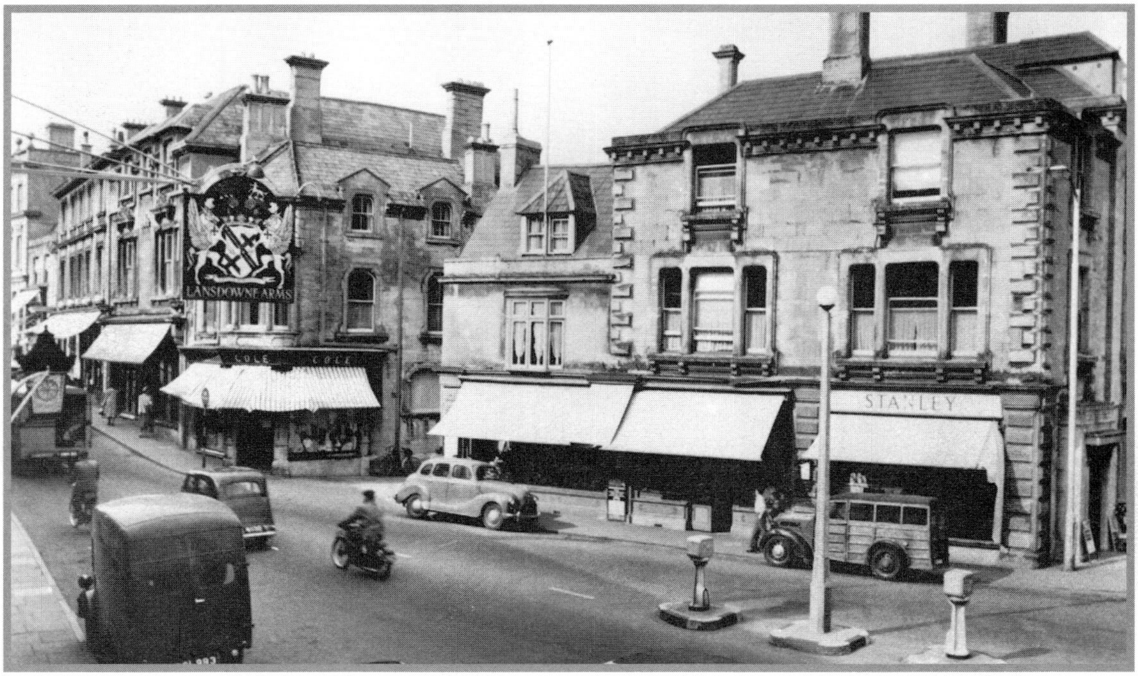

CALNE, THE STRAND c1955 C228060

This view of the bottom of the Strand in Calne is now much changed. The building in the centre has gone and a massive redevelopment is under way, although the Lansdowne Arms Hotel has been spared so far.

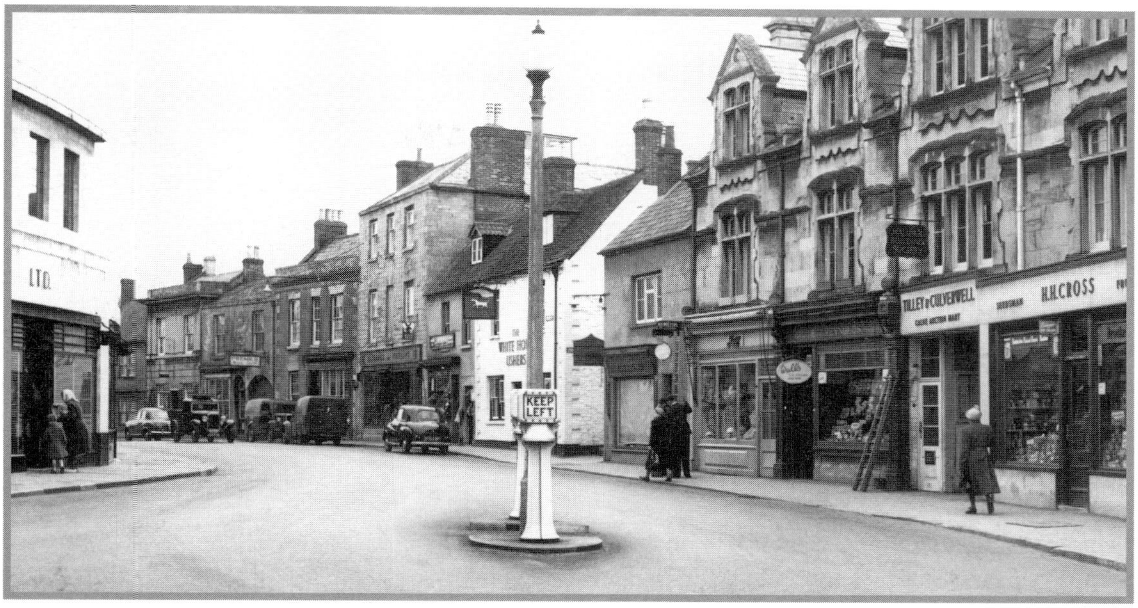

Calne, Wood Street c1955 C228052
The main differences between this picture of Calne and the town today is that there is room to park and no yellow lines. Note the rather quaint street furniture in this and the preceding picture. The terrace of shops on the right is an example of how the Victorians delighted in creating facades which did not necessarily harmonise with existing vernacular buildings.

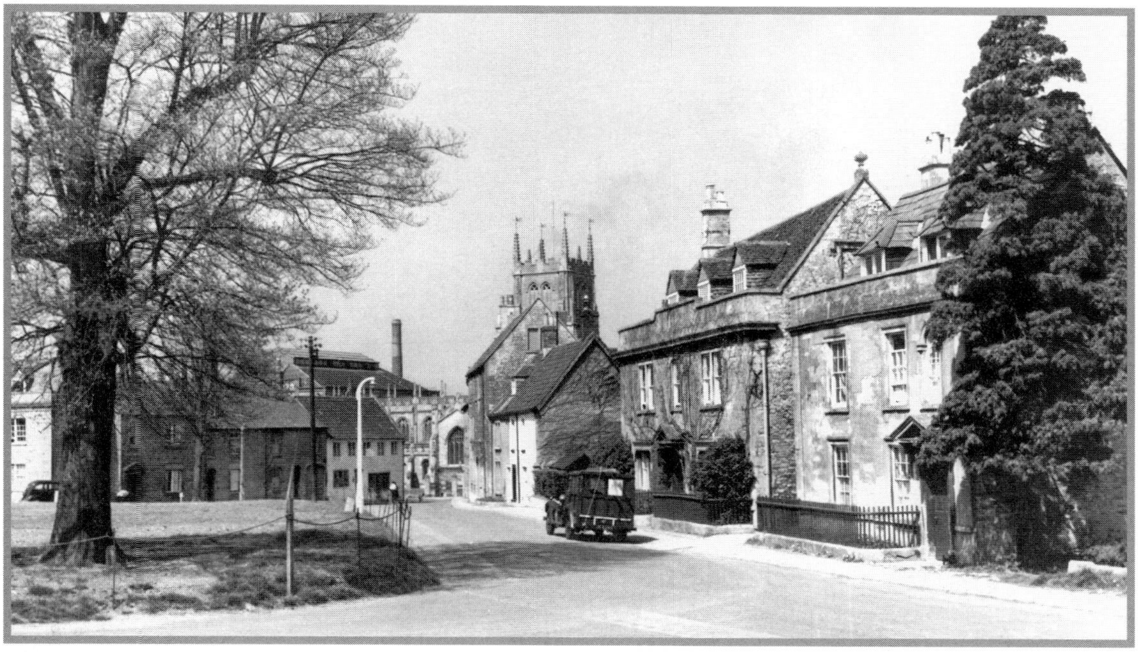

Calne, The Green c 1955 C228032
Once, wool dominated Calne: then it was pigs. The Harris bacon factory (in the background) was established as one of the main industries in this town. Calne can also boast of having a market for over a thousand years: some record. This photograph shows some of the town's best Georgian buildings, with St Mary's church in the centre.

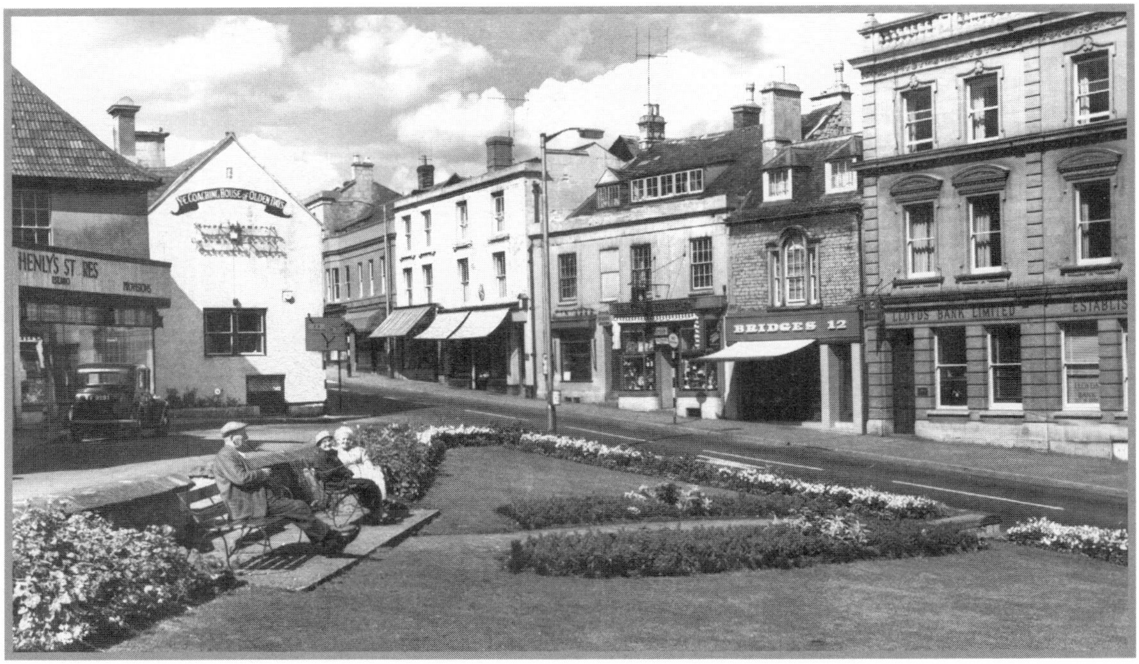

CALNE, THE CENTRAL GARDENS c1960 C228081
Unfortunately these gardens are now gone: the site has been turned into a car park. Wood Street - to the right of the gable - is now traffic free, and the road goes through where the photograph shows a white building on the right.

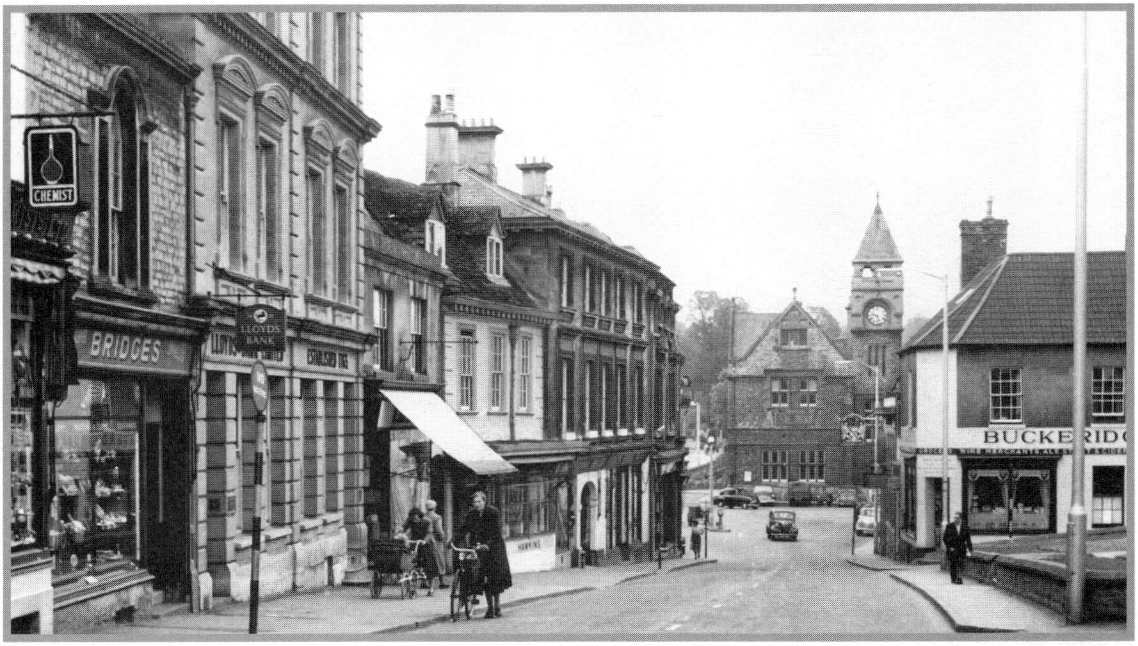

CALNE, HIGH STREET c1955 C228053
This view looks down the High Street towards the Strand. The delightfully ornate building at the bottom is the Town Hall, and the Central Gardens seen in the previous picture are on the extreme right. The Lloyds Bank building on the left is a typically grand and solid structure, clearly designed to impress clients.

Calne
Station Road c1955
This view simply does not exist any longer. The railway is closed, and private housing dominates this view today. To the right of the car is now the location of the town's fire station.

Chippenham
New Road from the Viaduct c1960
A fine overview of Chippenham. On the left is the road to the station, with the High Street ahead. Little has changed in the intervening years. Brunel's viaduct was built in 1841 and widened in 1848.

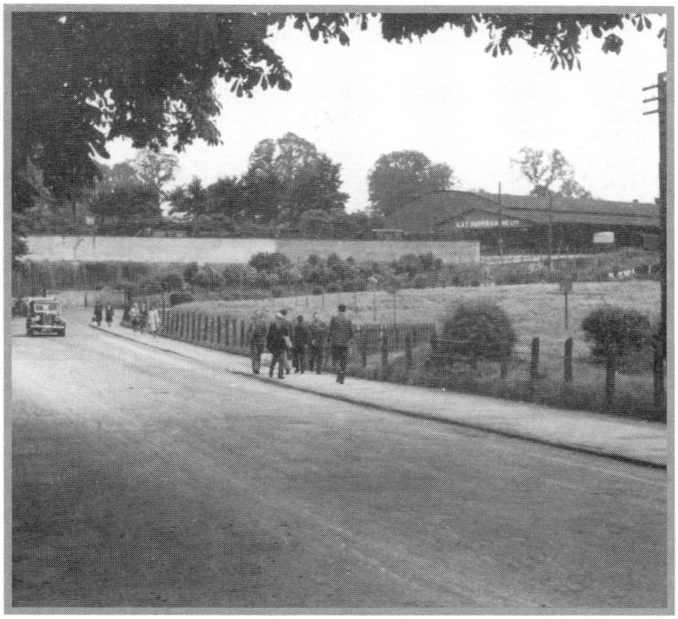

Calne, Station Road c1955 C228003

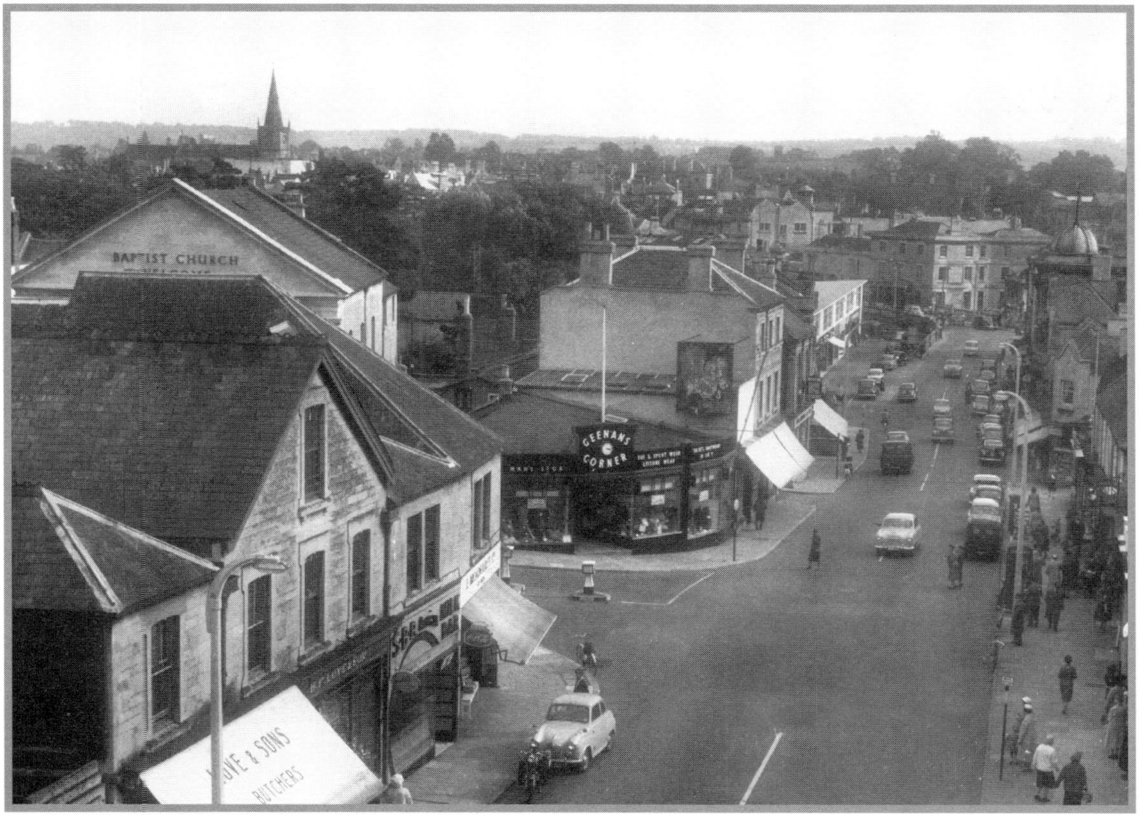

Chippenham, New Road from the Viaduct c1960 C294056

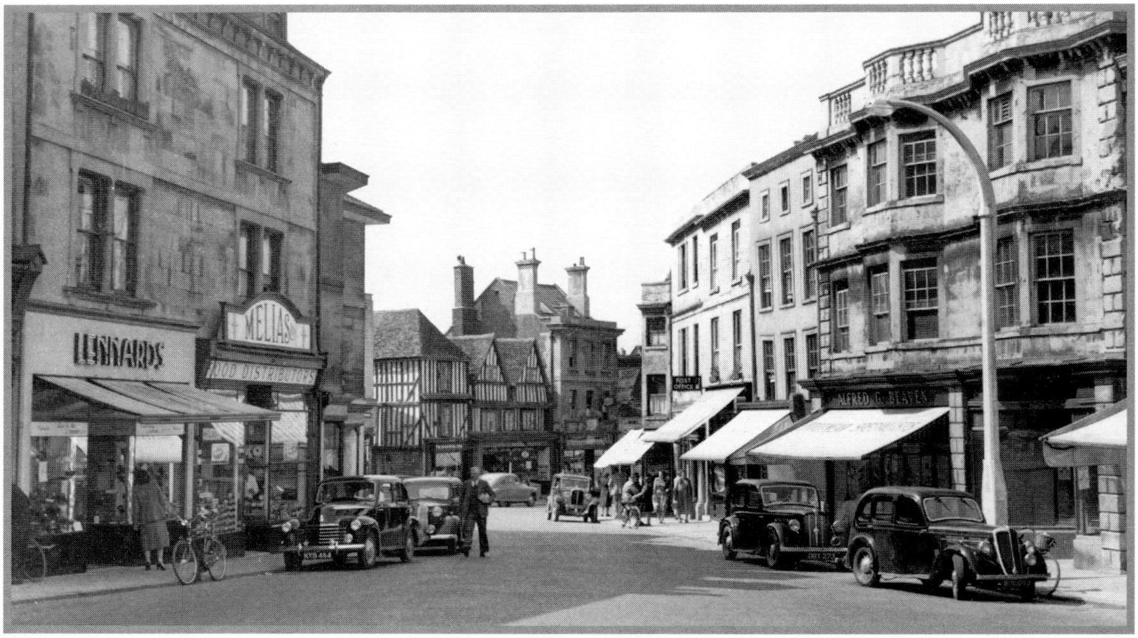

CHIPPENHAM, HIGH STREET c1955 C294032
Chippenham High Street is much changed today. The street is closed to traffic, Lennards on the left is now a solicitors and the drab building to the right has been spruced up. The striking half-timbered buildings in the centre no longer exist. Melias' decorative shop sign is a fine example of the sign-writer's art.

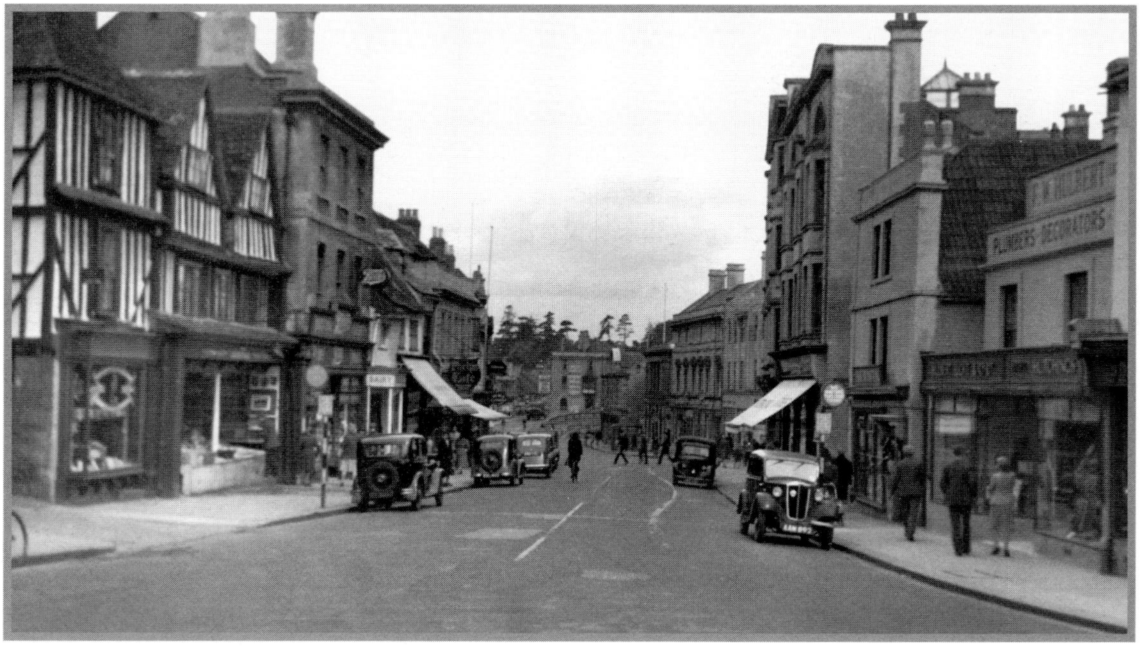

CHIPPENHAM, HIGH STREET c1955 C294004
A closer view (taken at the same time) of the timber-framed buildings in the High Street which have now disappeared. The bridge over the Avon is in the distance. On the right, a shop front has been added to an earlier building. From the pavement the change would be almost invisible.

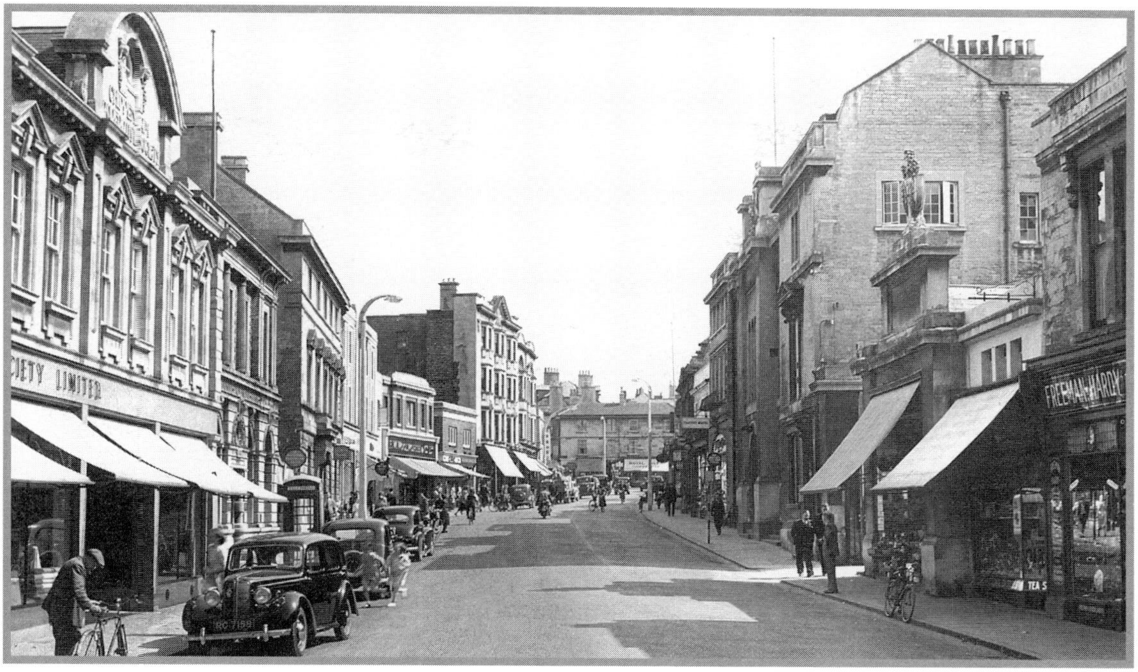

CHIPPENHAM, HIGH STREET c1955 C294038

CHIPPENHAM
High Street c1955

Another view of the High Street, looking in the opposite direction. The ornate building on the left is no longer The Chippenham Co-operative Society, but a department store. On the right is a grand stone shopfront, with decorative carving at the top.

CHIPPENHAM
Market Place c1960

The wide street indicates its use as a market place. The half-timbered building is the Old Yelde Hall, the former Town Hall; it is now a museum. This island of buildings is known as The Shambles. Note the impressive Doric pediment of the white building in the background.

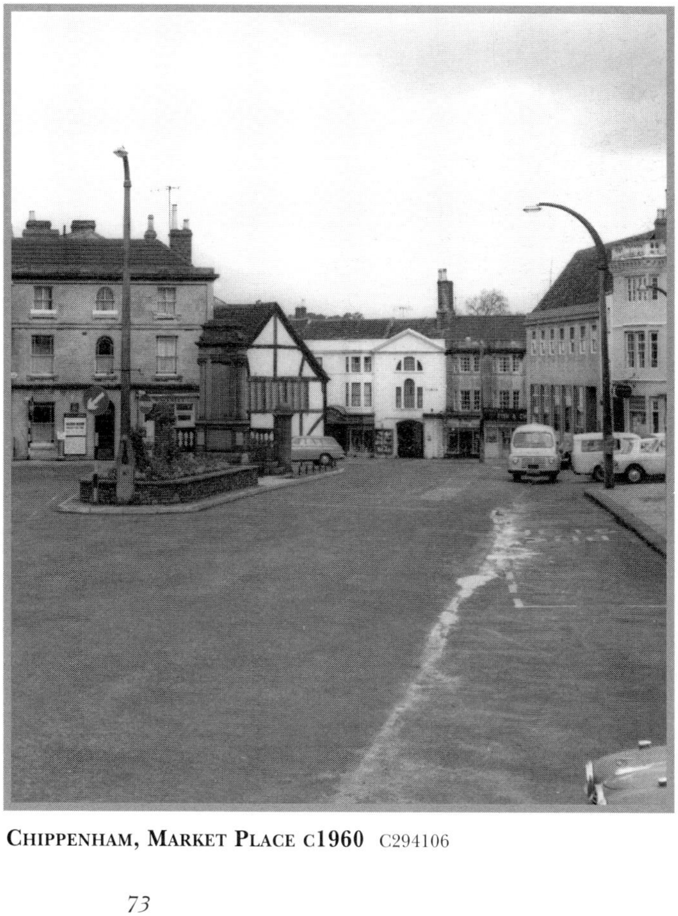

CHIPPENHAM, MARKET PLACE c1960 C294106

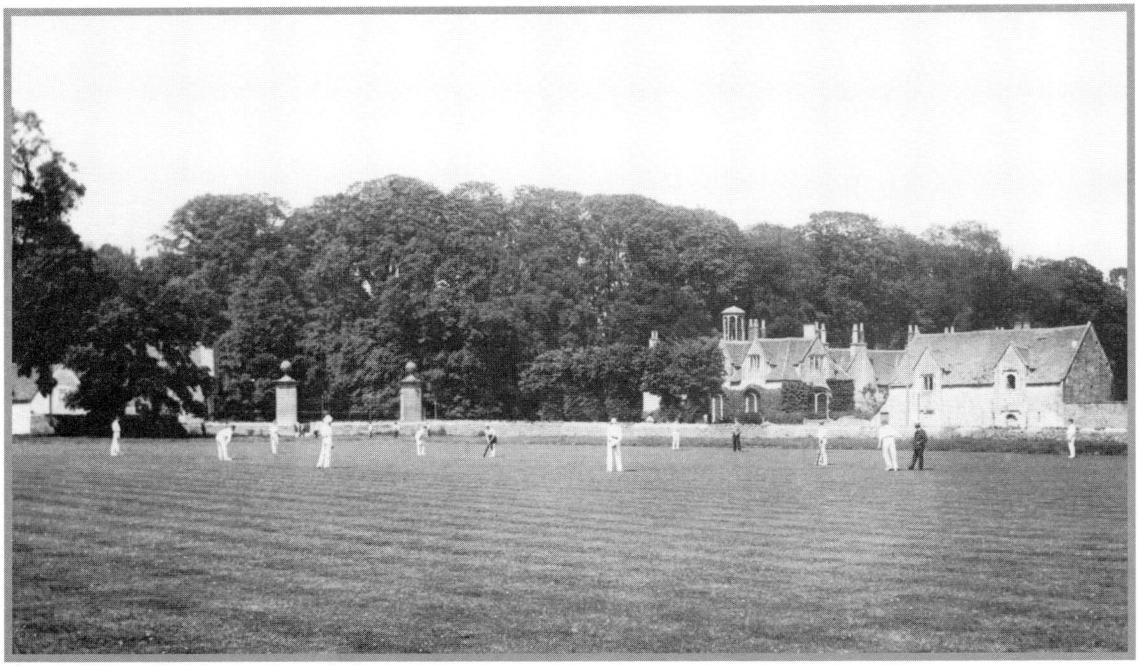

CORSHAM, THE CRICKET MATCH 1904 51479A
This possibly romantic view of rural England is balanced by the Hungerford Almshouses, built during the Jacobean period in 1668, which were charitable institutions to house the poor, and which overlook the cricket field.

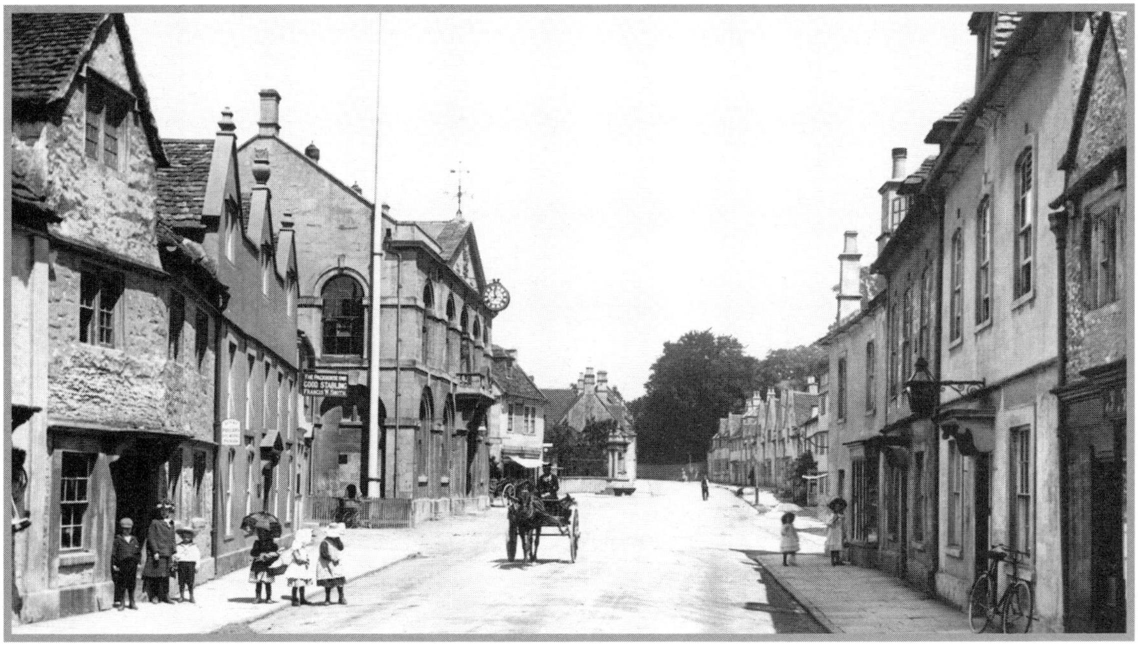

CORSHAM, HIGH STREET 1904 51469
Much of this area is unchanged today: it is an attractive combination of golden stone buildings from the 17th and 18th centuries. The Town Hall with its clock is on the left. In the distance on the right, the delightful Flemish weavers' cottages still exist today.

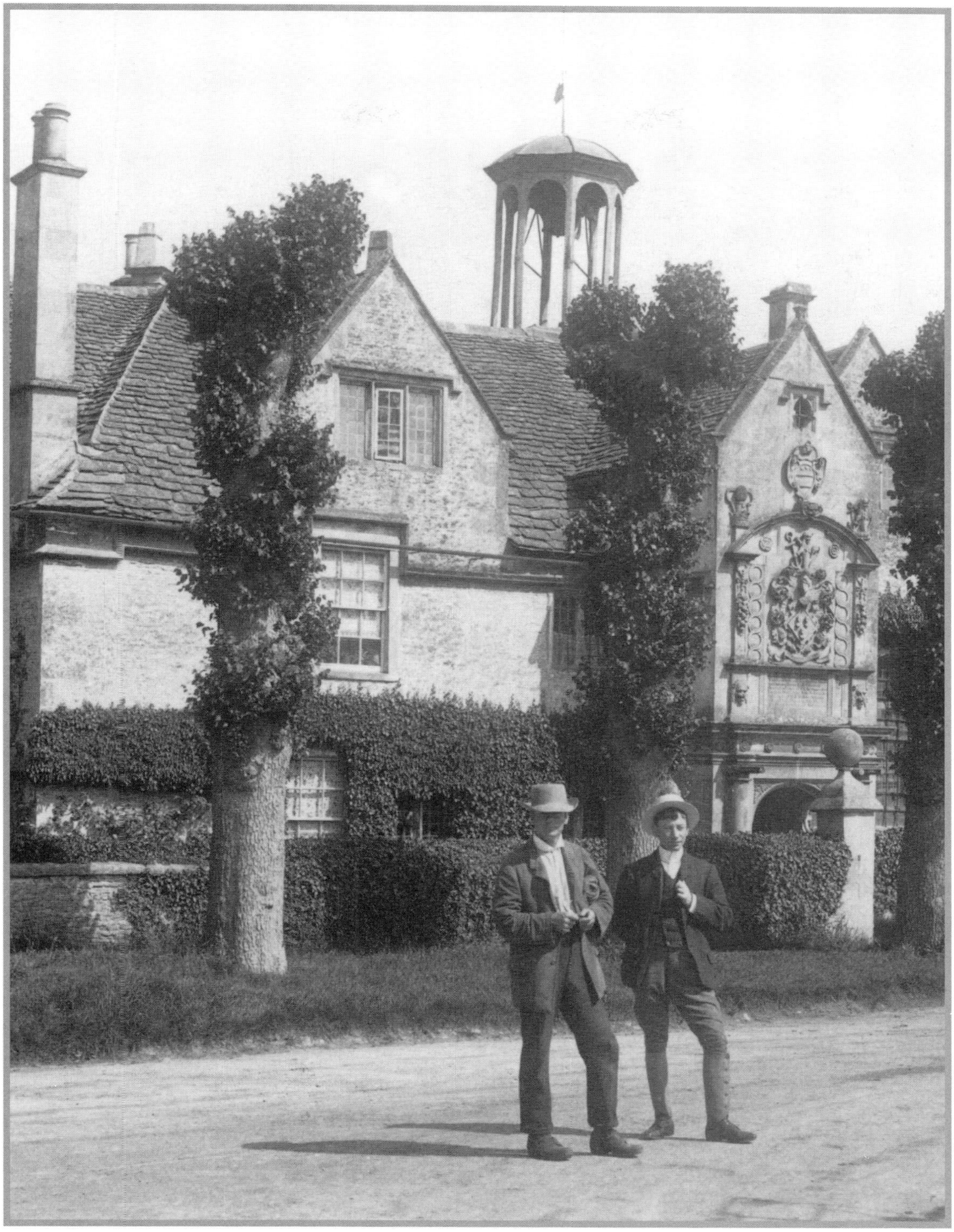

Corsham, The Almshouses 1906 54353
One of the architectural treasures of Corsham is the Hungerford Almshouses and their school. Note the Baroque pediment and coat-of-arms over the entrance. Two jauntily-dressed young men pose for the camera.

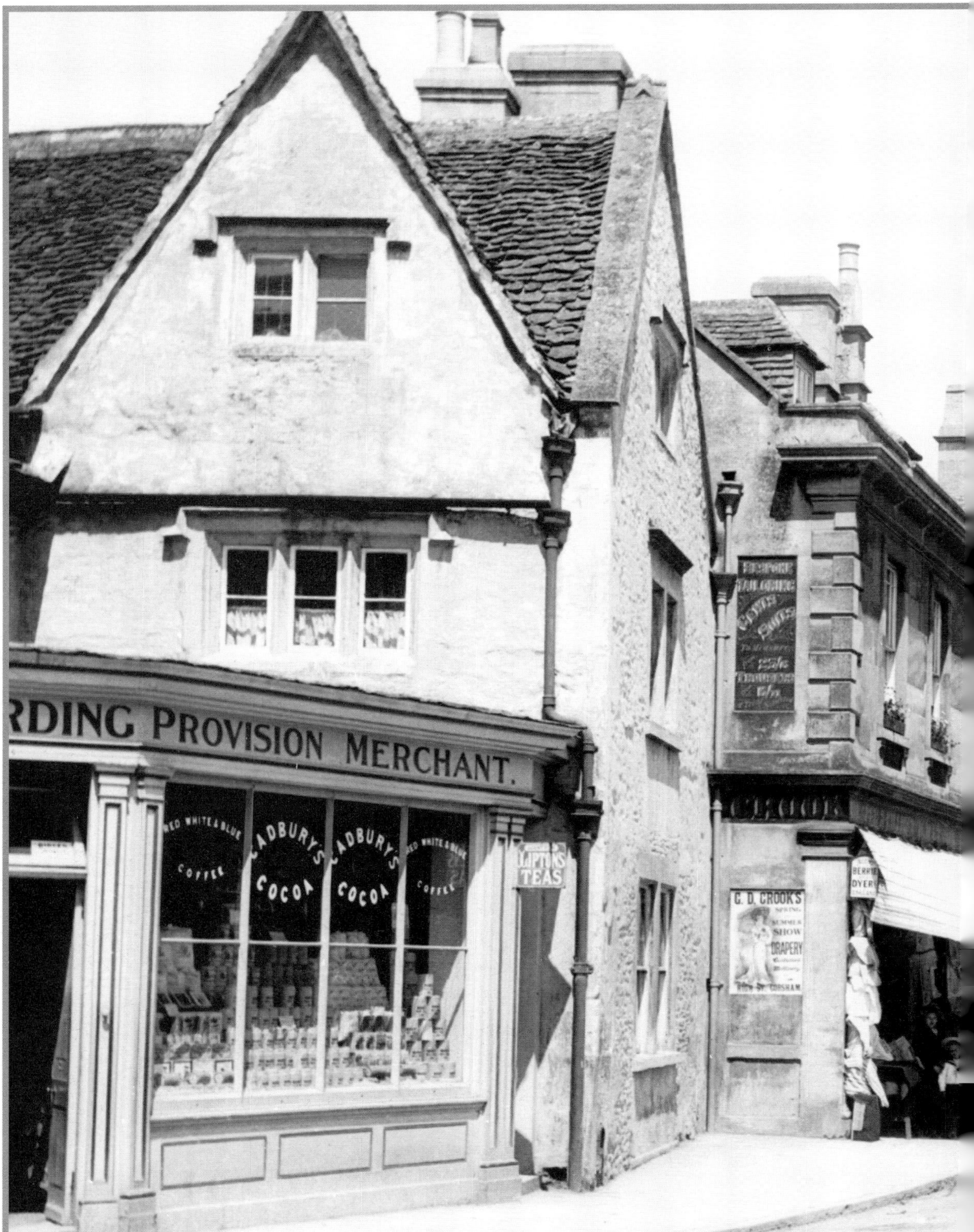
RDING PROVISION MERCHANT.
RED WHITE & BLUE COFFEE
ADBURY'S COCOA
ADBURY'S COCOA
RED WHITE & BLUE COFFEE
LIPTON'S TEAS
G. D. CROOK'S
SHOW
DRAPERY

Corsham

High Street 1904 51471

This view shows the top of the High Street at a time when horse transport was the norm. The busy shop window on the left advertises Cadburys Cocoa and Liptons Teas. The awnings are down over the shop window next door. A family, one of the children in a smart sailor suit, shelters from the sun.

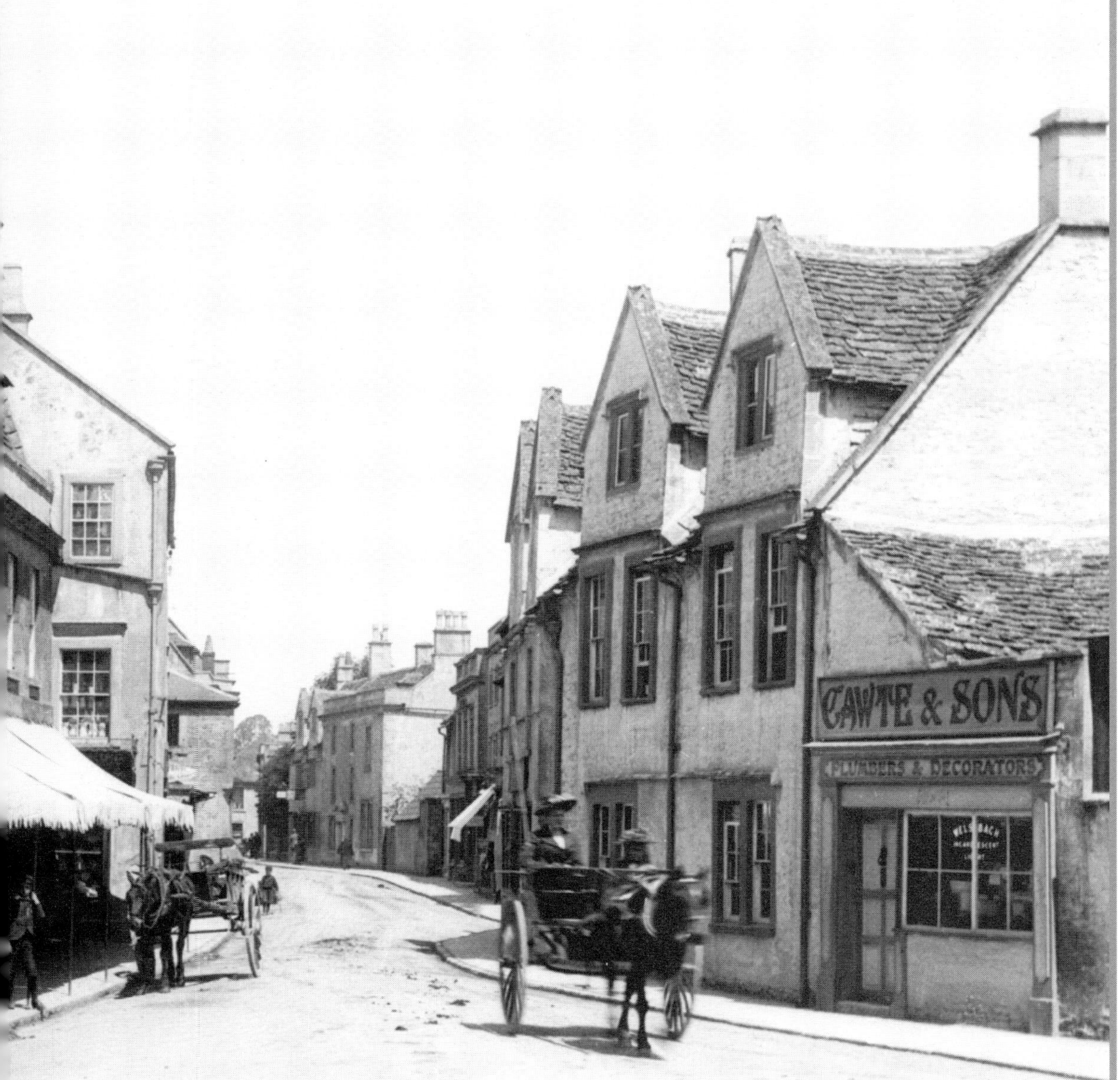

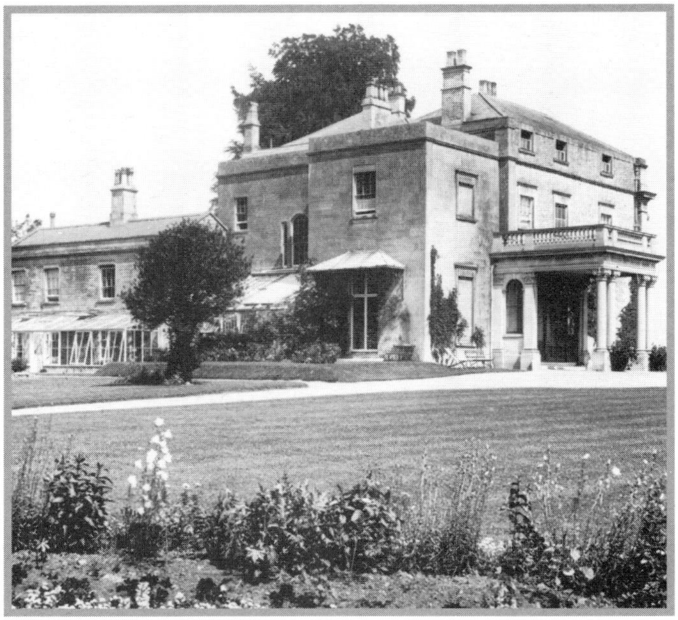

CORSHAM, MONKS PARK 1906 53924

CORSHAM, MONKS PARK 1906 53924
When this photograph was taken, Monks Park was on its own to the south of Corsham. Today, the village has become a town, the road alongside carries traffic and the scene has dramatically changed.

DEVIZES, THE CASTLE 1898 42309
Devizes Castle was originally a Norman motte and bailey fortification, but was rebuilt in 1120, possibly by Bishop Osmund of Salisbury. It then fell into ruin. The castle today, with its round towers, oriel windows and battlemented walls, belongs to the 19th century.

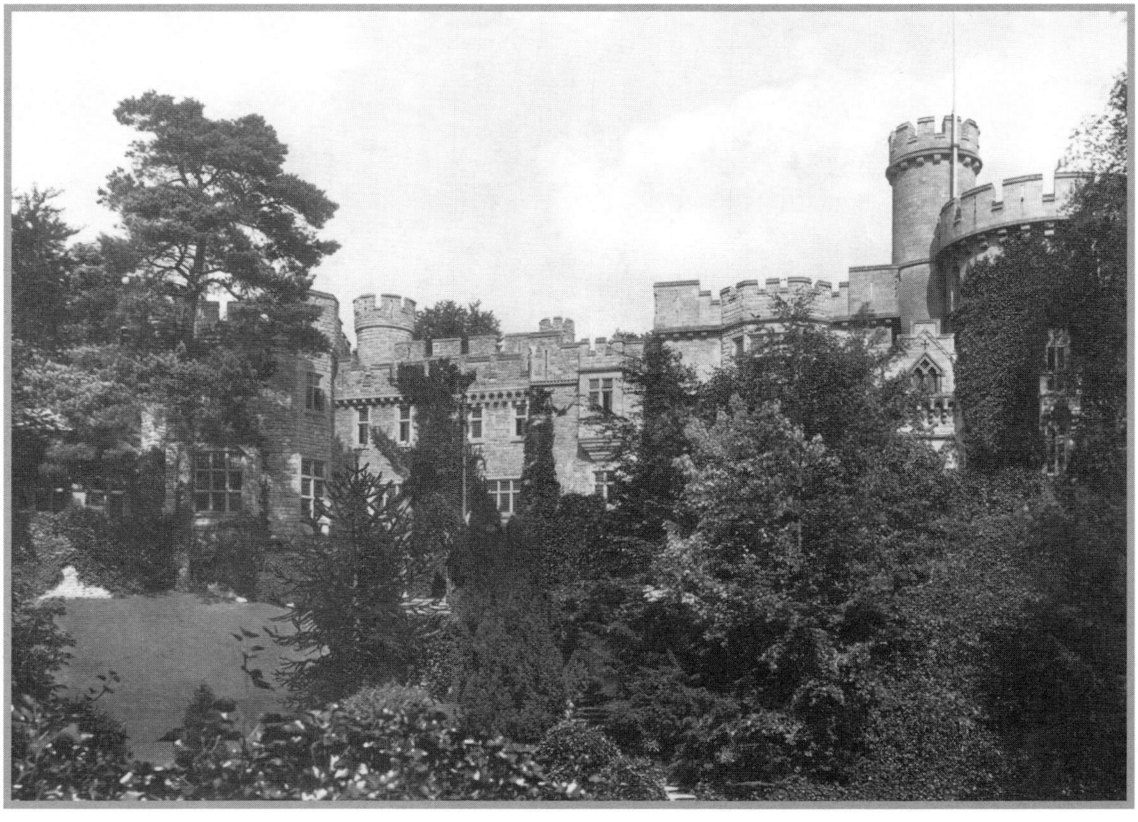

DEVIZES, THE CASTLE 1898 42309

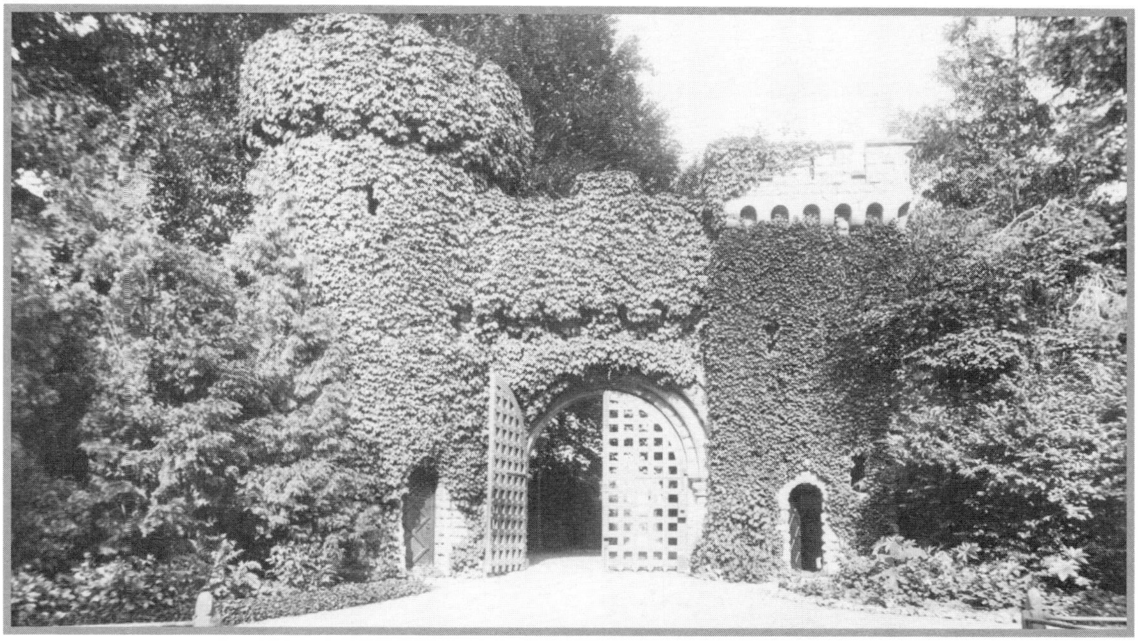

Devizes, The Castle 1898 42307

Devizes Castle today is a Victorian reconstruction by a Bath architect, H E Goodridge. The foliage-covered walls and gate present an attractive and imposing building. However, it has never played a significant part in the history of the town.

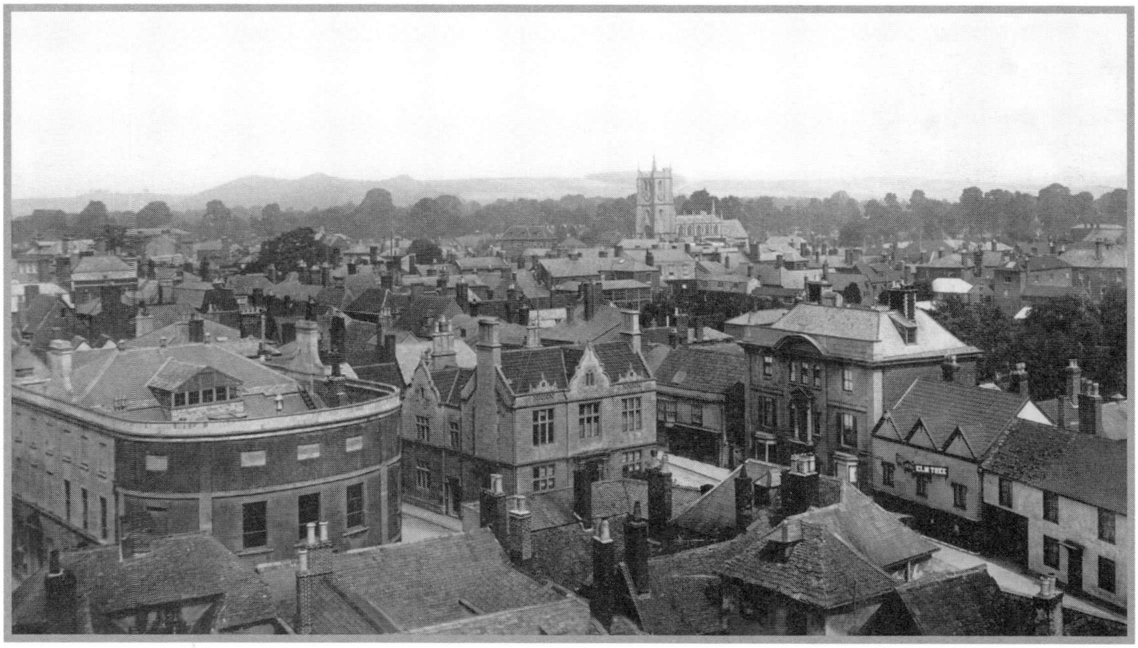

Devizes, View from St John's Church 1898 42306

Gothic, Jacobean, classical and domestic architecture testify to the history of the town's development. Note the attractive, almost Flemish gabling of the building in the centre of the picture. The impressive tower of the church rises over the town roofs.

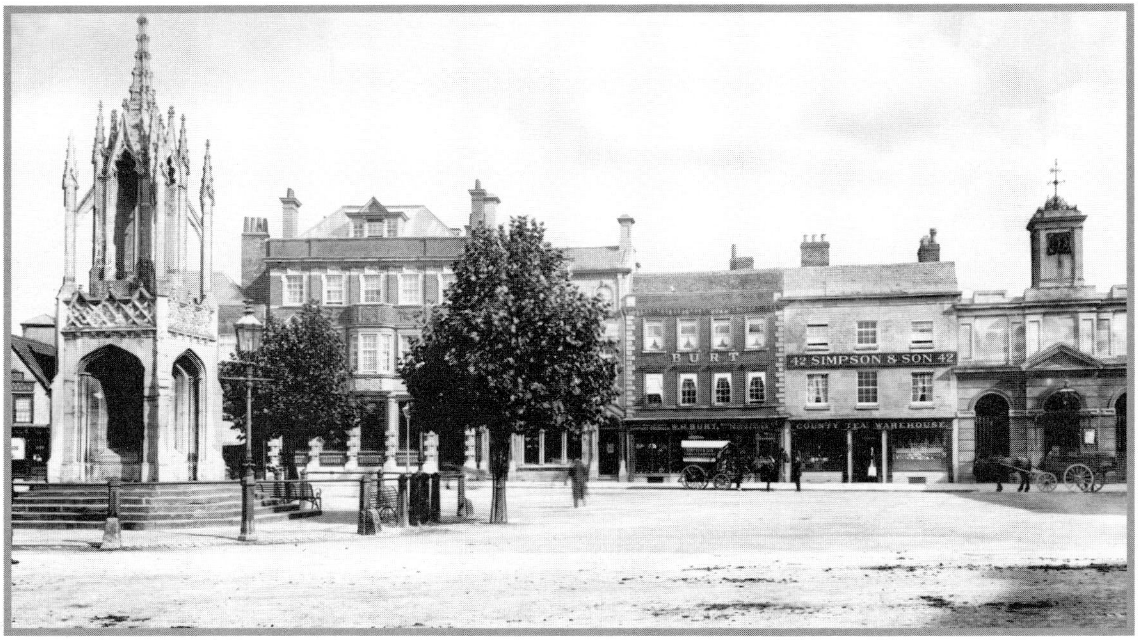

DEVIZES, MARKET PLACE 1899 44845
The large Market Place, with many fine Georgian buildings, is the central feature of Devizes. Benjamin Wyatt's 1814 Market Cross is a delight. The inscription tells us that a Ruth Pierce asked heaven to strike her dead if she had lied about money. Heaven did what she asked - as the inscription tells, 'She instantly fell and expired'.

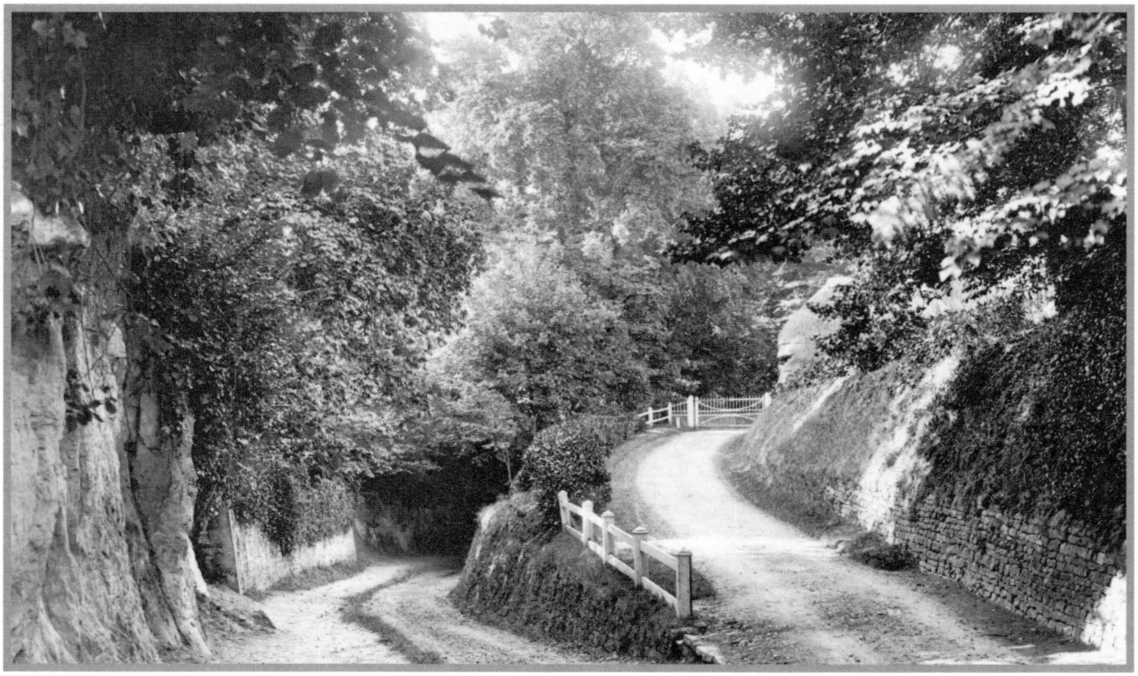

DEVIZES, HARTMOOR 1899 44846
The Hartmoor area of Devizes lies to the south. This photograph is a revealing view of old England. The unsurfaced roads and thickly wooded banks climb down the steep slopes at the end of the Vale of Pewsey.

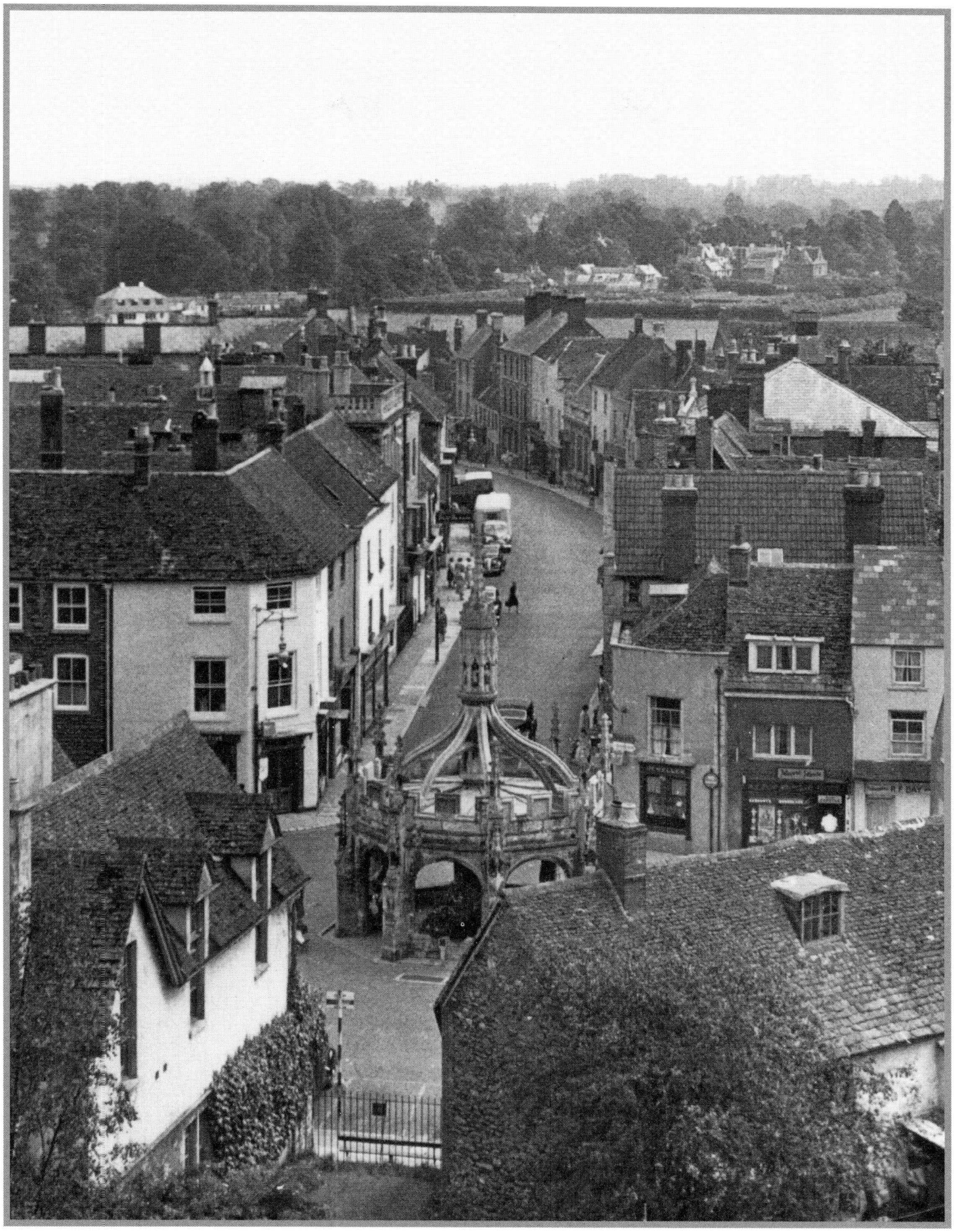

MALMESBURY, c1955 M13020

An overview of one of the oldest boroughs in England, looking towards the High Street from the abbey. The octagonal Gothic market cross is 16th century, the remains of the abbey itself are largely Norman.

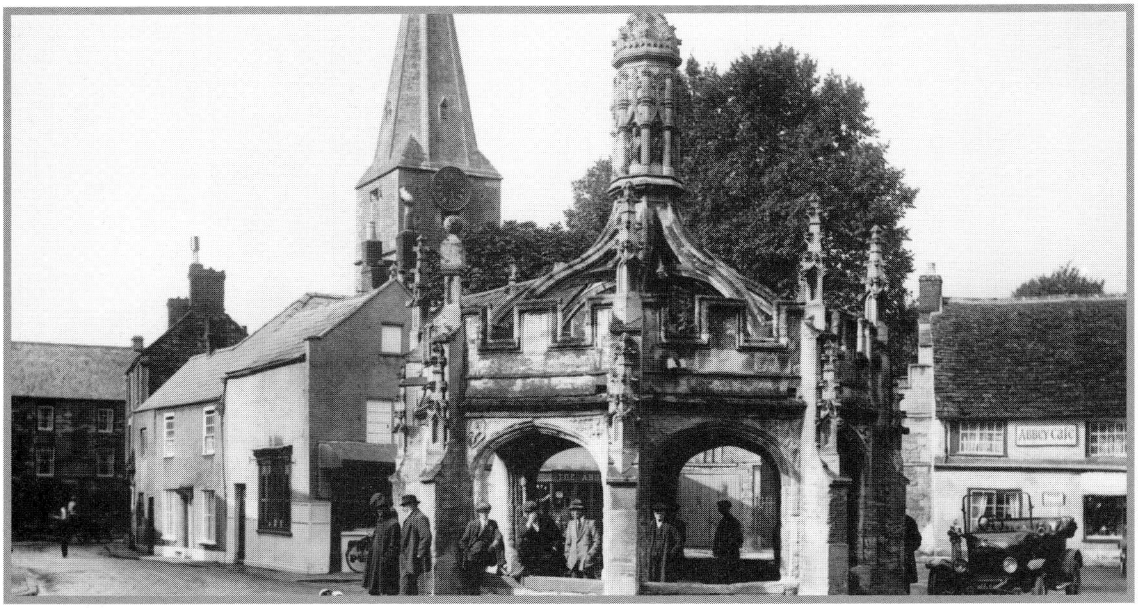

MALMESBURY, MARKET CROSS 1924 76145
The market cross was showing its age when it was completely restored in 1980 as part of the celebrations marking the town's 1100th anniversary. John Leland (c1506-1552) was King's Antiquary when he visited Malmesbury and described the cross as '...for poore folkes to stande dry when the rain cummeth'. The tower of St Paul's church is behind the trees.

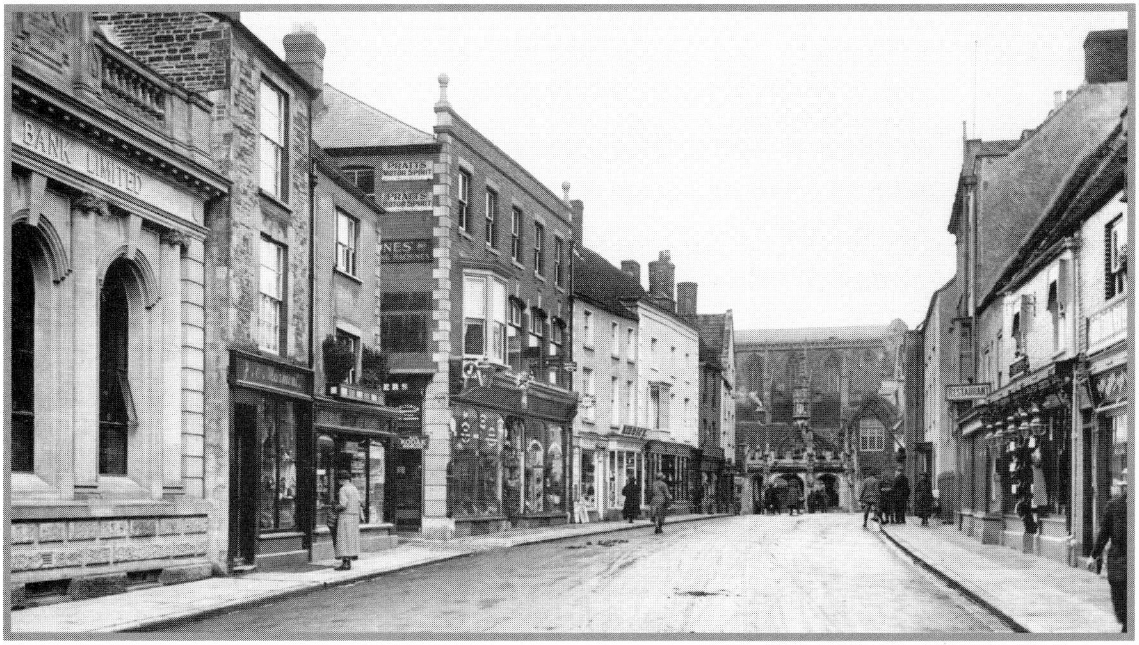

MALMESBURY, MAIN STREET 1924 76144
A view of the High Street, looking towards the abbey and market cross. Everybody is wearing either a hat or cap, the road is not surfaced, and there is a virtual absence of street lighting. The massive bulk of the ancient abbey walls rise close the vista in the distance.

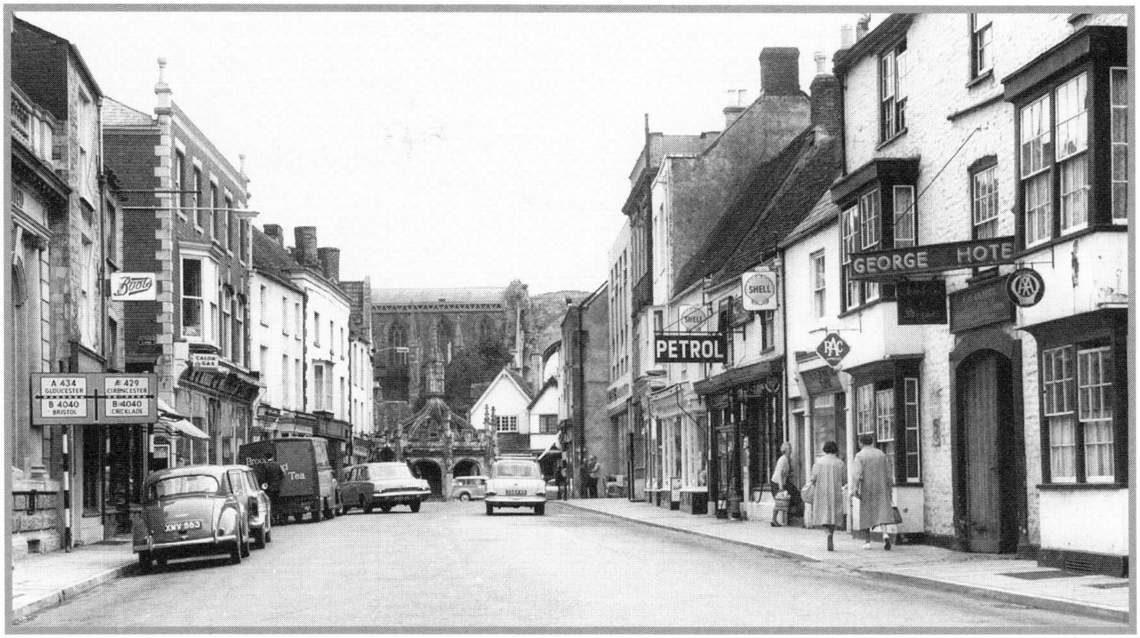

MALMESBURY, HIGH STREET c1960 M13070
Consider the visual impact made by the motor car in forty years by comparing the traffic, the signs, the shop fronts and the street furniture. Note the quaint petrol station on the right. Also on the right is the arched coach entrance to the George Hotel.

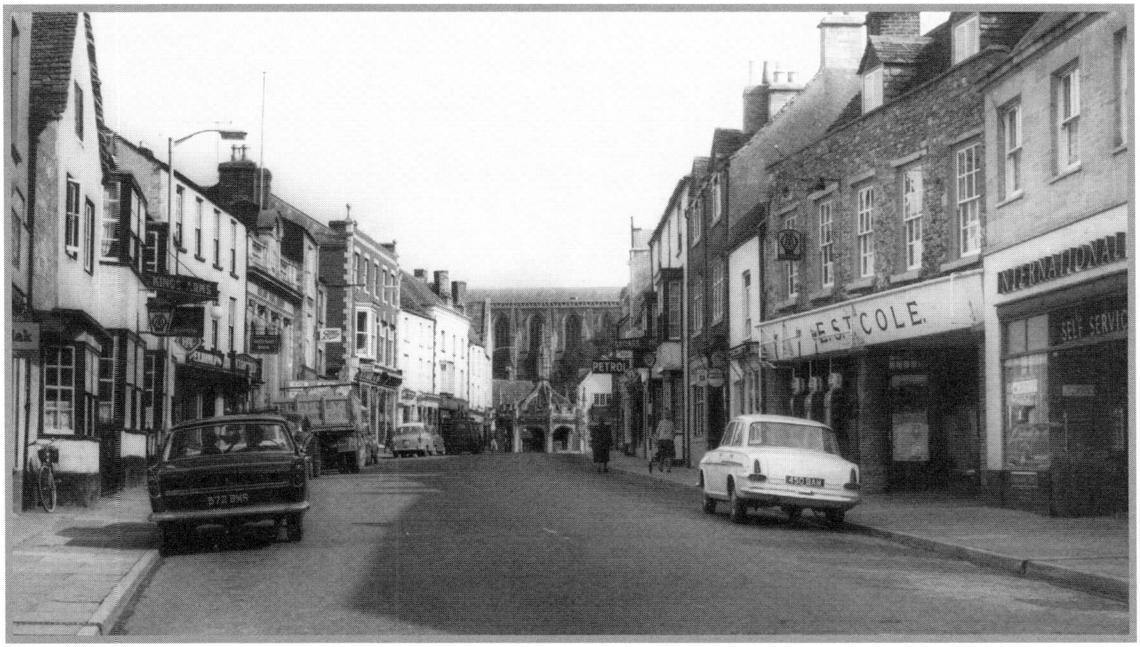

MALMESBURY, HIGH STREET c1960 M13063
This view reveals the piecemeal alterations to buildings that are so characteristic of our small country towns. On the right a flat façade has been added to an earlier cottage-style building, probably in the late Georgian period. The lower half of the building has been unsympathetically altered more recently to accommodate petrol pumps.

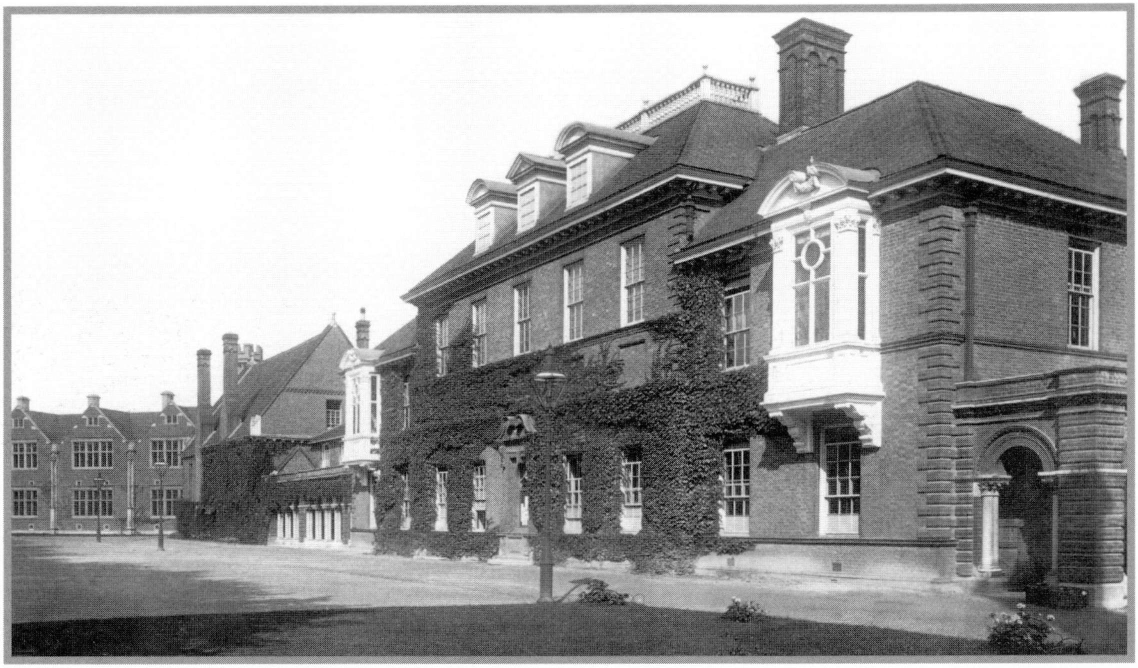

MARLBOROUGH, THE COLLEGE, MUSEUM BLOCK 1901 47659
Marlborough College, the prestigious public school, was founded in 1843 close to the river Kennet and the site of the old castle. One of the houses was located in a 1700 mansion built by the Duke of Somerset.

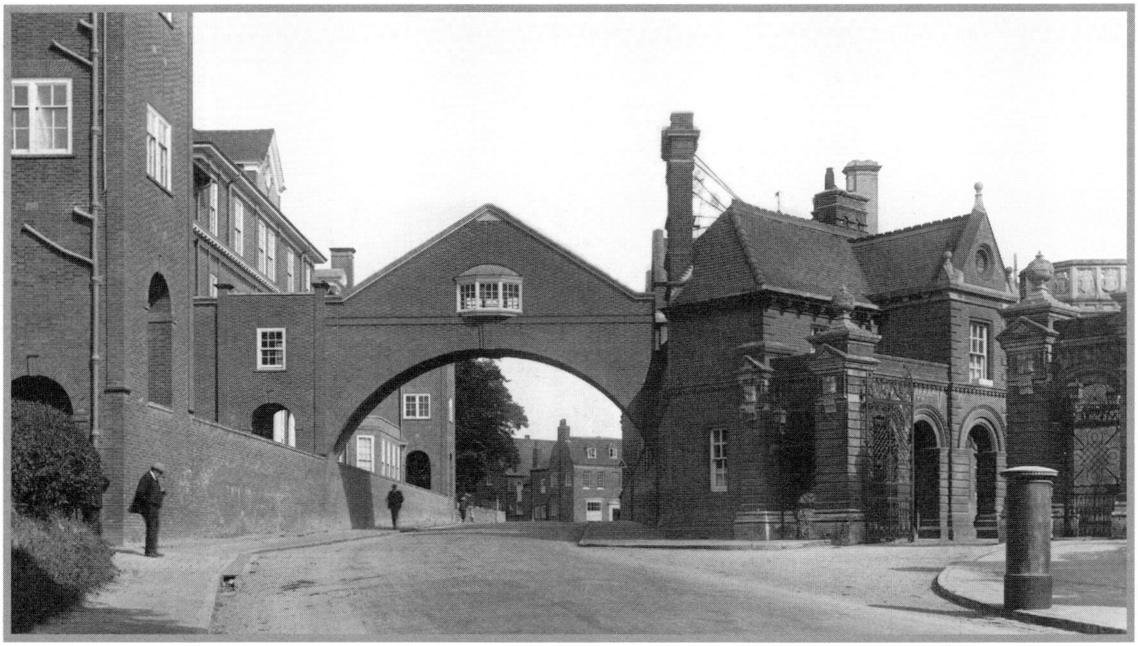

MARLBOROUGH, THE COLLEGE 1923 74456
An enclosed bridge crosses the A4 Bath road. The entrance to the College is to the right. The dark red brick gives the college buildings a serious and imposing air. The pillar box still exists, although it has been moved back against the wall.

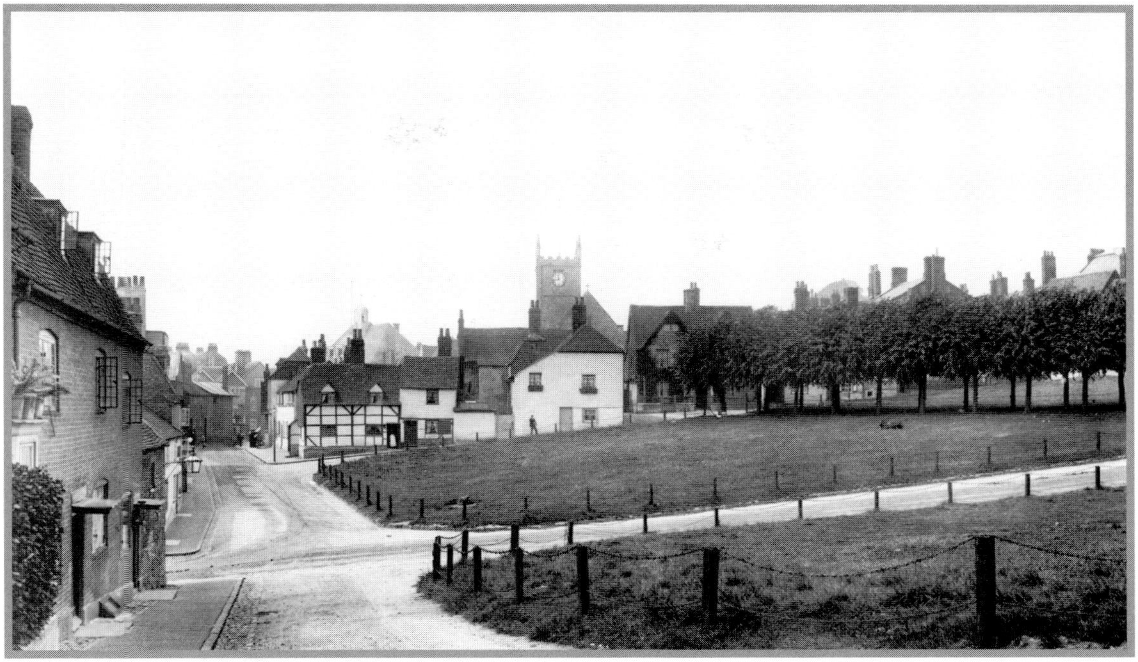

Marlborough, The Green 1902 48638
Today, nearly a century later, the view is instantly recognisable, with the tower of St Mary the Virgin's church in the centre and the Town Hall a little to the left. The trees still stand, although now they are pollarded.

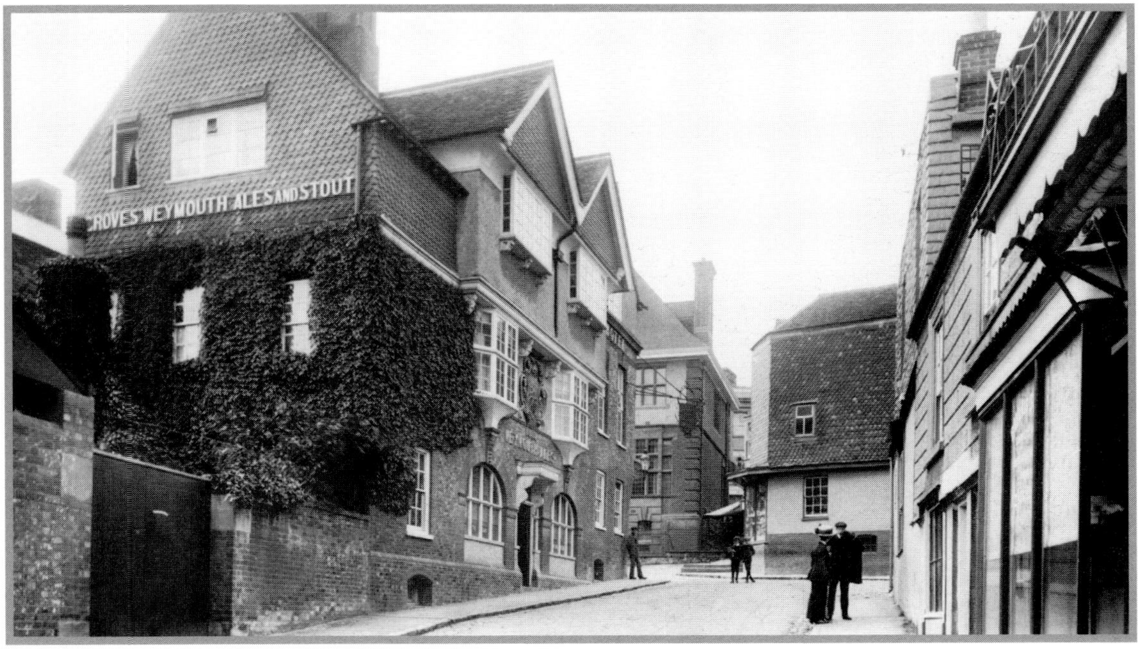

Marlborough, The Parade and Bear and Castle Hotel 1910 62456
The central feature - The Bear - still trades today, but Groves Weymouth Ales and Stouts do not. The tall chimney in the middle of the picture is the rear of the Town Hall. Pupils at Marlborough College were then expected to wear boaters.

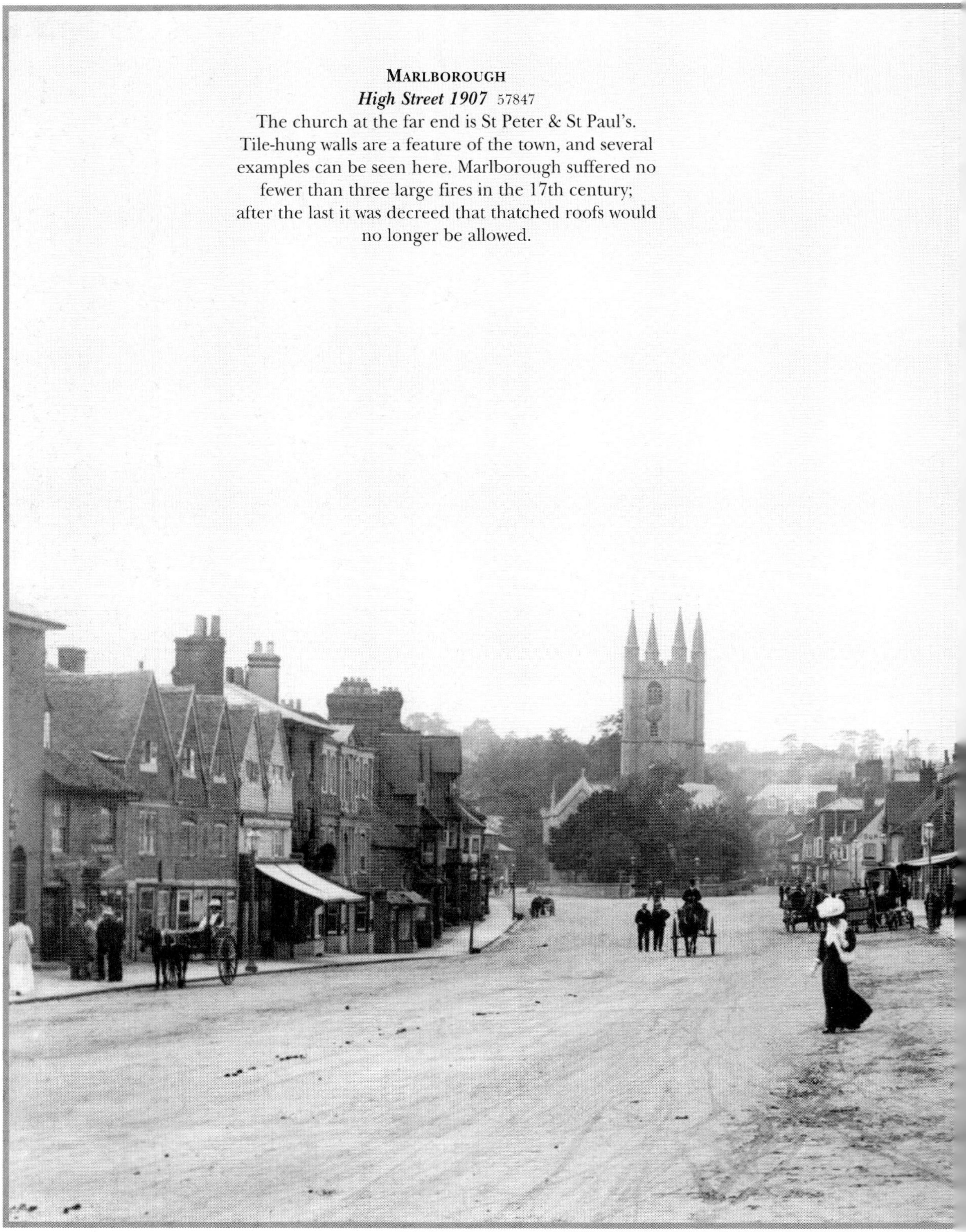

MARLBOROUGH
High Street 1907 57847
The church at the far end is St Peter & St Paul's. Tile-hung walls are a feature of the town, and several examples can be seen here. Marlborough suffered no fewer than three large fires in the 17th century; after the last it was decreed that thatched roofs would no longer be allowed.

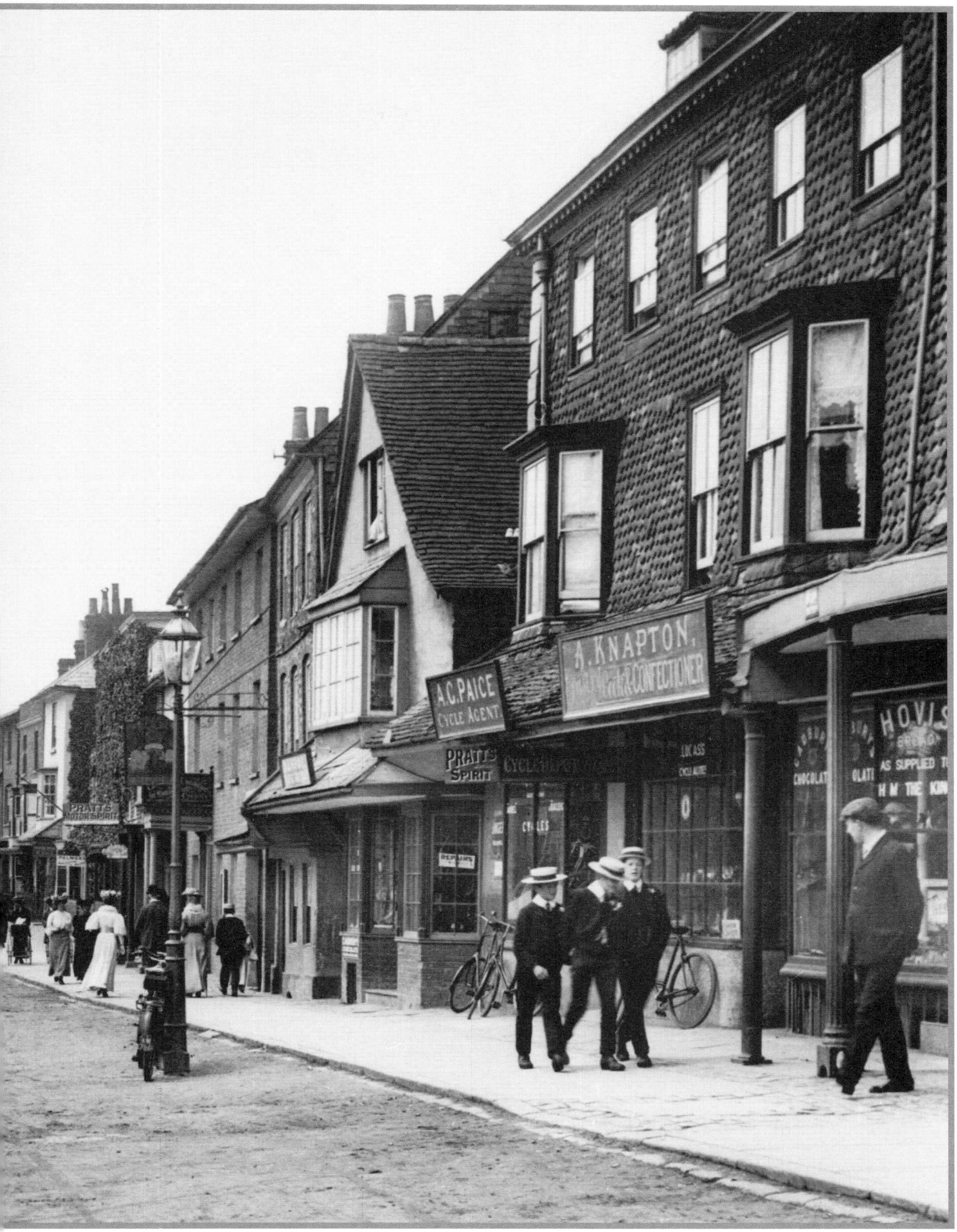
A.C. PAICE
CYCLE AGENT
A. KNAPTON,
CONFECTIONER
PRATTS
SPIRIT
HOVIS
AS SUPPLIED TO

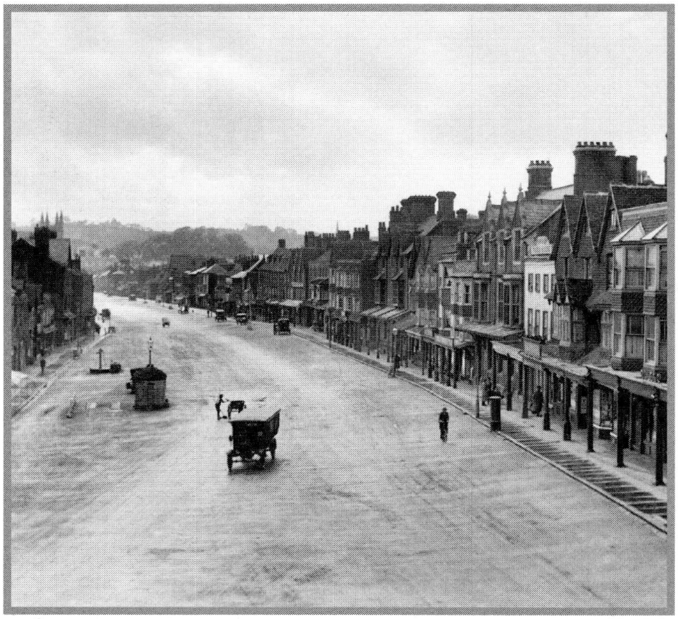

MARLBOROUGH, HIGH STREET 1923 74453

MARLBOROUGH
High Street 1923

A wide High Street was essential for the movement of sheep on market days. The unmetalled road shows that despite the presence of some motorised vehicles, the age of the car was still distant. The south-facing colonnaded Georgian shops form an attractive feature.

MARLBOROUGH
High Street 1907

The High Street, this time looking east towards the (then) new Town Hall. The church building in the distance is St Mary's, whose north wall still carries scars said to be of a lesser civil war skirmish fought here. During restoration work on the building, a Roman statue to the goddess Fortuna was discovered.

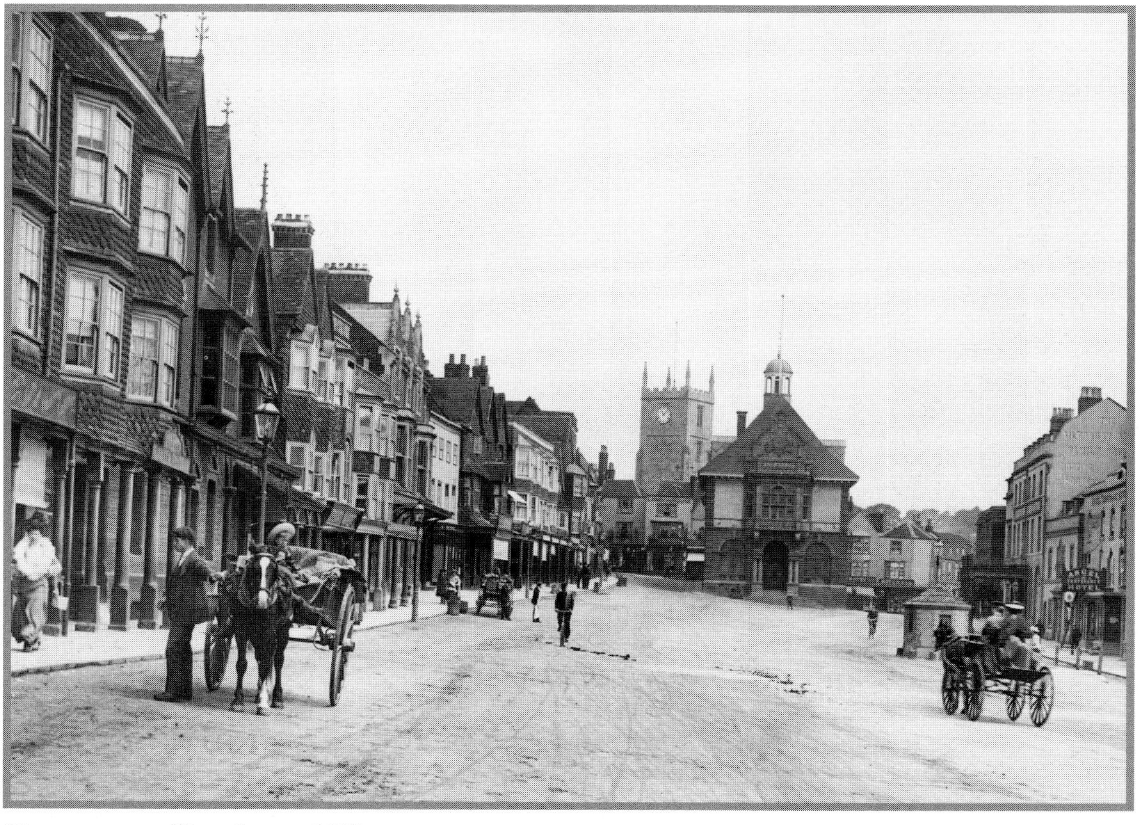

MARLBOROUGH, HIGH STREET 1907 57846

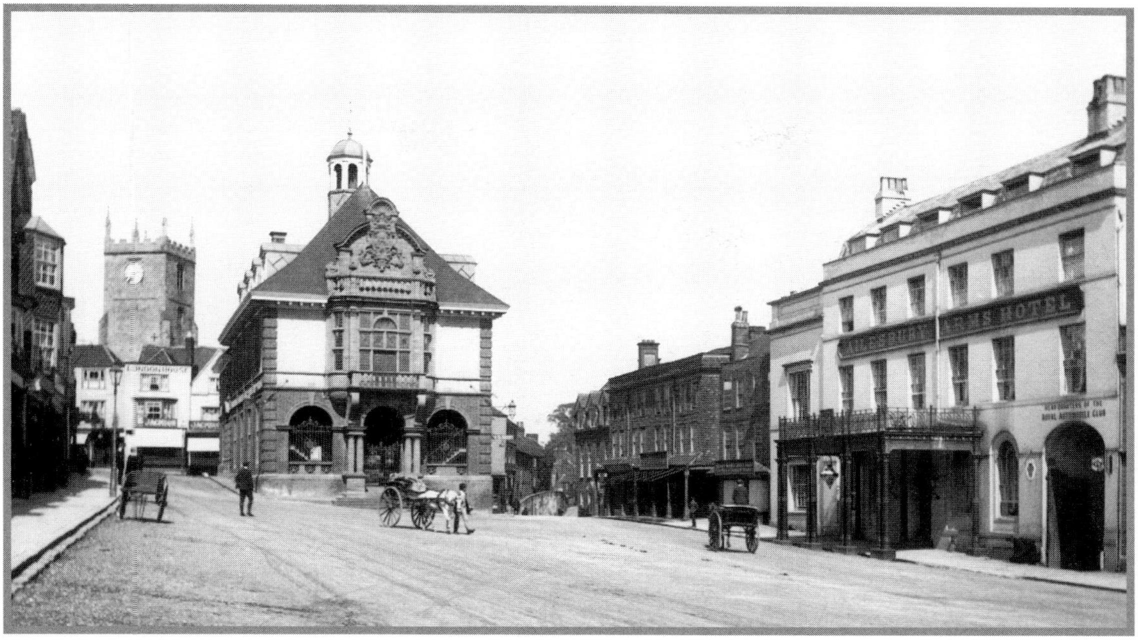

Marlborough, High Street 1910 62455
The present Town Hall building is the latest in a succession located at the top of the wide High Street on the site of the old Market Cross. The Ailesbury Arms hotel is still on site, although much changed and renamed Ailsebury Court.

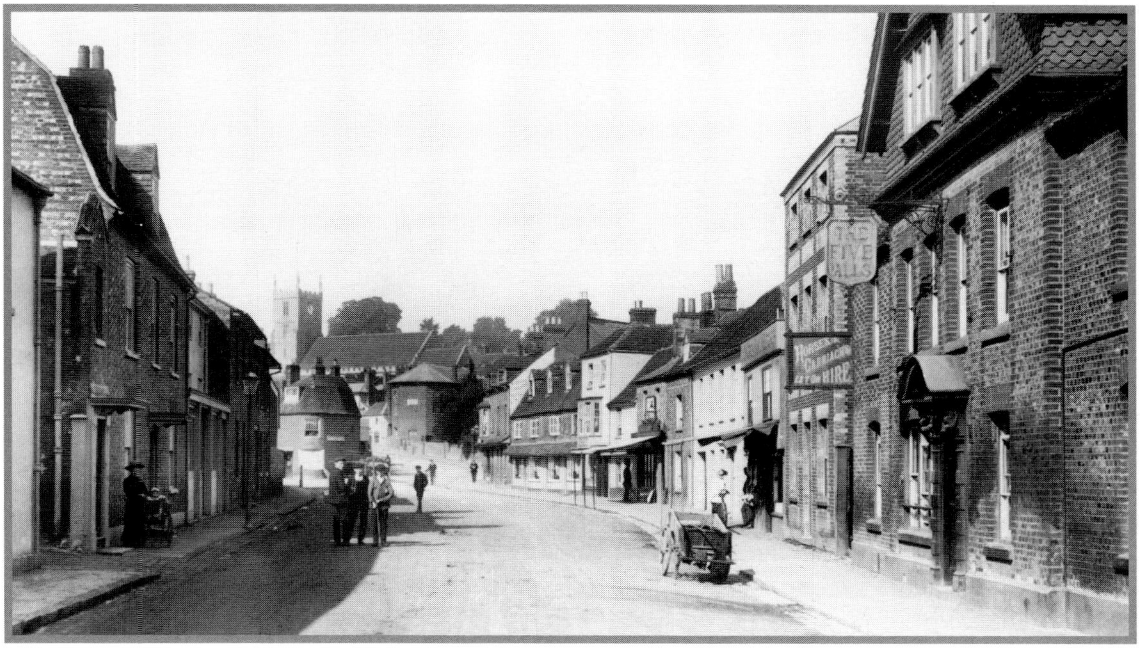

Marlborough, Street Scene 1908 60943
The Five Alls Pub in New London Road can still be seen with the same interesting name . The central figure is a king with the legend ' I rule for all'. Others are a lawyer: 'I plead for all', a soldier: 'I fight for all', a priest: ' I pray for all' and a labourer: 'I work for all'.

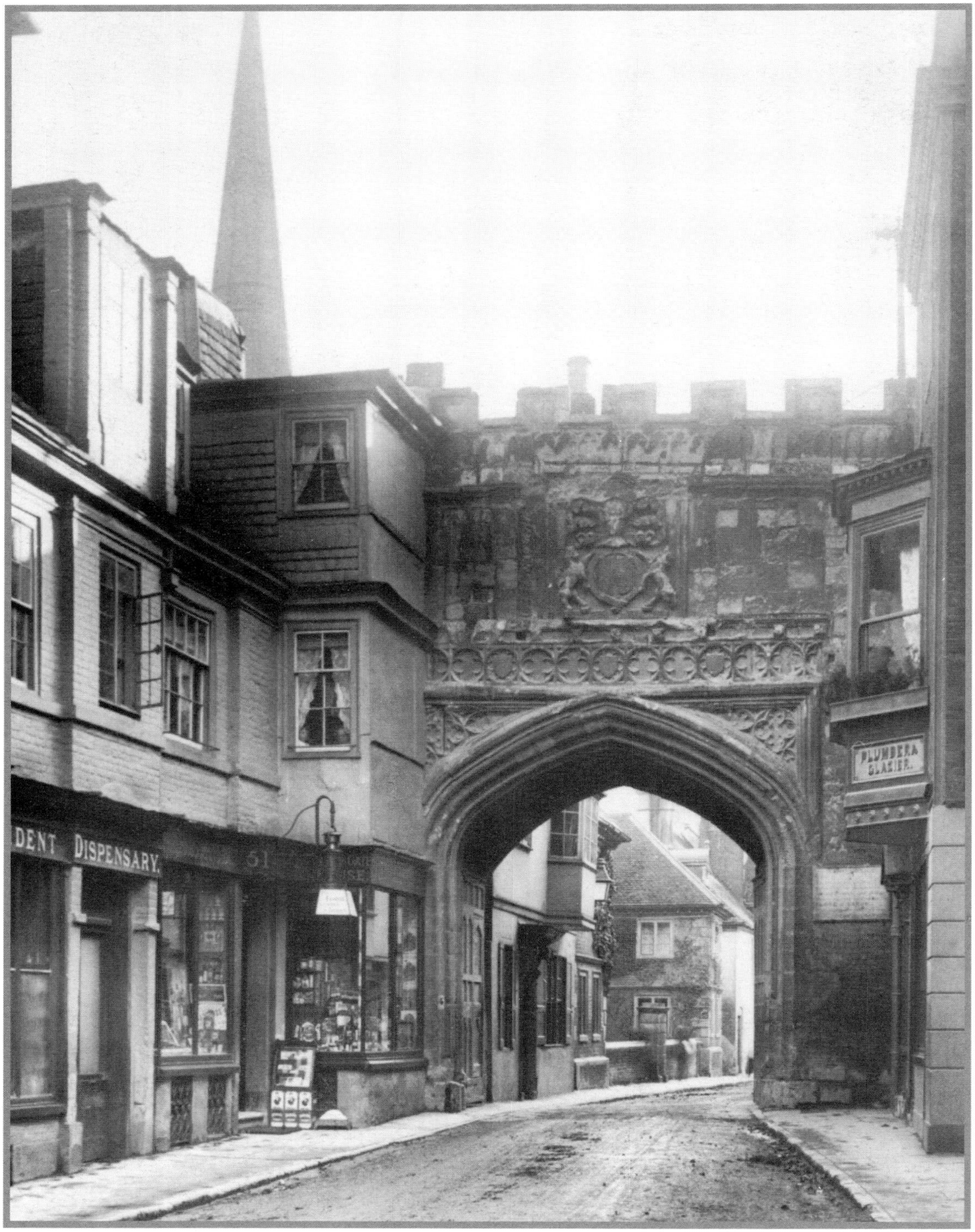

SALISBURY, HIGH STREET GATE 1894 34871
High Street Gate, also known as the North Gate, is a reminder that the city and Cathedral Close live two different lives. The 14th-century gate is shut every night, marking the boundary between city and church. Looking through the gate, the Porters Lodge and Matrons' College can be seen.

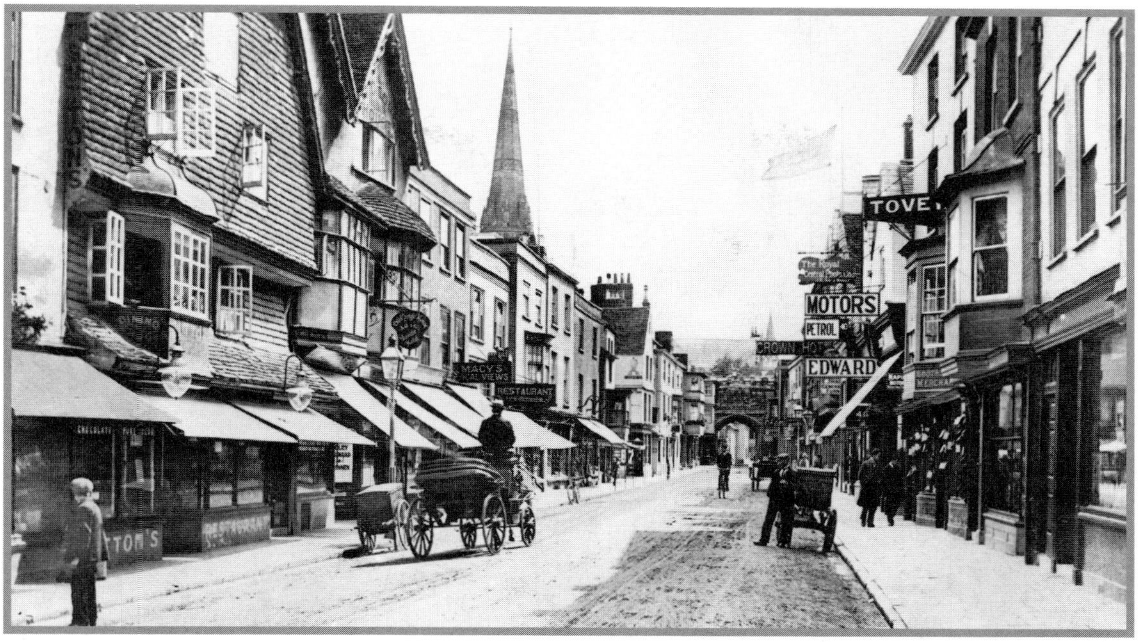

Salisbury, High Street 1906 56354

Looking towards the North Gate. It is surprising to see how quickly motor cars became available during the transition from horse to combustion engine. It was only two years earlier that the law required a man with a red flag to precede all motorised vehicles. On the left street lighting has appeared.

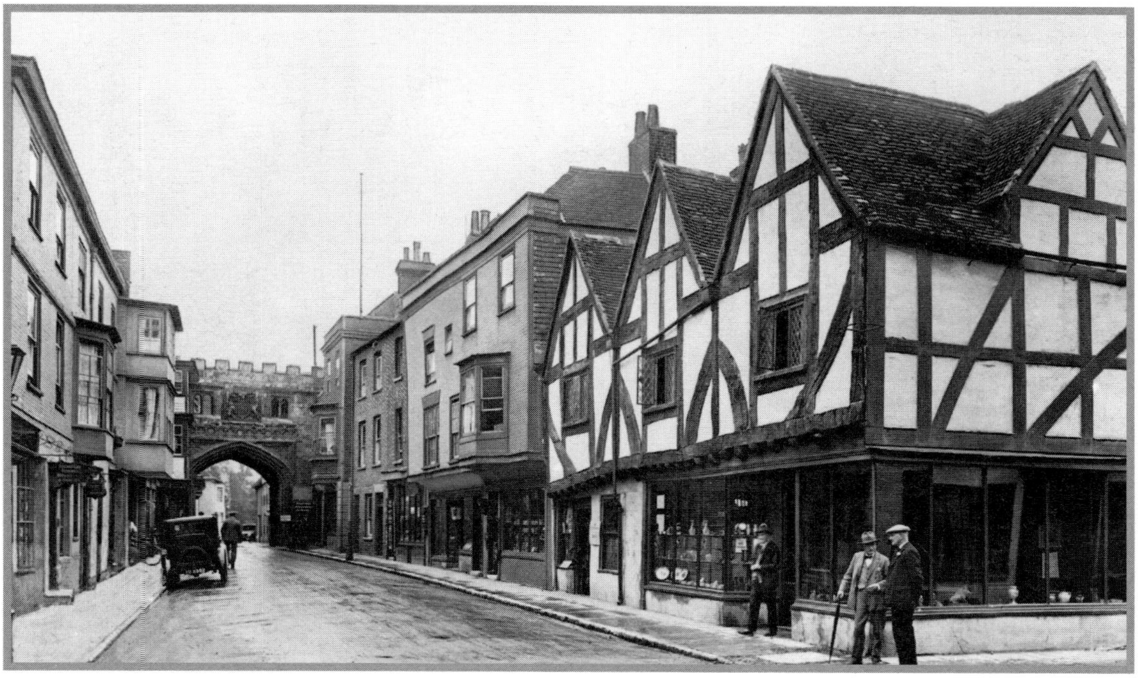

Salisbury, Old House in High Street 1928 80923

This picture shows the junction of High Street and Crane Street. The three-gabled timber-framed building on the right is 14th century, and until recently was the well-known antiquarian bookshop, Beach's.

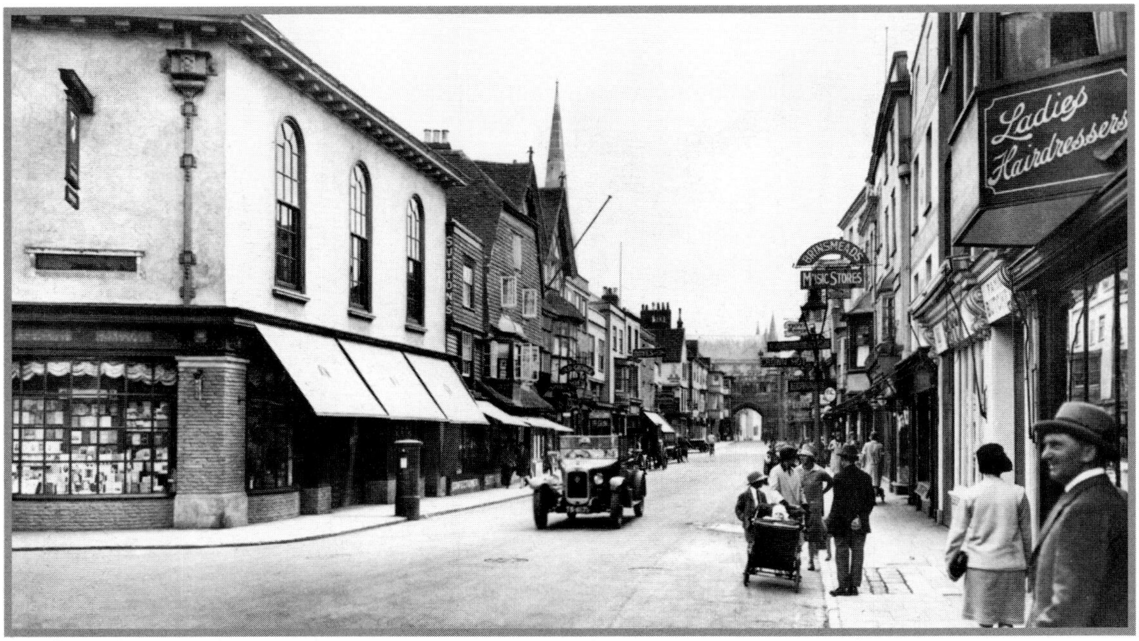

SALISBURY, HIGH STREET 1928 80922

Compare the detail of this photograph of the High Street with the one taken in 1906. Apart from the car having replaced the horse, little has changed. Even the tile-hung building on the left still has its sun blind unfurled, although the small shop next door has had the render removed.

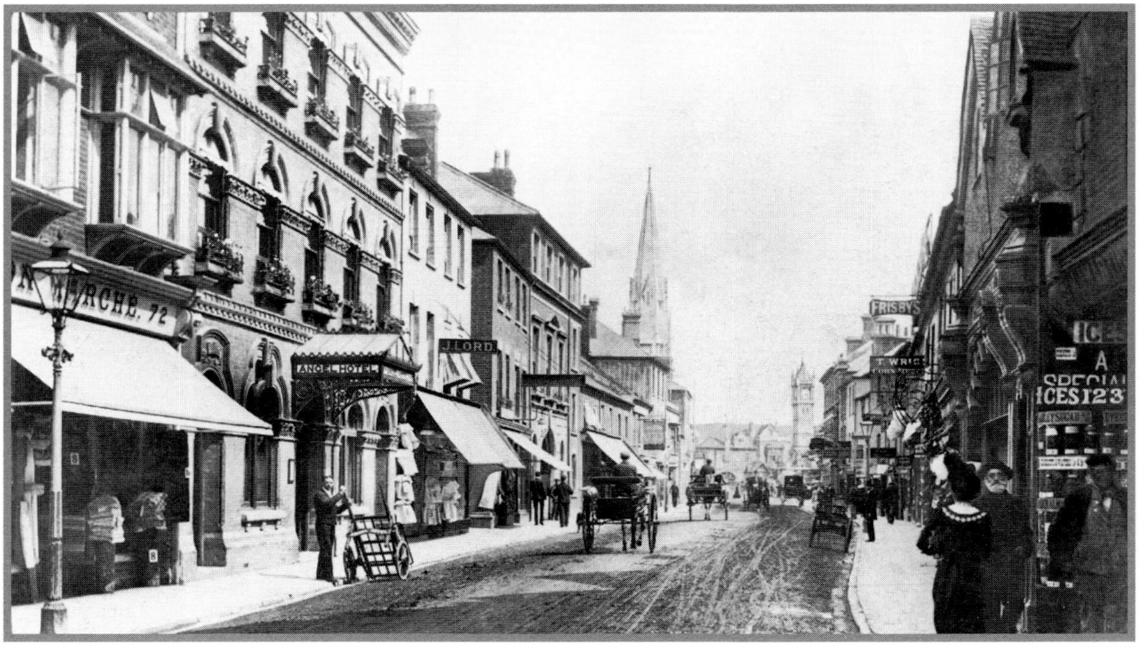

SALISBURY, FISHERTON STREET 1906 56360

The elegant Angel Hotel is no more, but at least the road is now surfaced. The ladies' long frocks in this photograph must have been impossible to keep free of stains. The spire is of the Congregational (now United Reformed) church, with the Victorian clock tower opposite on the bridge over the Avon.

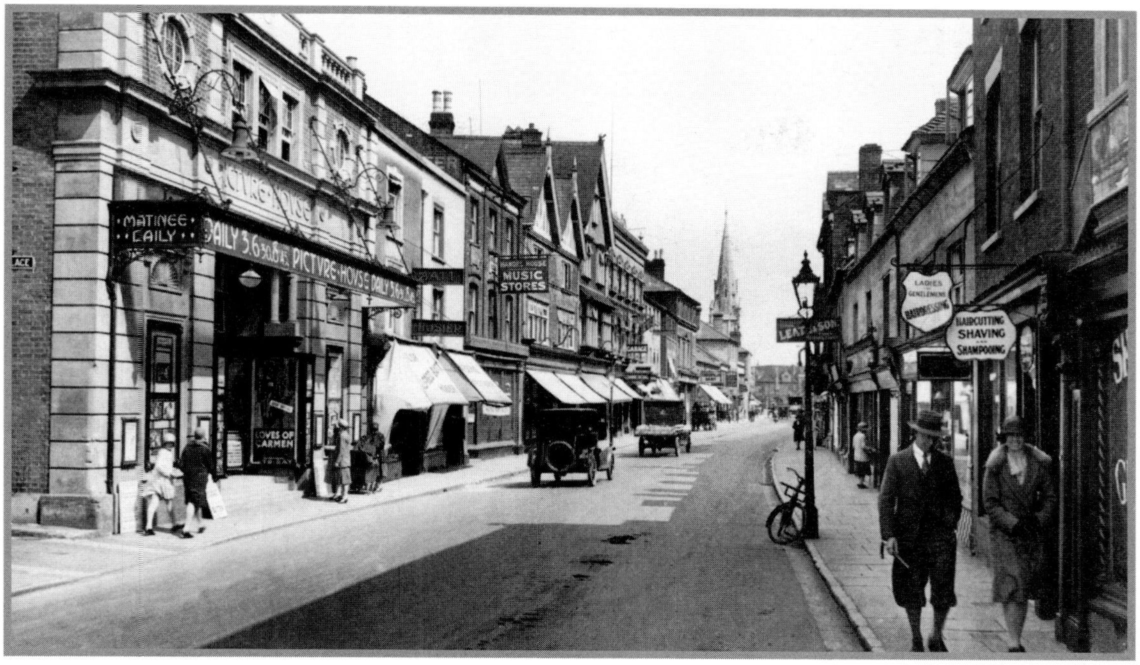

SALISBURY, FISHERTON STREET 1928 80924
The glorious Picture House is no more. After becoming the City Hall just after the last war, it was demolished, and is now occupied by a new building. That week cinema goers were enjoying 'Loves of Carmen'.

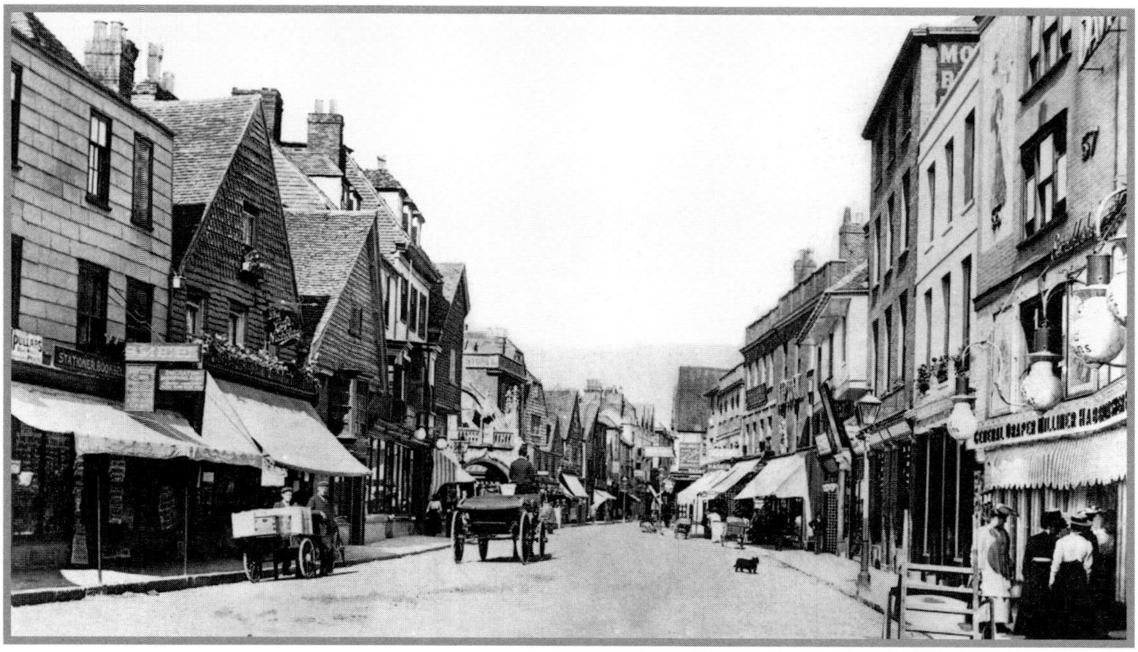

SALISBURY, SILVER STREET 1906 56357
This picture looks towards Butchers Row. The shop fronts and the general street scene have changed considerably since this picture was taken. The Poultry Cross is just visible, left of centre. Delivery boys lean on their handcart. The shop on the extreme right boasts some highly ornate gas lamps over its frontage.

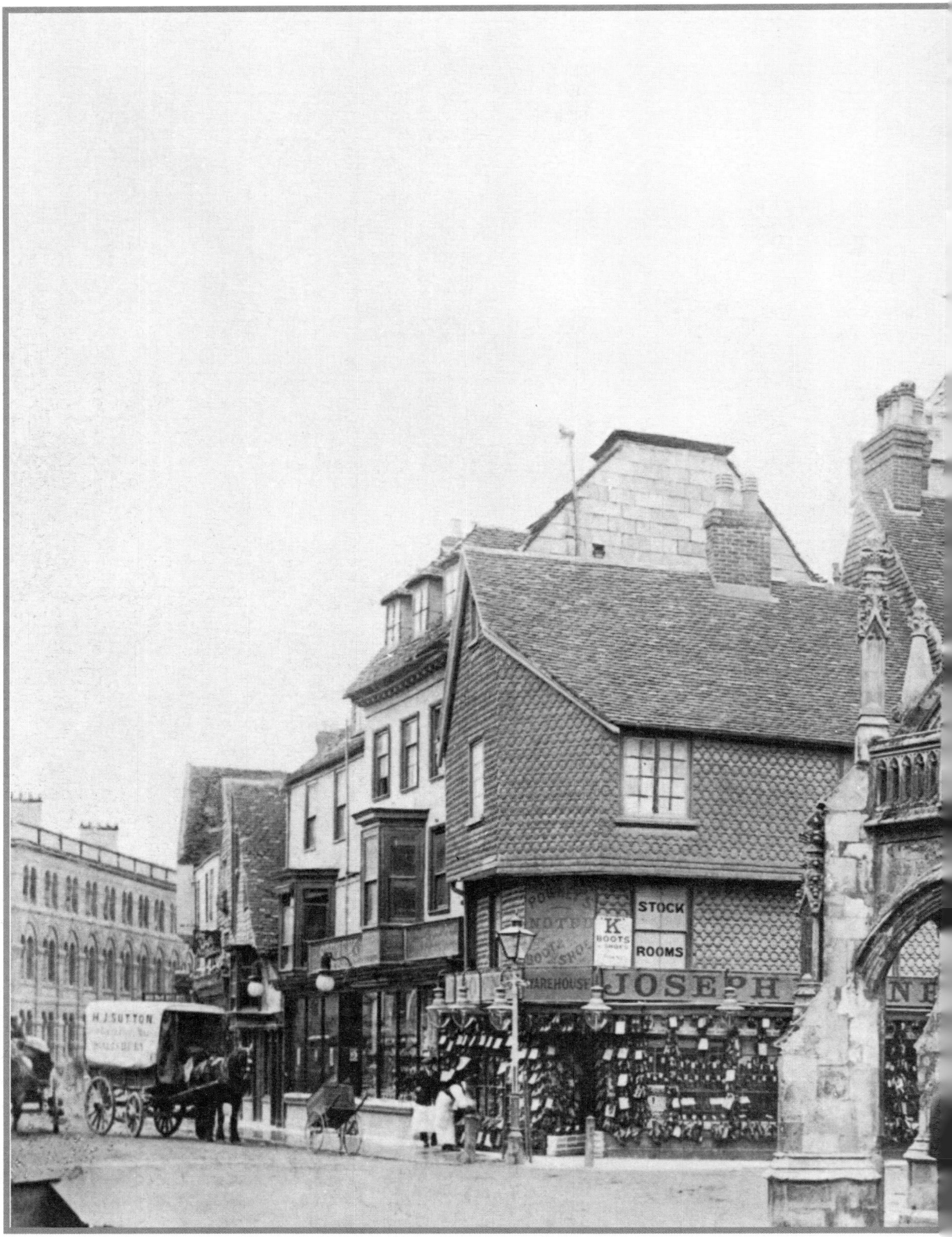
H.J.SUTTON
STOCK
ROOMS
K
BOOTS
JOSEPH

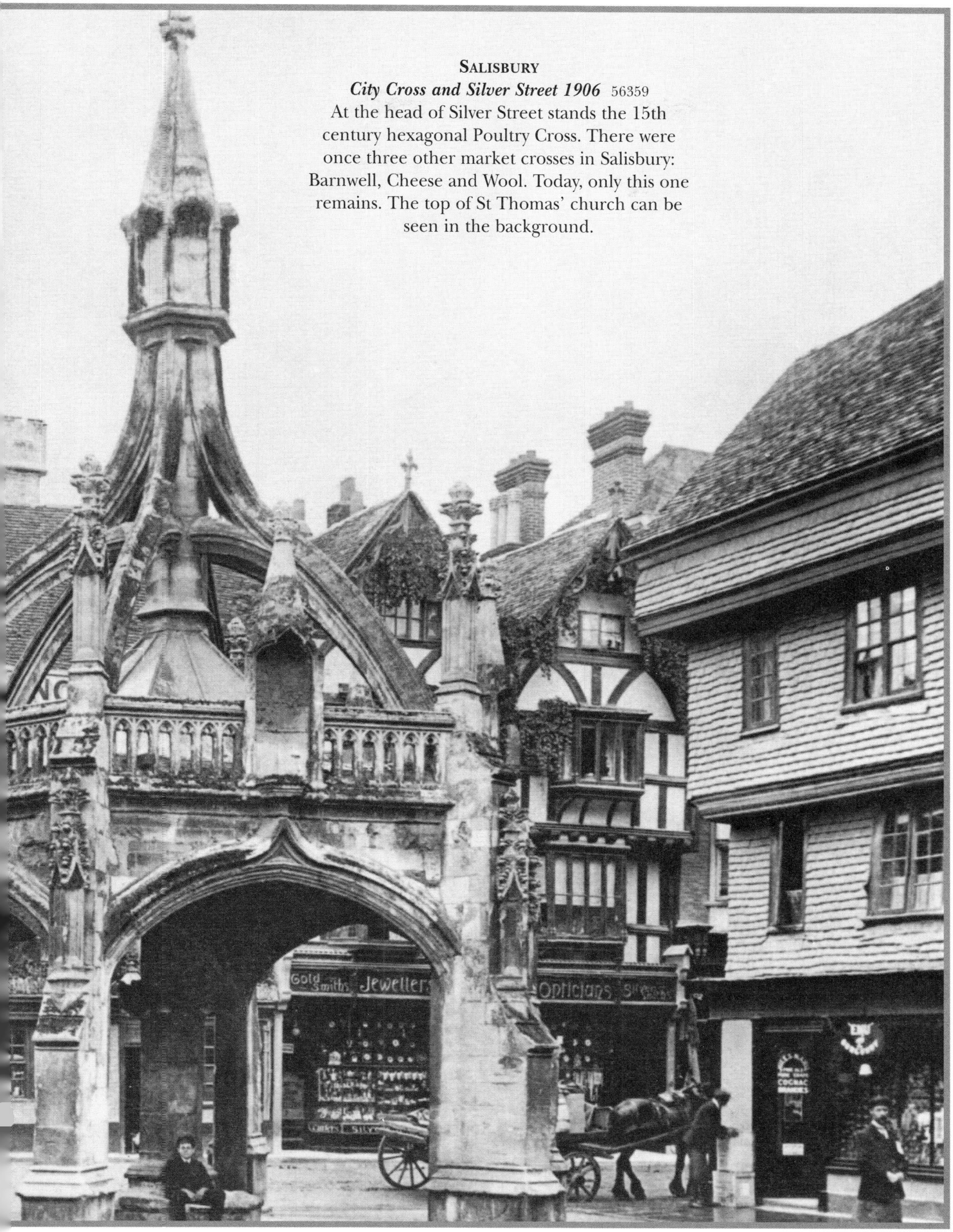

Salisbury

City Cross and Silver Street 1906 56359

At the head of Silver Street stands the 15th century hexagonal Poultry Cross. There were once three other market crosses in Salisbury: Barnwell, Cheese and Wool. Today, only this one remains. The top of St Thomas' church can be seen in the background.

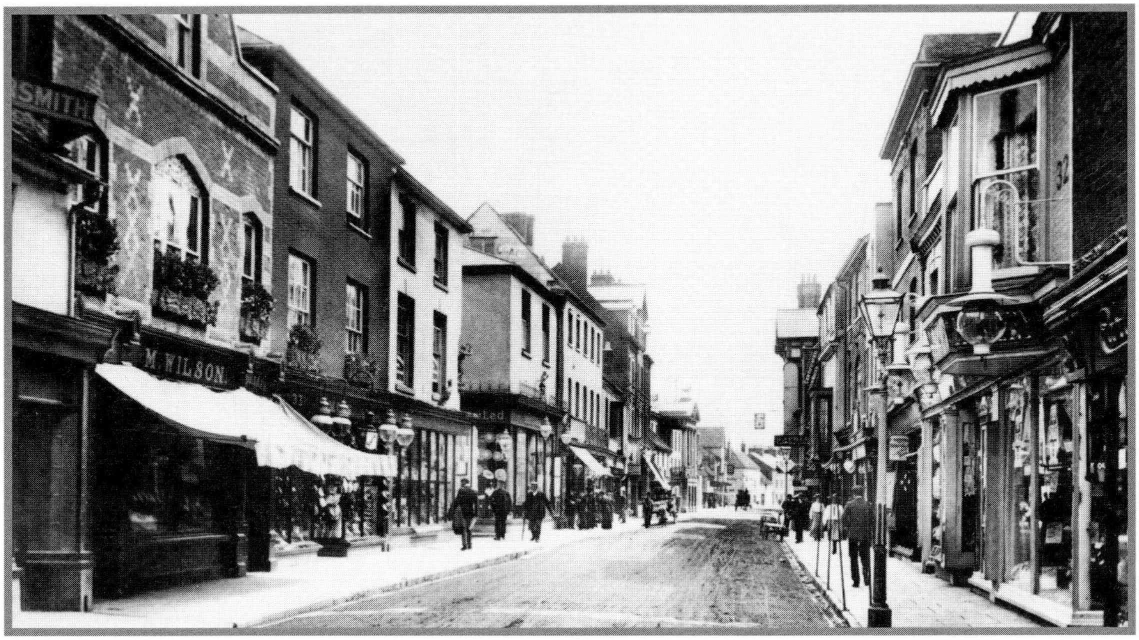

SALISBURY, CATHERINE STREET 1906 56356
Salisbury was founded in the 13th century: there was no earlier settlement here, consequently the wide streets were laid out on a grid pattern. The medieval grid pattern remains, but here the shops and houses are late Georgian and Victorian. To the left, Wilson's façade is a fine example of Victorian decorative brick work.

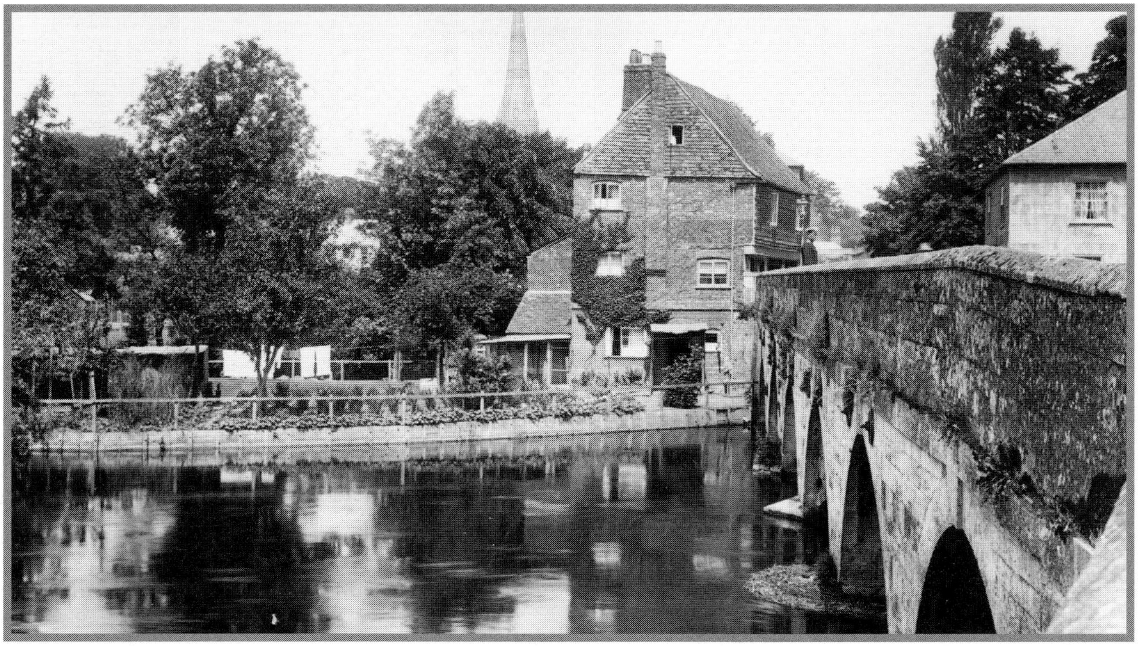

SALISBURY, HARNHAM BRIDGE 1928 80937
Harnham Bridge was first erected about 1230. Then, it carried all the traffic from the south over the Avon into Salisbury. This traffic reached such levels that it could not cope, and a new one was built a short distance downstream. This leaves the old one still in use, but not congested with lorries. The cathedral spire is in the background.

Swindon

High Street 1880

The High Street is part of Old Swindon, which was the extent of the town before the railway arrived. Then, it was a small town serving an agricultural area, but the arrival of the iron road changed all that. This picture was taken when the railways were at the height of their popularity.

Swindon

High Street and Goddard Arms c1955

Another view of the High Street. The ivy-covered 18th-century Goddard Arms had been a coaching inn and is a reminder of pre-railway days. Now the RAC and AA signs shows that it has successfully adapted itself to the age of the motor car.

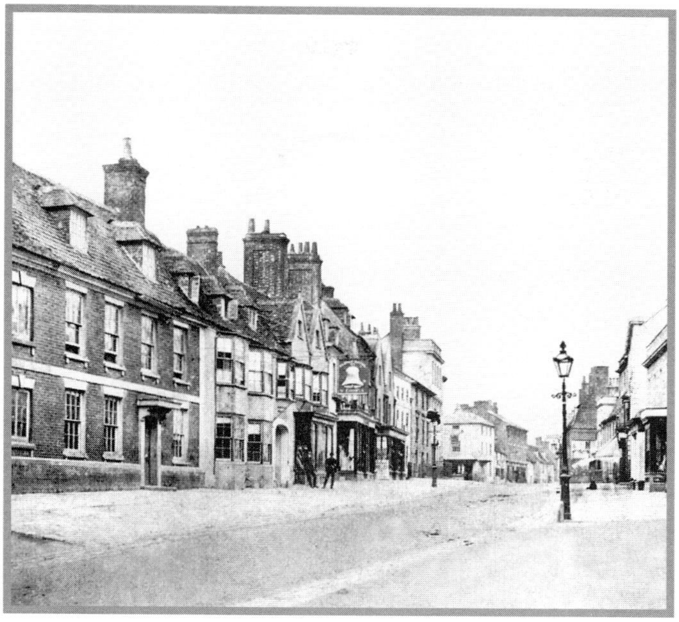

Swindon, High Street 1880 S254606

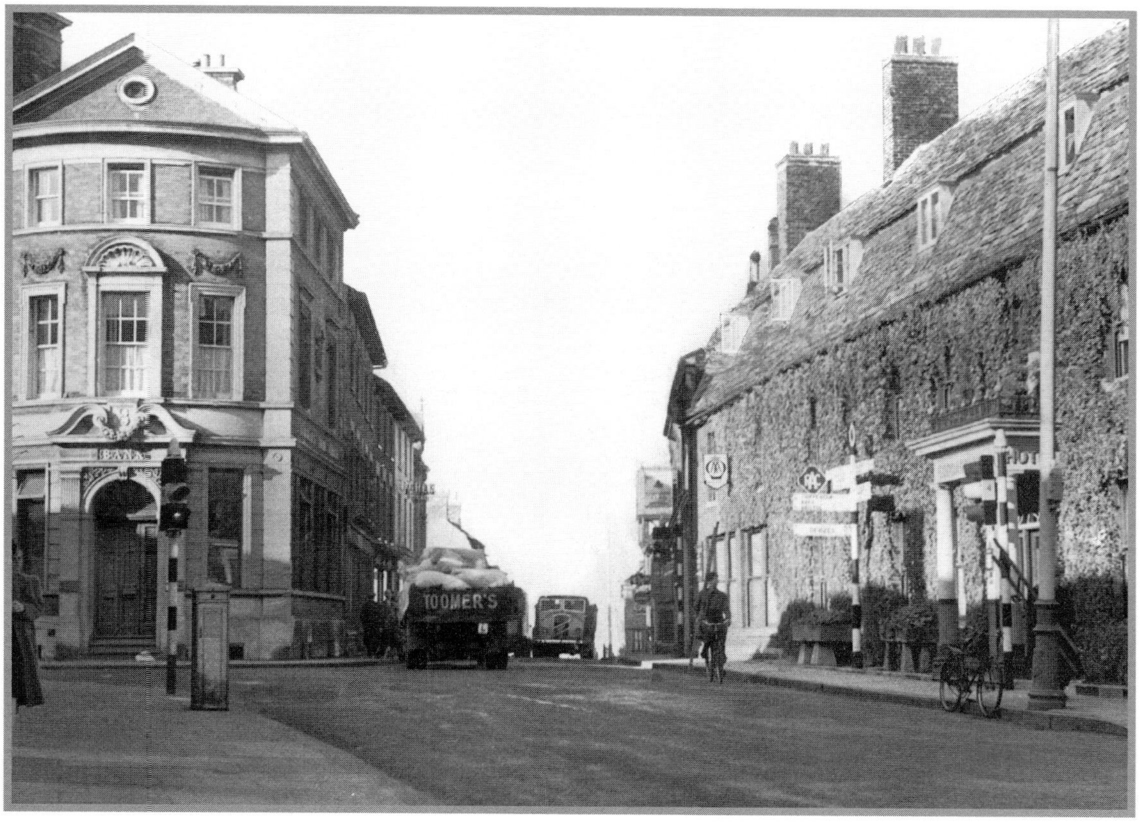

Swindon, High Street and Goddard Arms c1955 S254023

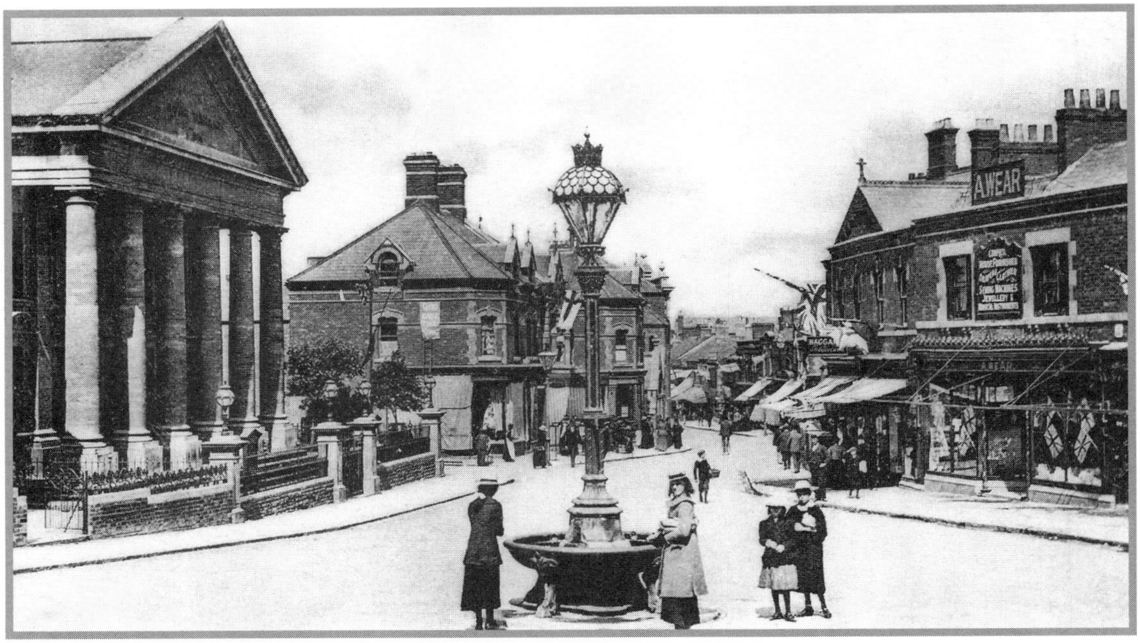

SWINDON, REGENT CIRCUS 1902 S254523
This photograph reflects the prosperity and commerce which the Great Western Railway yards brought to the town. The Baptist Tabernacle building on the left comprises six Tuscan columns with a pediment and was built in 1886.

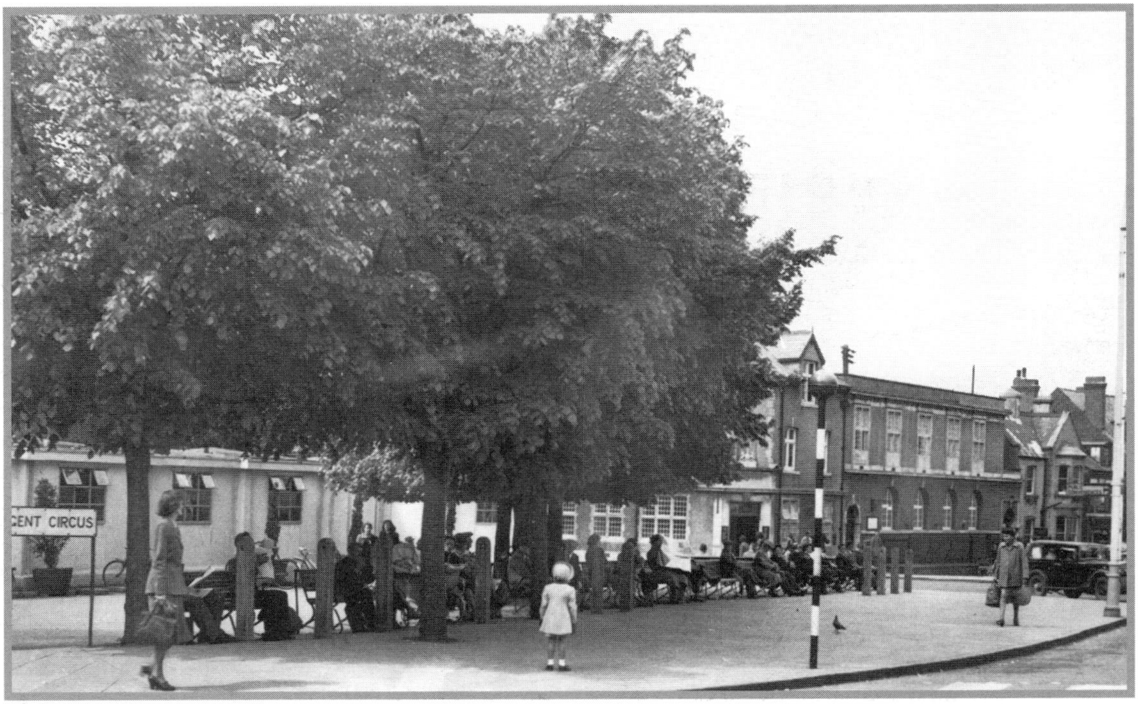

SWINDON, REGENT STREET 1961 S254063
Shoppers shelter from the sun under the trees in Regent Circus. Note the very tall pole of the Belisha beacon.

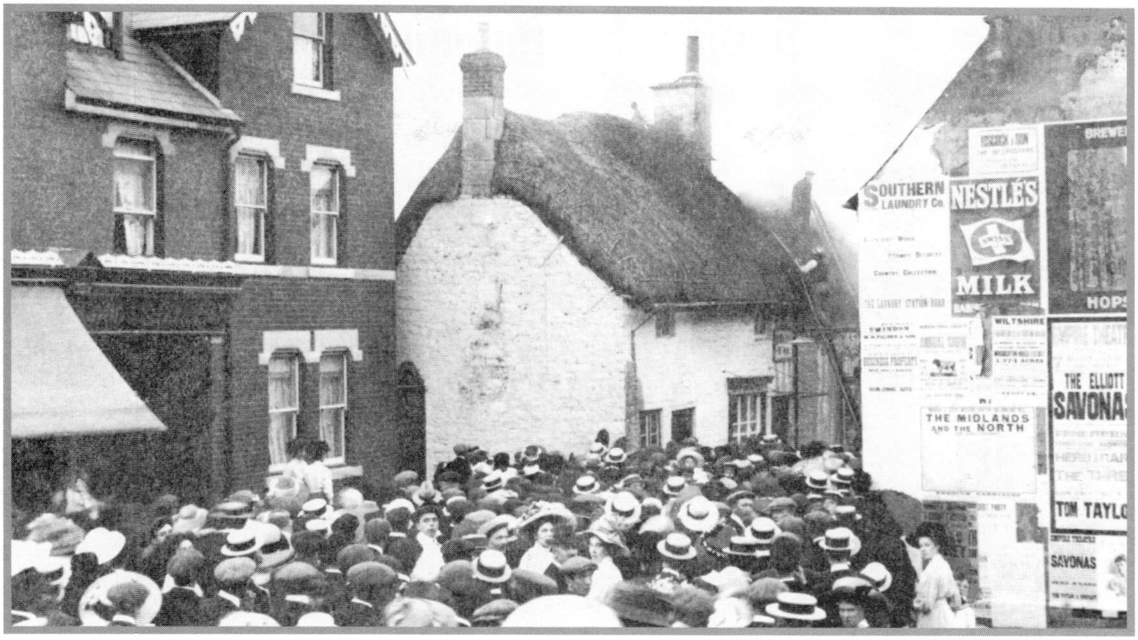

SWINDON, NEWPORT STREET 1910 S254517
A large crowd has gathered in Newport Street, part of the Old Town of Swindon. The cause of the excitement is not clear, but it could be a fire at the thatched building round the corner. The wall of the house on the right is smothered in trade posters and advertisements for the forthcoming attractions at the Empire Theatre.

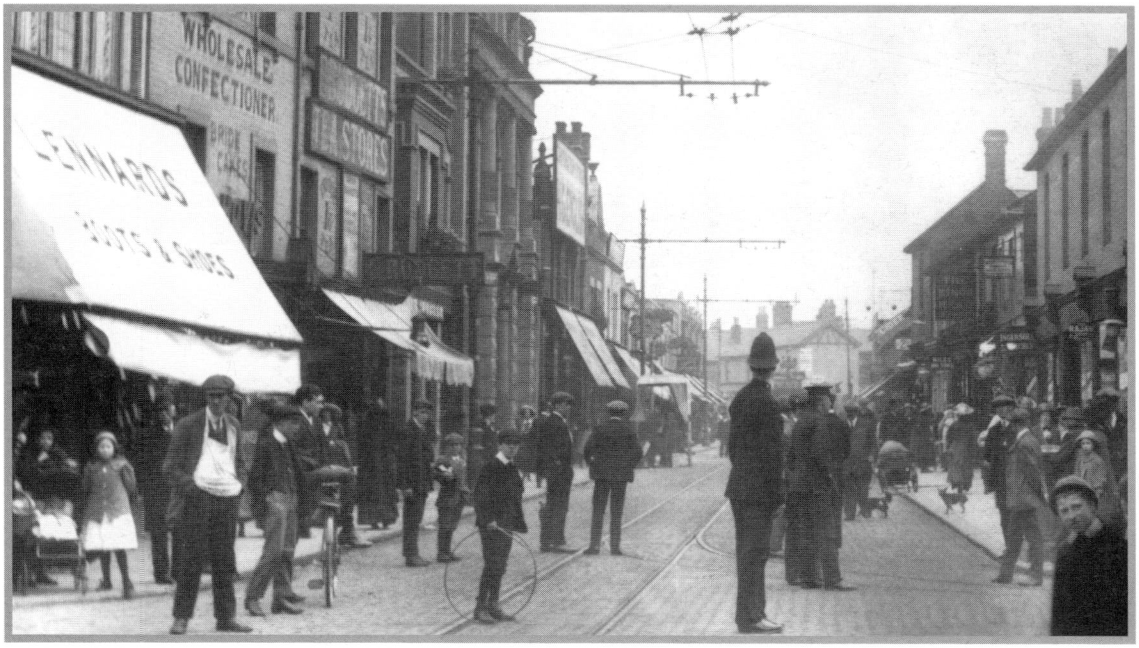

SWINDON, FLEET STREET 1913 S254608
This is the New Town, the railway end of Swindon, quite close to the GWR works and their workers' housing. Note the tram lines, overhead wires and the boy with his hoop. The policeman is standing in the middle of the road - was a parade about to begin?

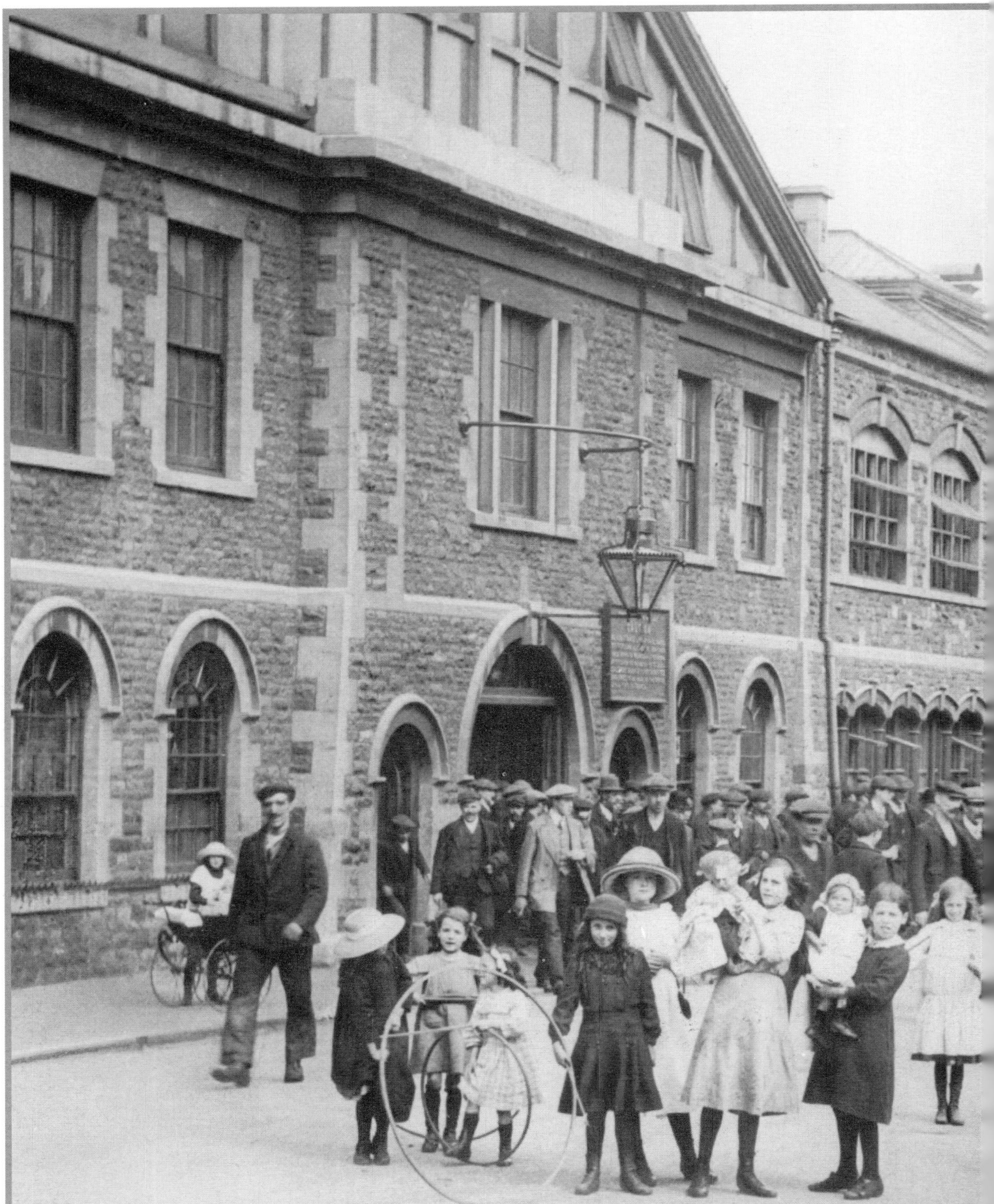

Swindon

Men Leaving GWR 1913 S254607

Here we see workers leaving the Great Western Railway yard, which, at one time, employed 12,000 people. The uniformity of dress amongst the men is striking. The sheer size of the building indicates the importance of the railway to the town. Gas street lighting is now common.

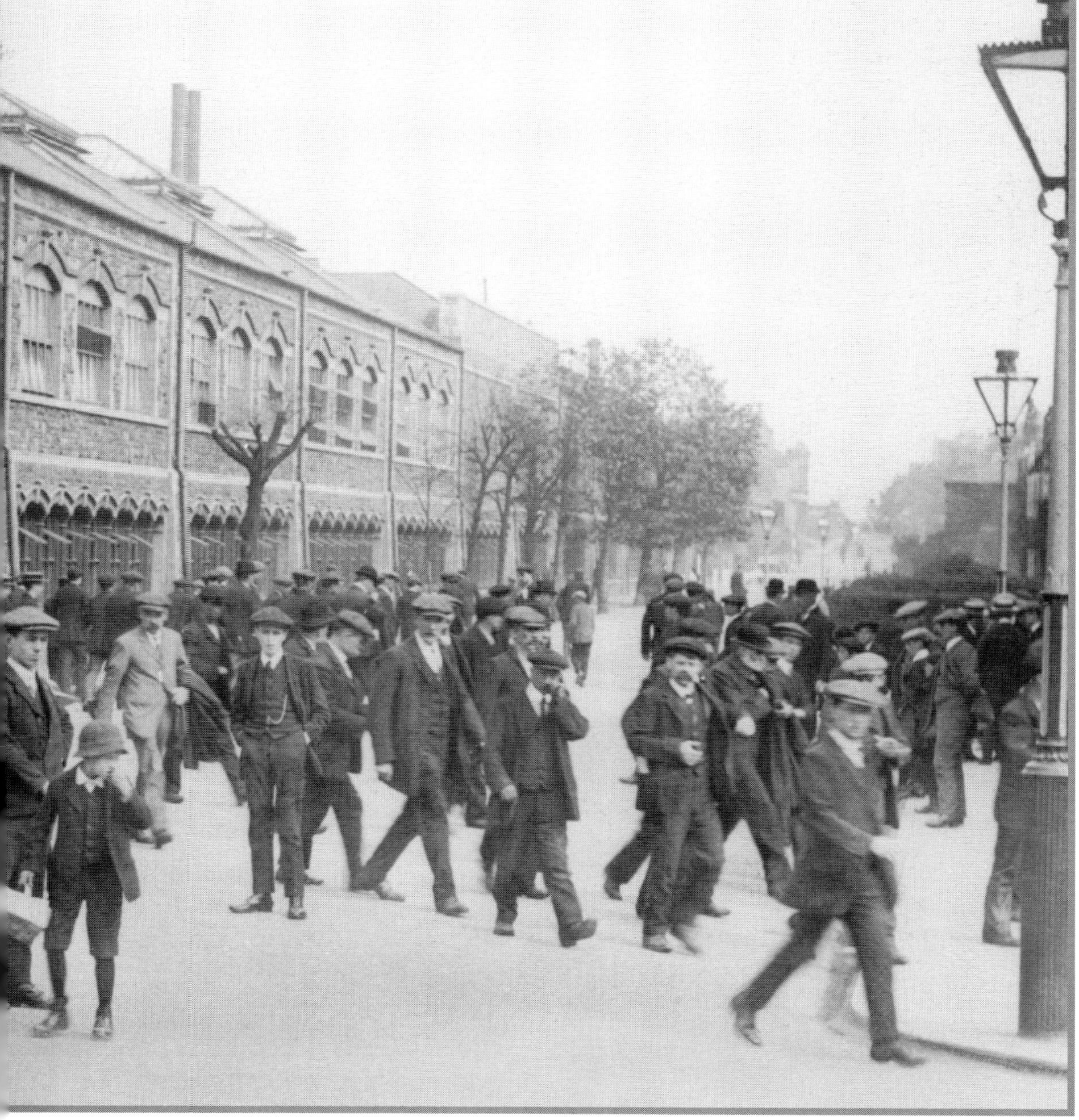

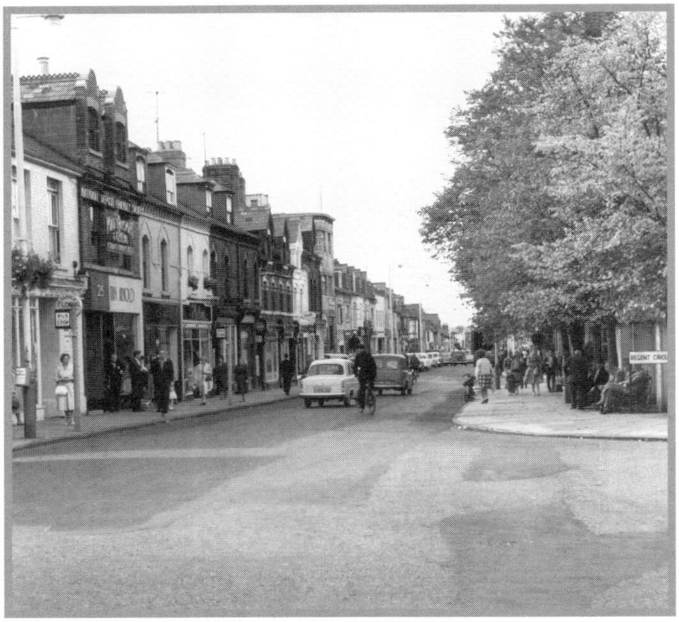

SWINDON, REGENT CIRCUS c1965 S254061

SWINDON
Regent Circus c1965
Although this picture was taken in the 1960's and is within living memory, it demonstrates how quickly fashion and styles change. The clothes appear almost drab, and the cars would now be collectors' items.

SWINDON
The Town Gardens c1955
The gardens offer a delightful green area of rest and relaxation, where the flower beds are bright and the trees shady. Opened in 1894, the bandstand featured here is still extant; so is a mini-Hollywood Bowl, called The Burmah Castrol Bowl, which is a venue for regular concerts in the Summer.

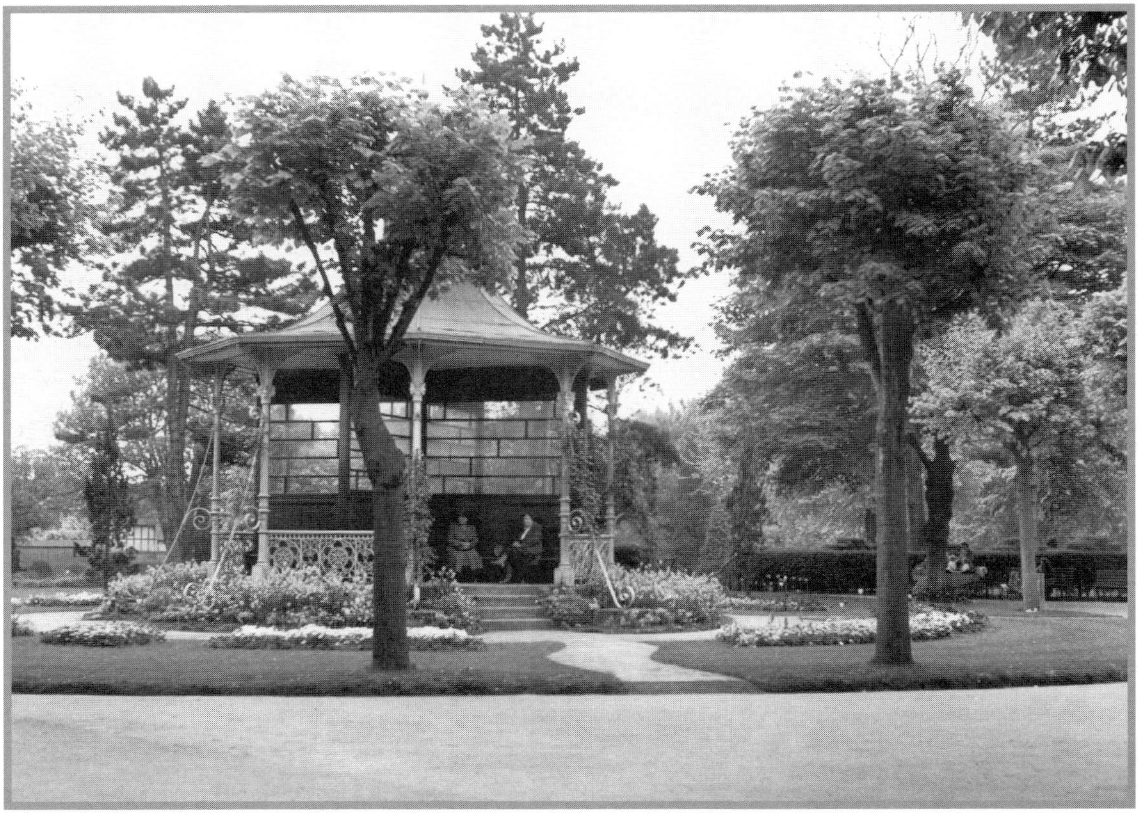

SWINDON, THE TOWN GARDENS c1955 S254039

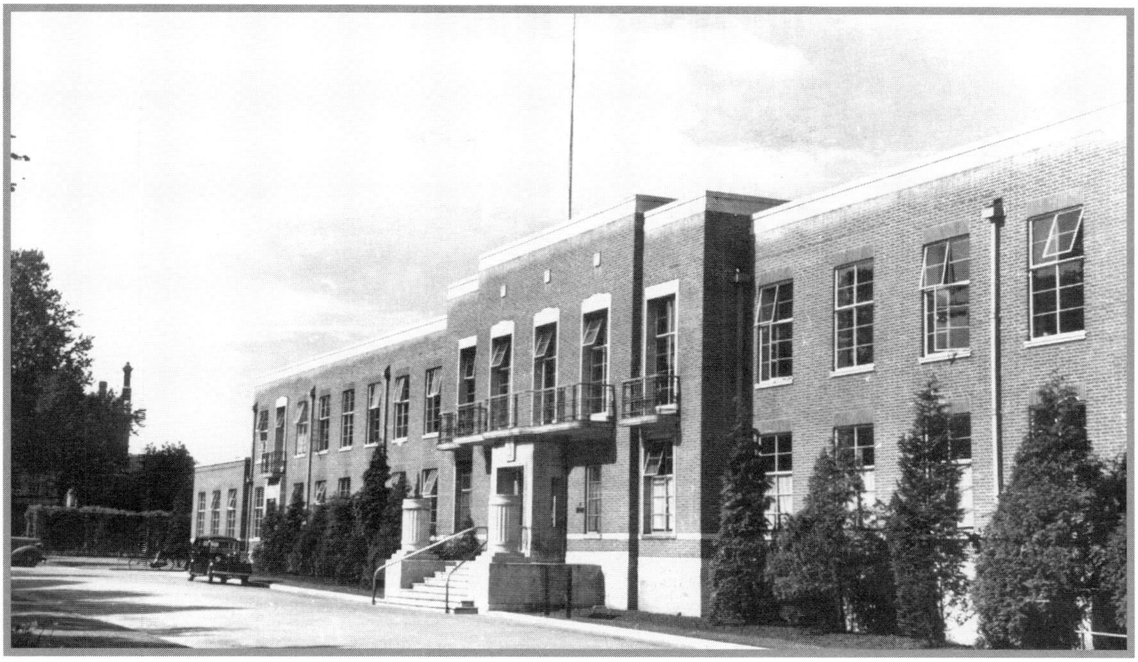

SWINDON, THE CIVIC OFFICES 1948 S254015
The old Civic Offices in Euclid Street, Swindon, built in 1936-38. The municipal architecture is a typical example of the most modern style of the day.

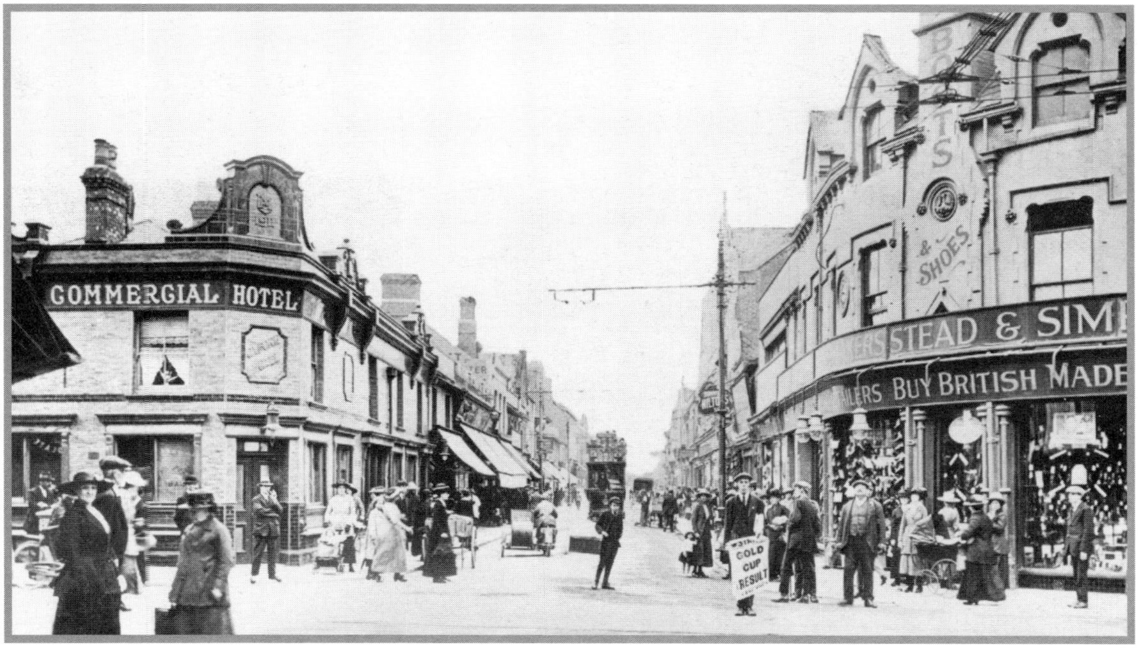

SWINDON, THE TRAM CENTRE c1919 S254518
Lots of bustle and business make this a delightfully atmospheric photograph, typifying the times just after the Great War. The billboard indicates that the only way to find out the racing results in those pre-radio and television days was by newsheet.

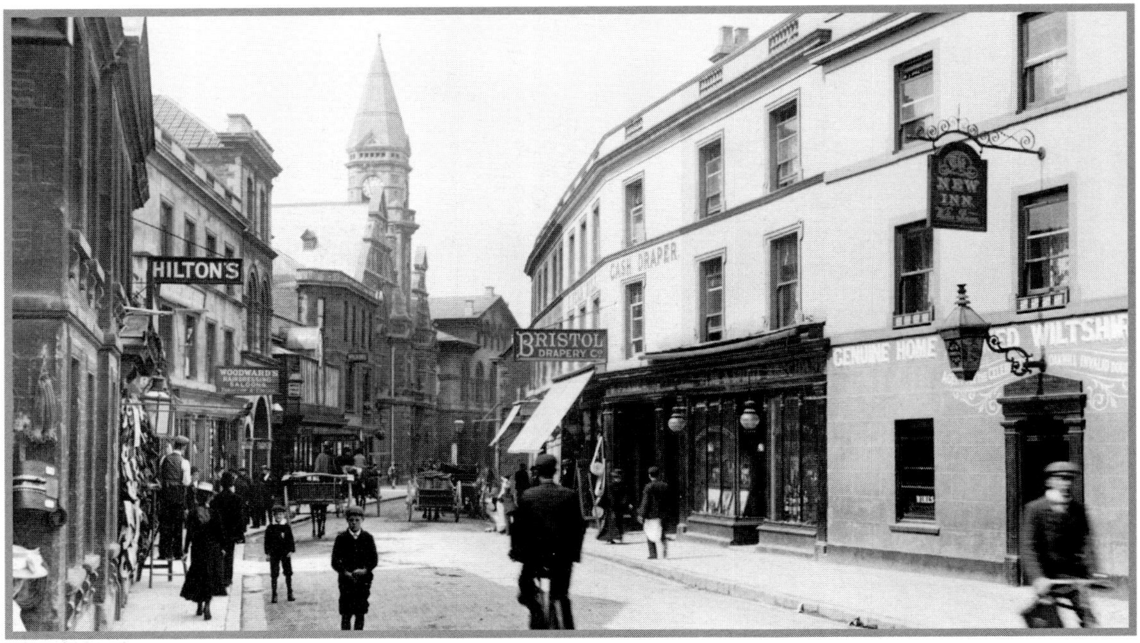

TROWBRIDGE, SILVER STREET AND THE TOWN HALL 1900 45343
A scene of undramatic terraced houses. In the background the tower of the Town Hall dominates the street. Trowbridge was famous for its cloth trade; the Bristol Drapery company is on the right. Home brewed Wiltshire Ales can be obtained at the New Inn, and Ushers Ales are still brewed today in the town.

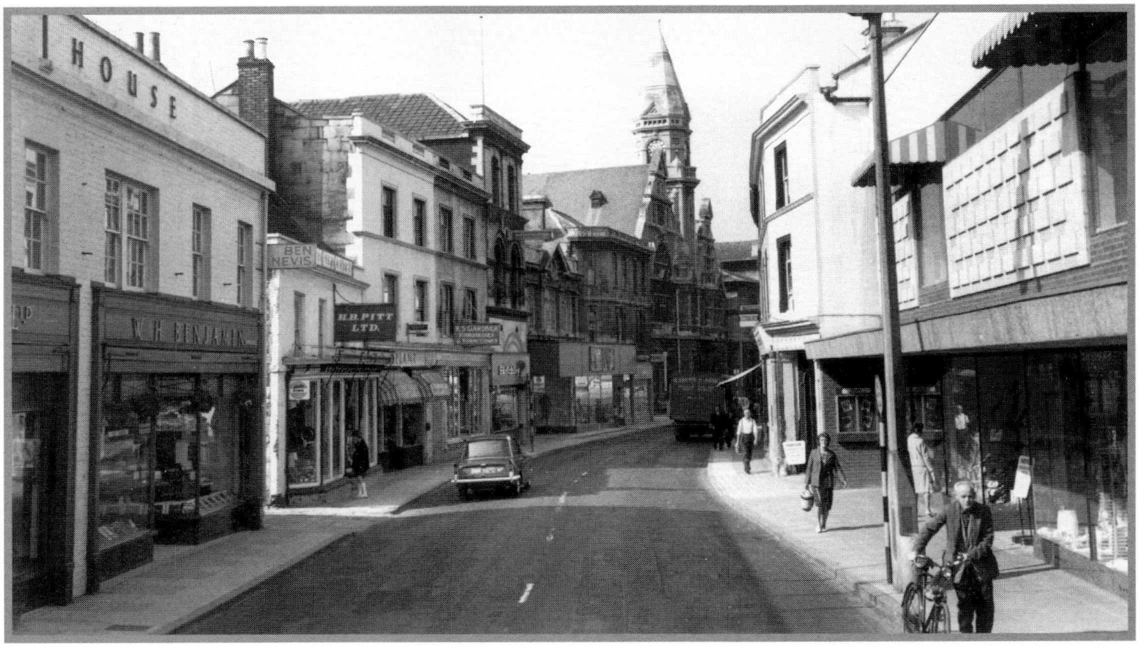

TROWBRIDGE, SILVER STREET c1965 T84068
In 1965, another photographer stood a few feet to the right of the man who took No 45343 to produce this view. The buildings further from the camera are untouched, but on the left, Hilton's has been replaced by a newer property, whilst the local Co-op have taken over the site of the New Inn for their business.

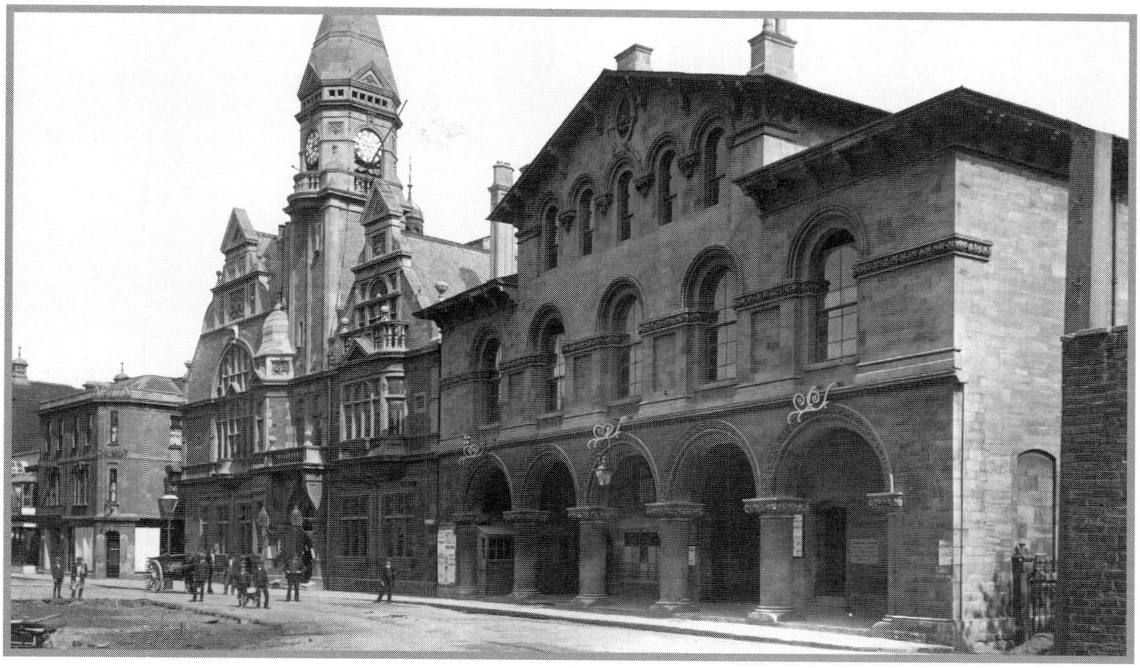

TROWBRIDGE, THE TOWN HALL AND MARKET HOUSE 1907 57697

The architecture of the Town Hall has been described as 'wild Franco-Elizabethan' and the Market House 'Victorian Italianate'. They create an exotic atmosphere to this traditional country town.

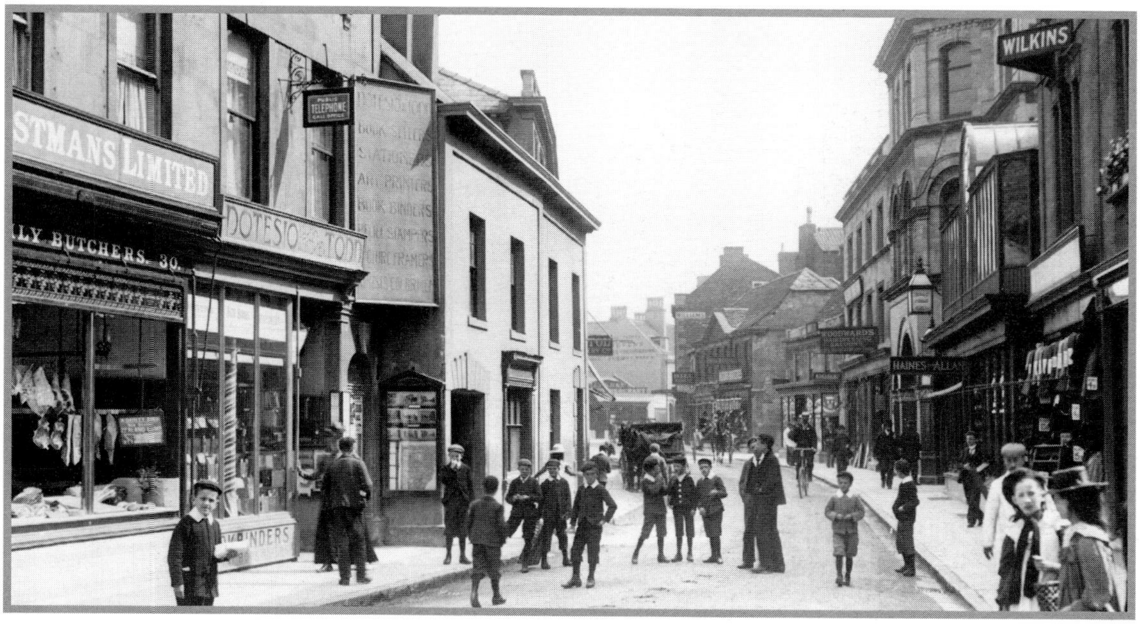

TROWBRIDGE, SILVER STREET 1900 45344

This photograph looks in the opposite direction to the previous pictures. Weaving was a trade that made Trowbridge wealthy. But it was not without its troubles, as recorded in St James' churchyard. Here there is a monument to Thomas Helliker, who was executed in 1809 at the age of 19 for leading the riots against the introduction of power looms.

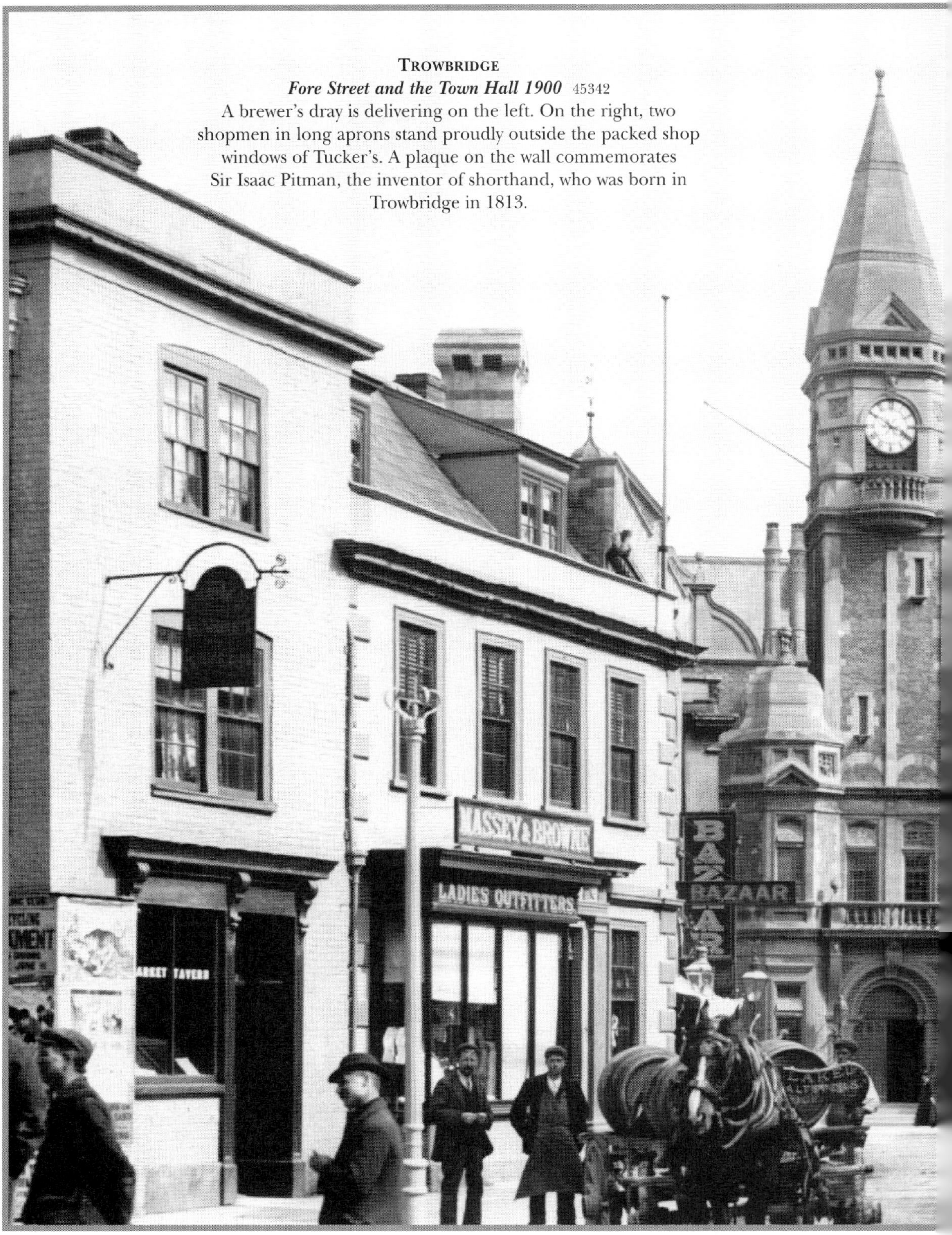

TROWBRIDGE

Fore Street and the Town Hall 1900 45342

A brewer's dray is delivering on the left. On the right, two shopmen in long aprons stand proudly outside the packed shop windows of Tucker's. A plaque on the wall commemorates Sir Isaac Pitman, the inventor of shorthand, who was born in Trowbridge in 1813.

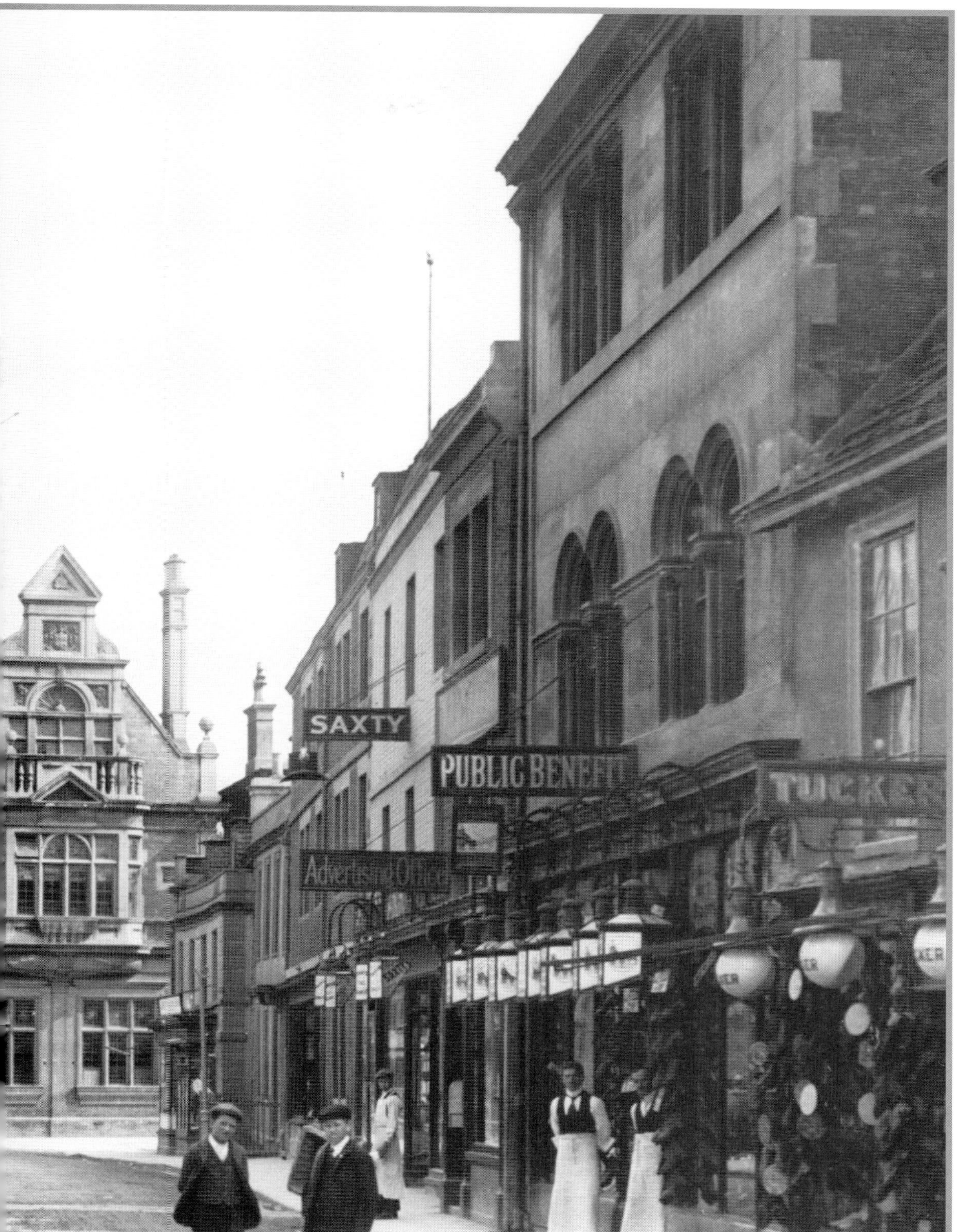
SAXTY
PUBLIC BENEFIT
Advertising Office
TUCKER

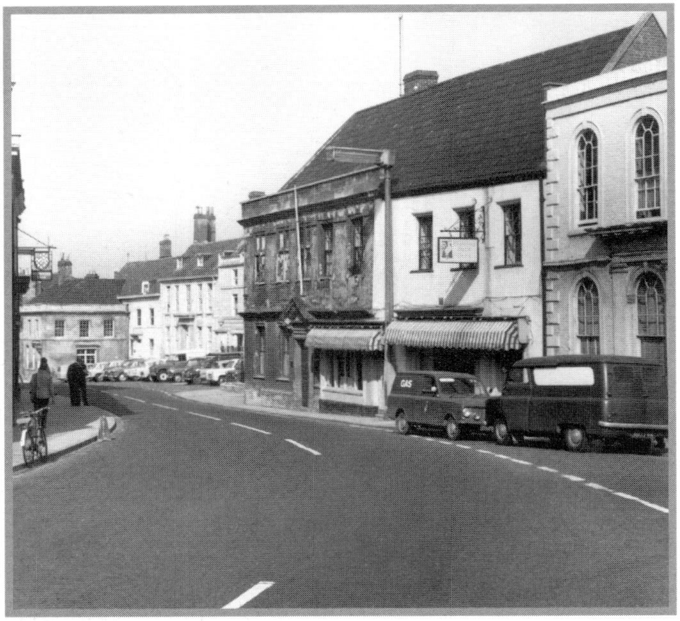

TROWBRIDGE, FORE STREET c1965 T84065

TROWBRIDGE
Fore Street c1965
Many of the fine 18th-century merchants' houses still stand in this road, some of them having been successfully converted to commercial uses.

WARMINSTER
High Street c1965
Warminster, on the A36 at the head of the Wylye valley, was an important market town and communication centre. Its broad street winds gracefully round towards the western reaches of the town.

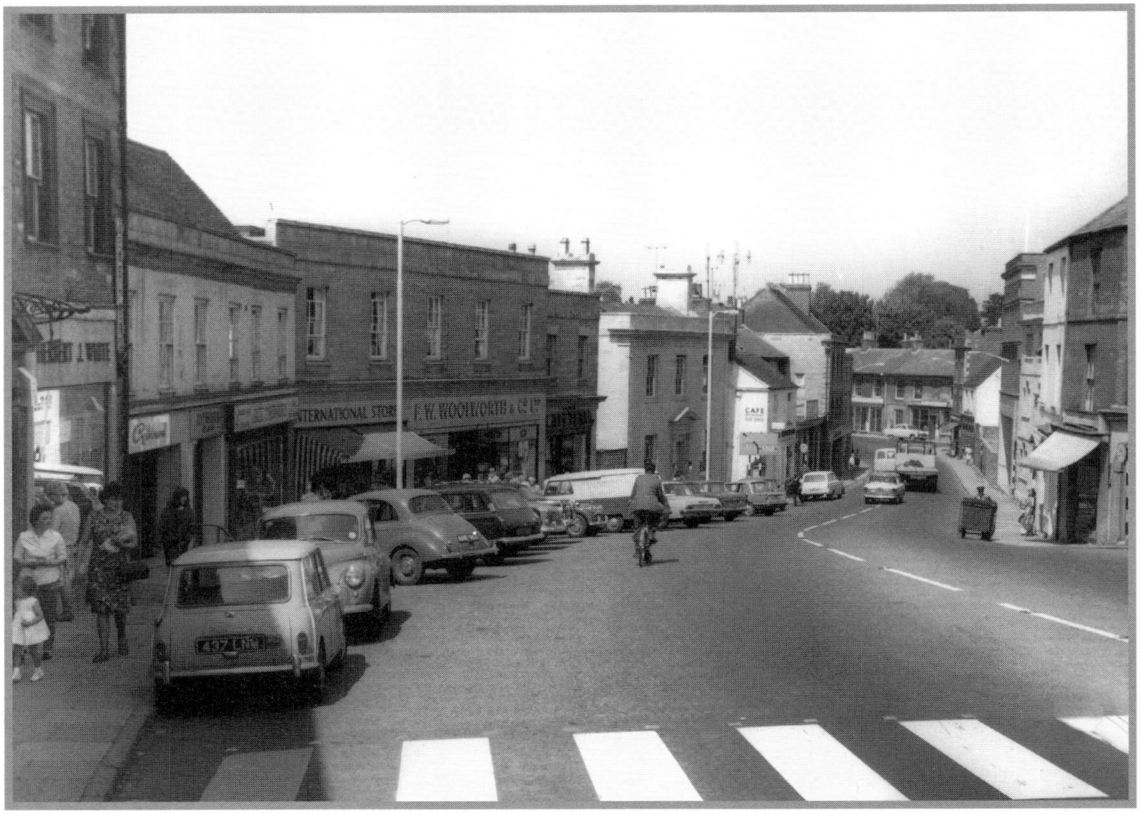

WARMINSTER, HIGH STREET c1965 W261058

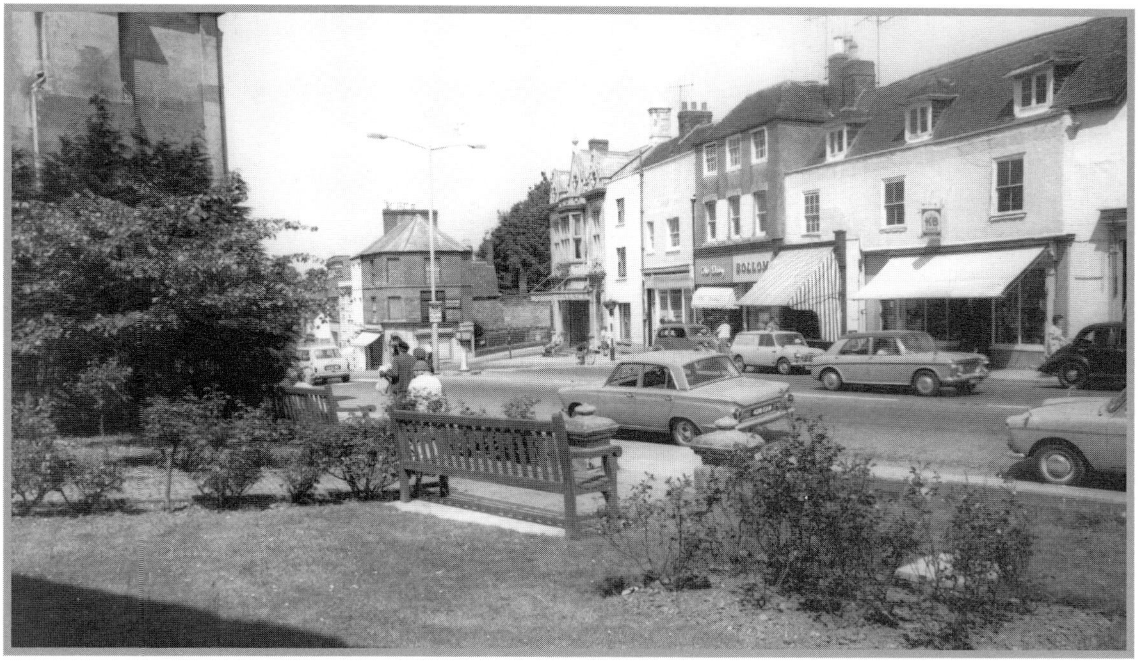

WARMINSTER, HIGH STREET FROM ST LAWRENCE'S c1965 W261065
Another view of the top of the High Street, taken from St Lawrence's church. The old Athenaeum Theatre is on the corner opposite.

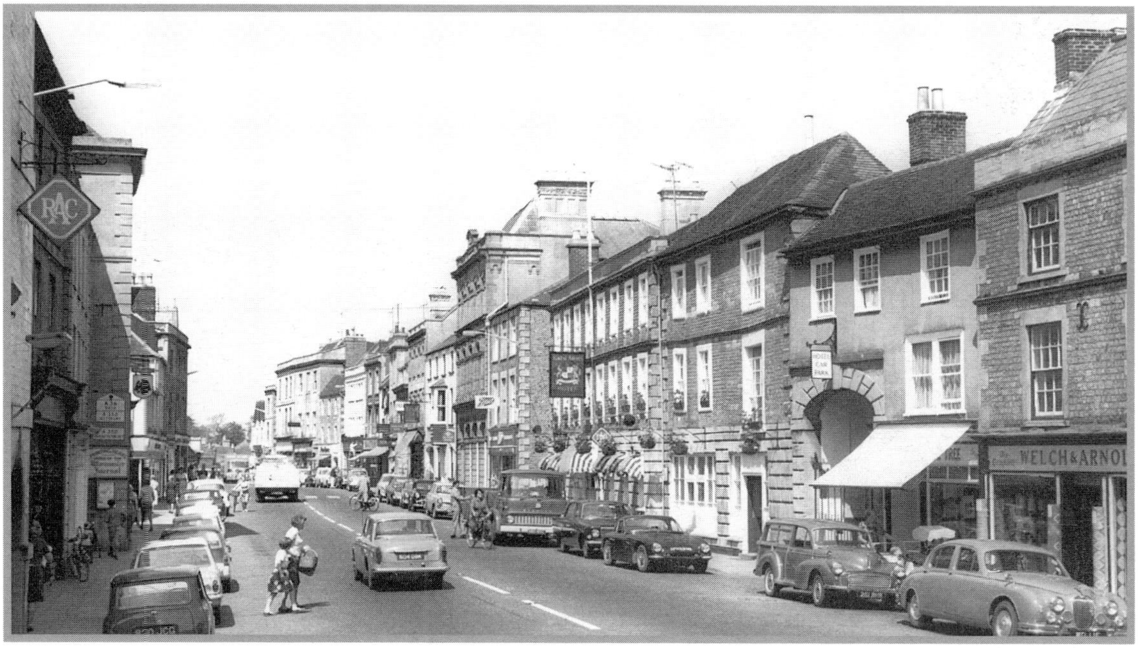

WARMINSTER, MARKET PLACE c1965 W261057
This photograph shows the Bath Arms Hotel, the old Literary and Scientific Institute, and the ever-increasing traffic. On the right is a heavily-rusticated arch leading through to the rear of the hotel, a reminder of the town's coaching days

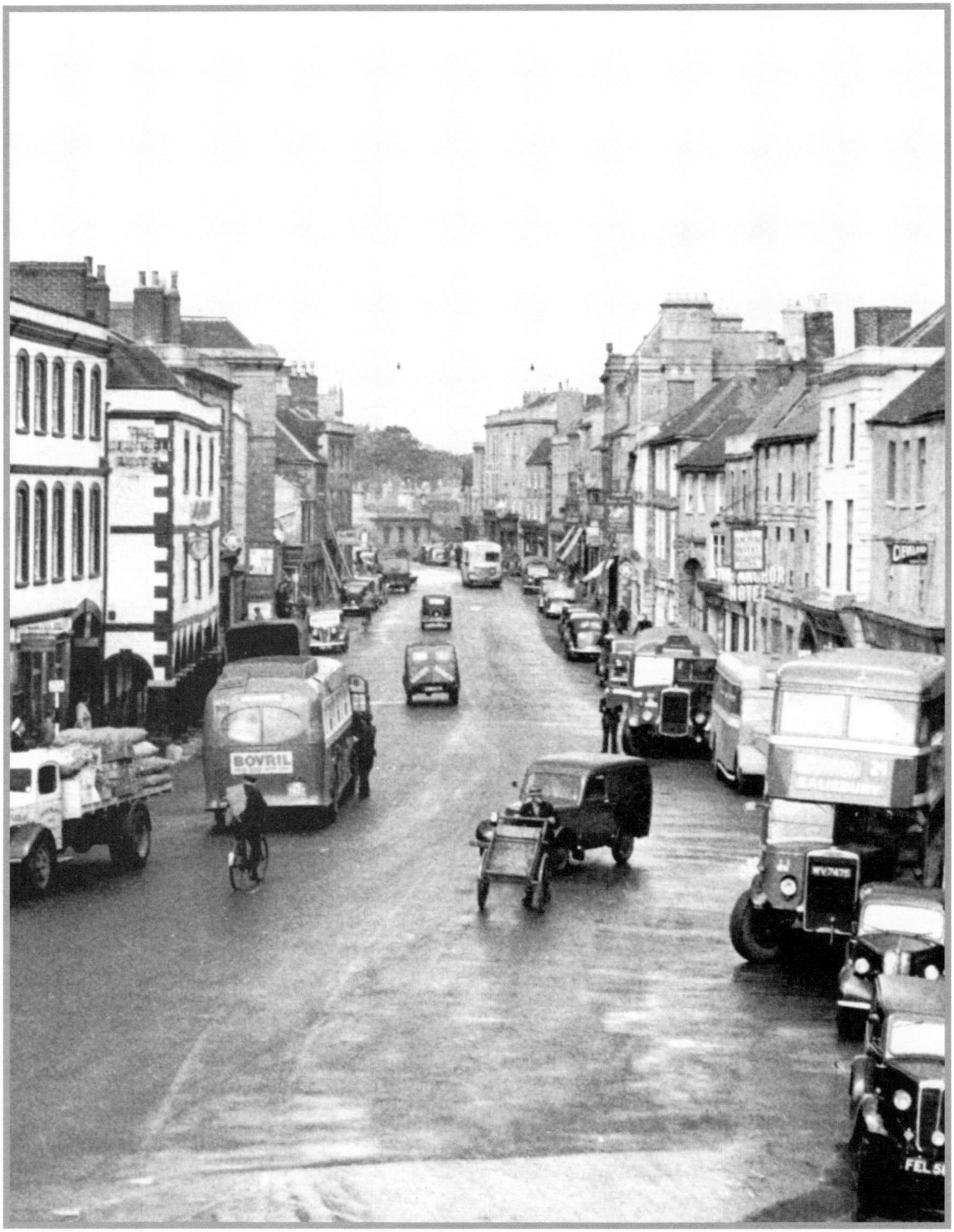

WARMINSTER, THE MARKET PLACE c1955 W261001

For many years Warminster had one of the largest corn markets in the west of England, and its prosperity is reflected in the many fine Georgian buildings in the Market Place.

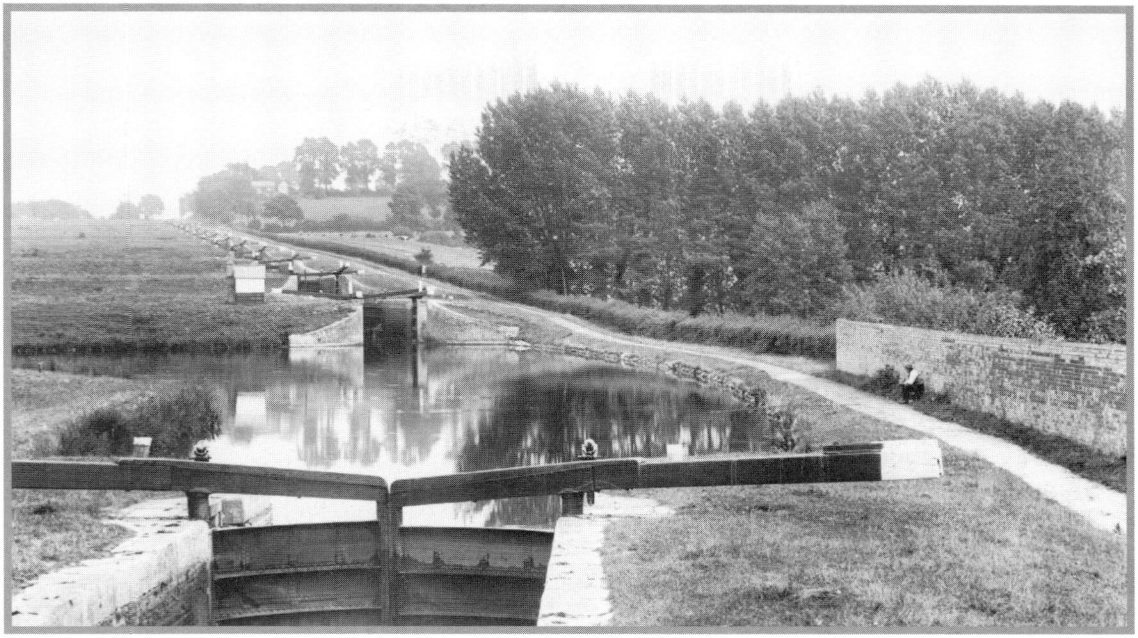

Devizes, The Canal Bridge & Lock 1898 42320

Few canal sights in Britain match the splendour of the Caen Hill flight of 29 locks which raises the Kennet and Avon canal 230 feet over a two mile stretch. The canal gently weaves its way from Bath through the idyllic countryside of the Vale of Pewsey until it completes its journey at Reading. It was built in 1801 by John Rennie.

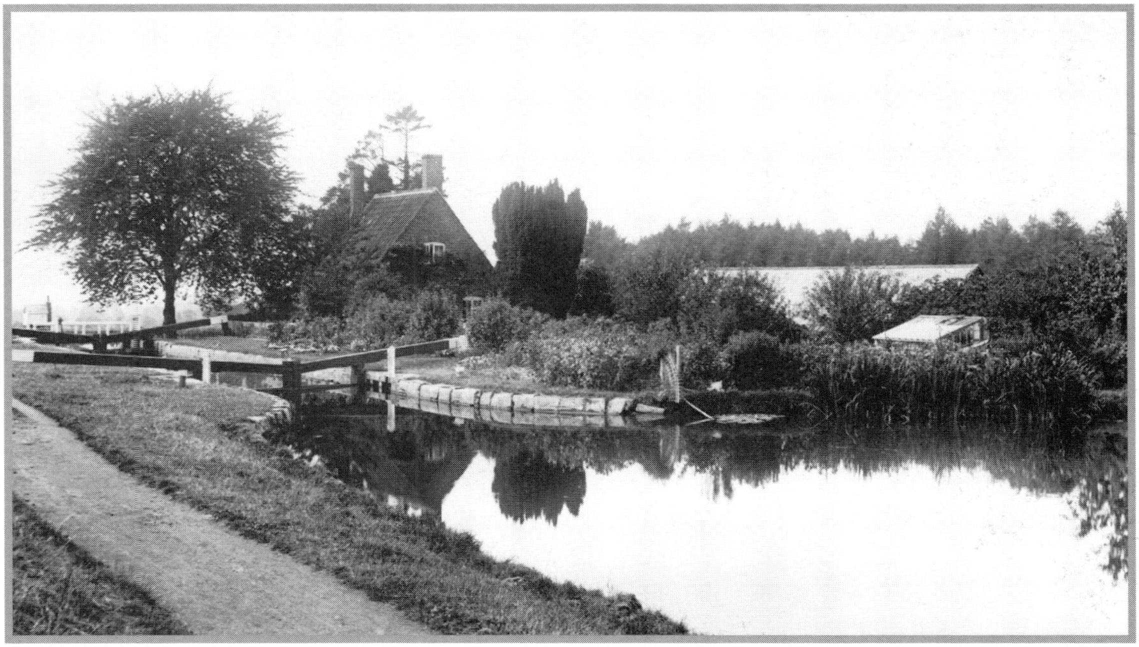

Devizes, On the Canal 1898 42318

Looking westward, this is the top lock of the Caen flight, which at one time had gas lighting installed for night time working. However, the economic life of the canal was short-lived. From the 1840s the steam railways proved to be the death-knell of the canal era.

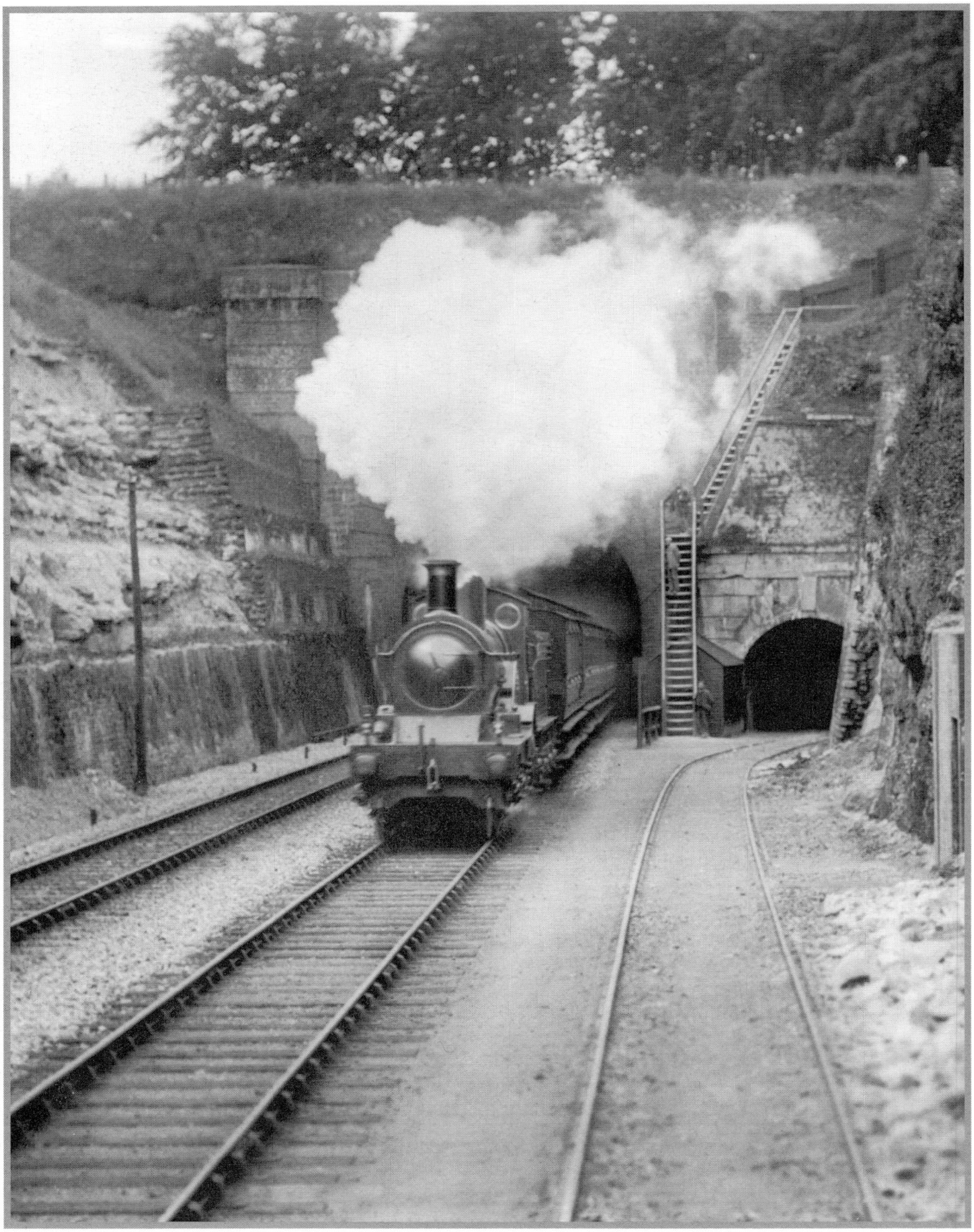

CORSHAM, THE BOX TUNNEL 1904 51492
Isambard Kingdom Brunel built the famous Box Tunnel in 1841 as part of the Great Western railway link between London's Paddington station and Bristol's Temple Meads. The 120 miles of railway line took five years to complete. Limestone from the excavated tunnel was used for building houses in nearby Corsham.

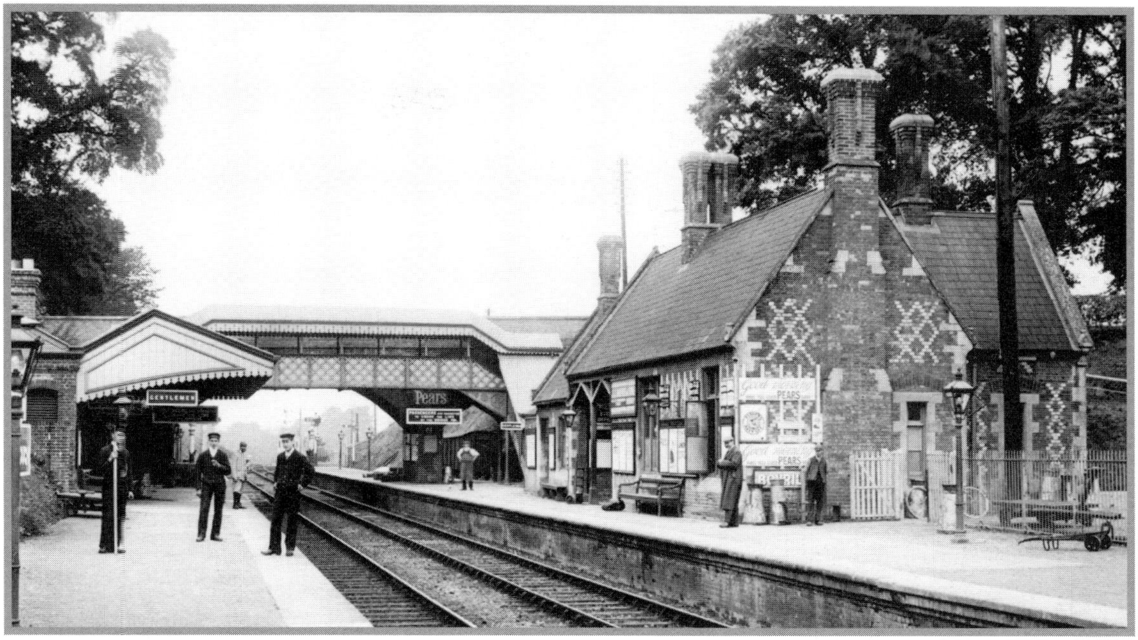

Savernake, Forest Station 1907 57217
There were two stations at Savernake, an Upper and Lower; one served the Great Western Company, the other the Midland SW Junction. Note the sack trolley on the right, the Gentlemen sign, the notice boards, the footbridge over the track: these functional items can still be seen today in some stations, ninety years later.

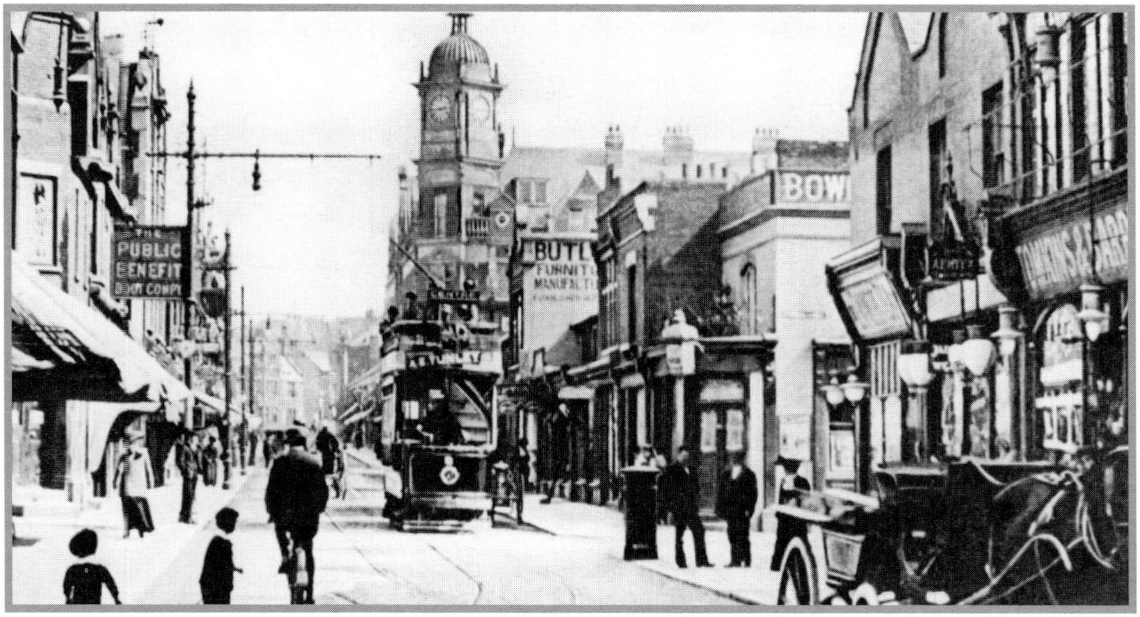

Swindon, Regent Street 1905 S254603
In 1905 Swindon was a busy manufacturing town which owed its wealth and commercial rise almost exclusively to the railway age in general and the inspiration of Sir Daniel Gooch in particular, who founded the Swindon Railway Works. Regent Street, in this picture, reflects the commercial activity. The post box on the right is the same style as is used today.

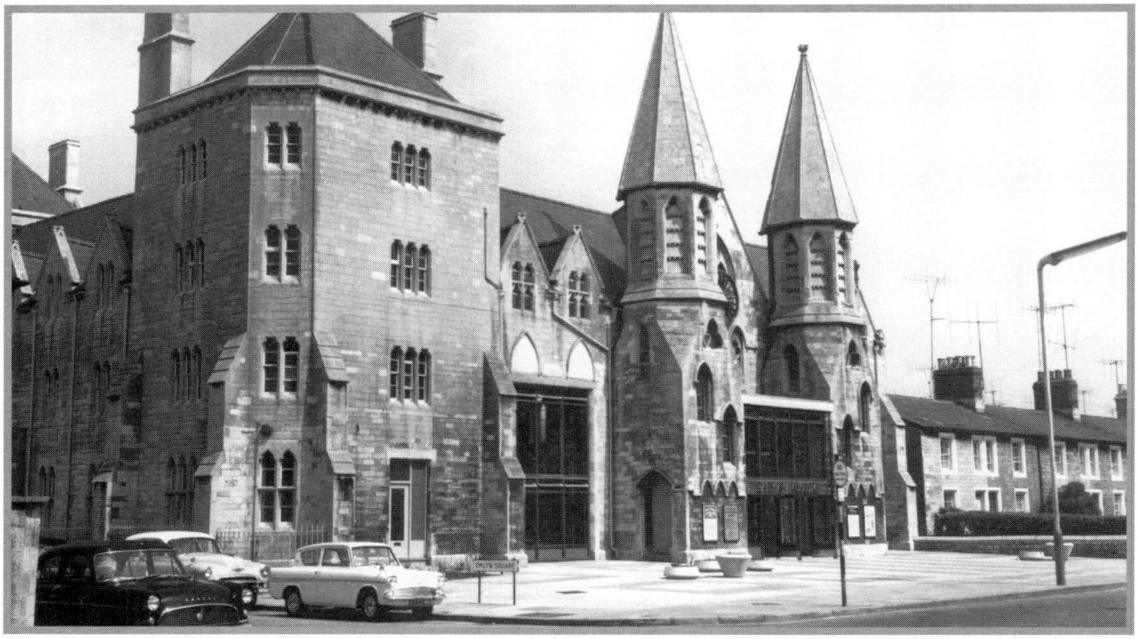

SWINDON, THE RAILWAY MUSEUM C1965 S254085
When the Great Western Railway came to Swindon, the company built accommodation for their Irish navvies. By 1960 it had been converted to a railway museum. Late in 1999, the collection will move elsewhere in the town, and the building will be used to house the town's art collection.

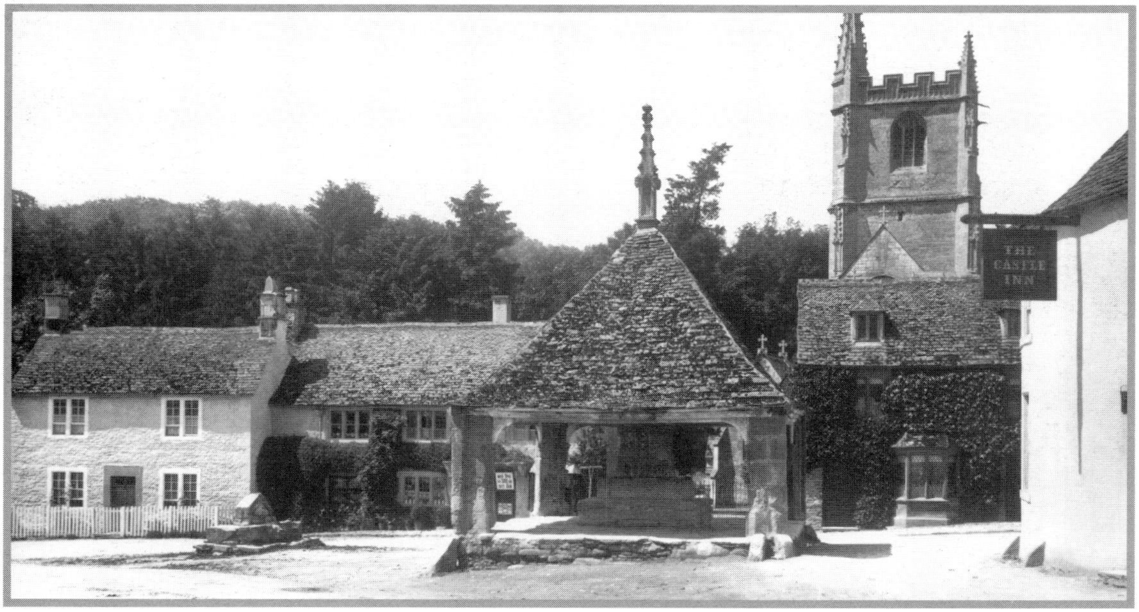

CASTLE COMBE, THE MARKET CROSS AND THE CHURCH 1906 53907
The grandeur and size of Perpendicular architecture owes its inception to the wealth created by the wool trade. The Cotswold stone tower of St Andrews Church stands fittingly adjacent to the Market Cross, the scene of Castle Combe's once famous sheep market. Nowadays, deemed the prettiest village in England, it relies on tourism for its income.

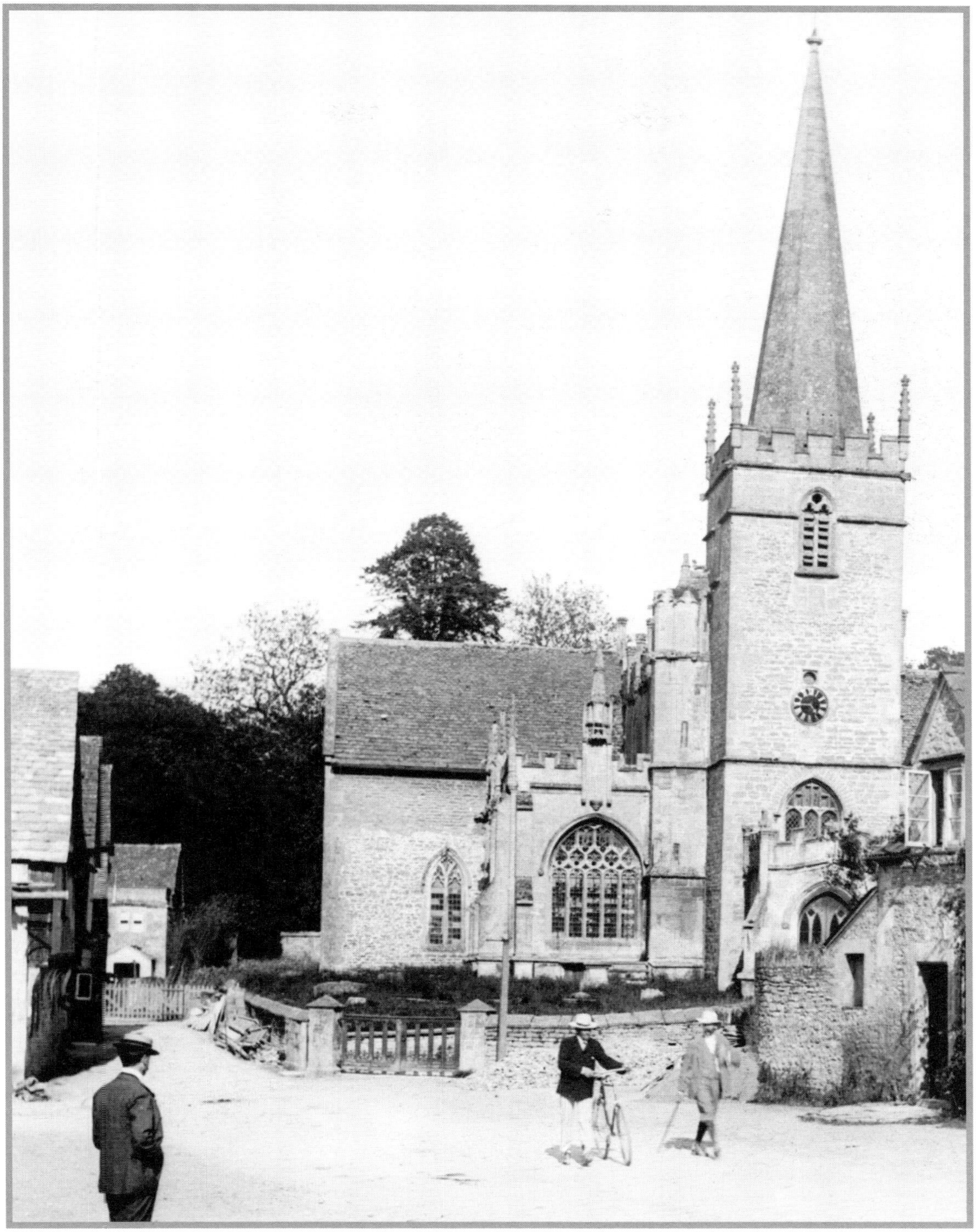

LACOCK, THE VILLAGE AND THE CHURCH 1904 51513

The church of St Cyriac is built largely in the Perpendicular style, and is full of interest. The nave has clerestory windows with battlements and pinnacles and some inventive and amusing gargoyles. Medieval stonemasons were allowed freedom of expression with gargoyles and some capitals.

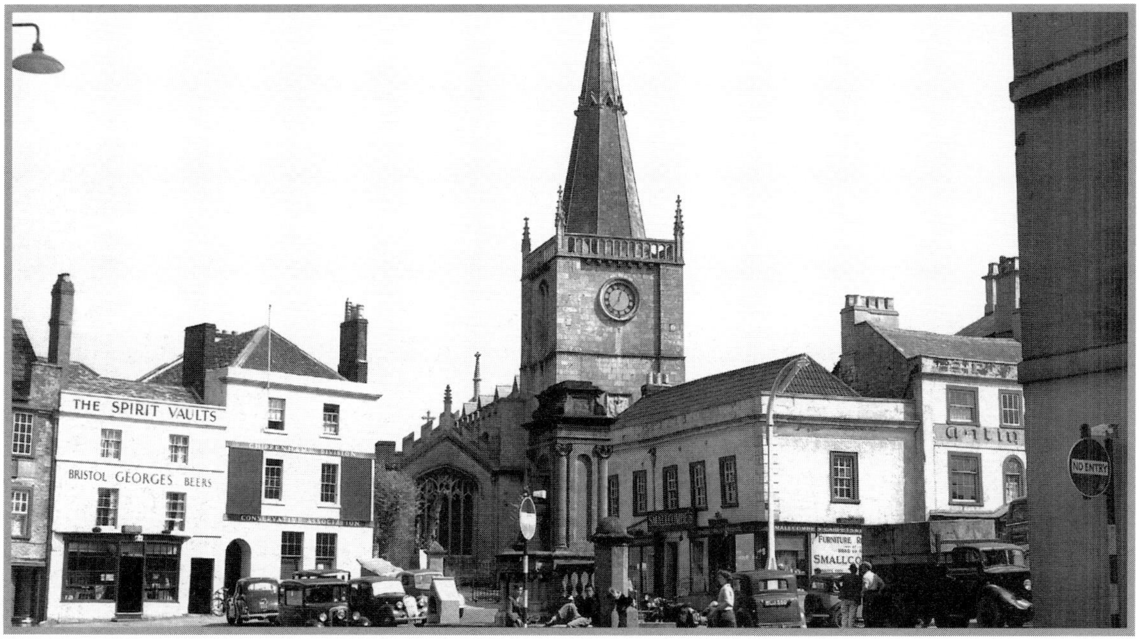

CHIPPENHAM, THE CHURCH c1955 C294029
St Andrews church, Chippenham, viewed from the market place. The church, partly medieval with some rebuilding over the centuries, dominates what was a busy three days a week market square surrounded by Georgian frontages, and the banks of the river Avon.

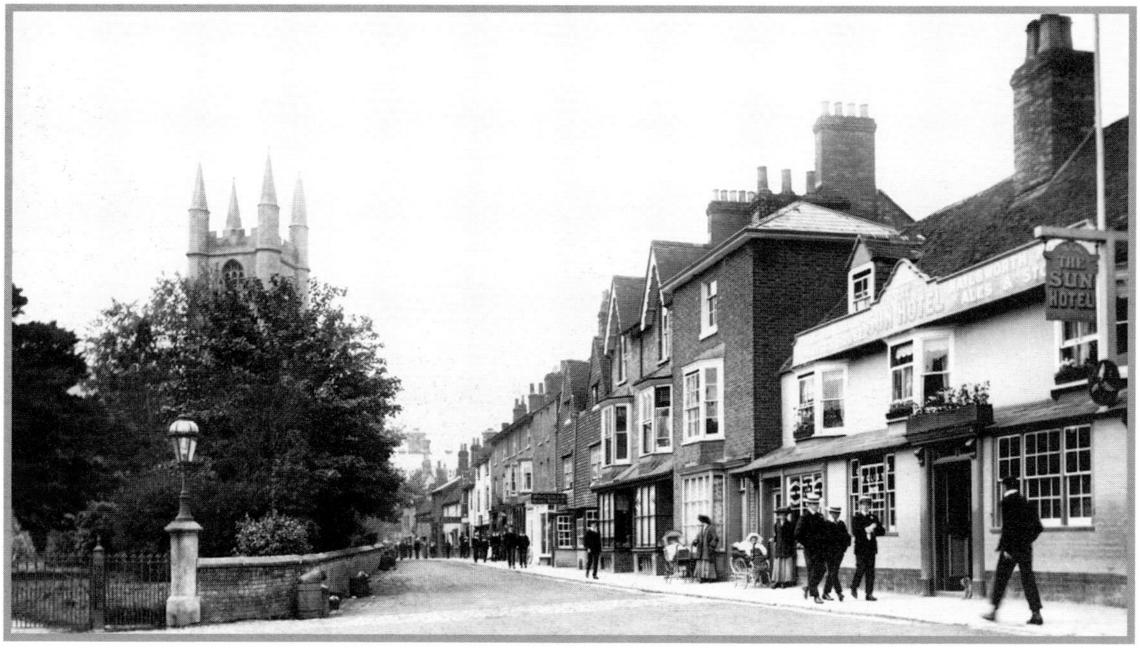

MARLBOROUGH, ST PETER'S 1907 57848
Little can be gleaned of the appearance of St Peter's church from this picture. It stands at the western end of the high street and is famous for the ordaining of Thomas Wolsey, Chancellor of England under Henry VIII. It has a magnificent 120ft tower. The Sun Hotel on the right is still trading today.

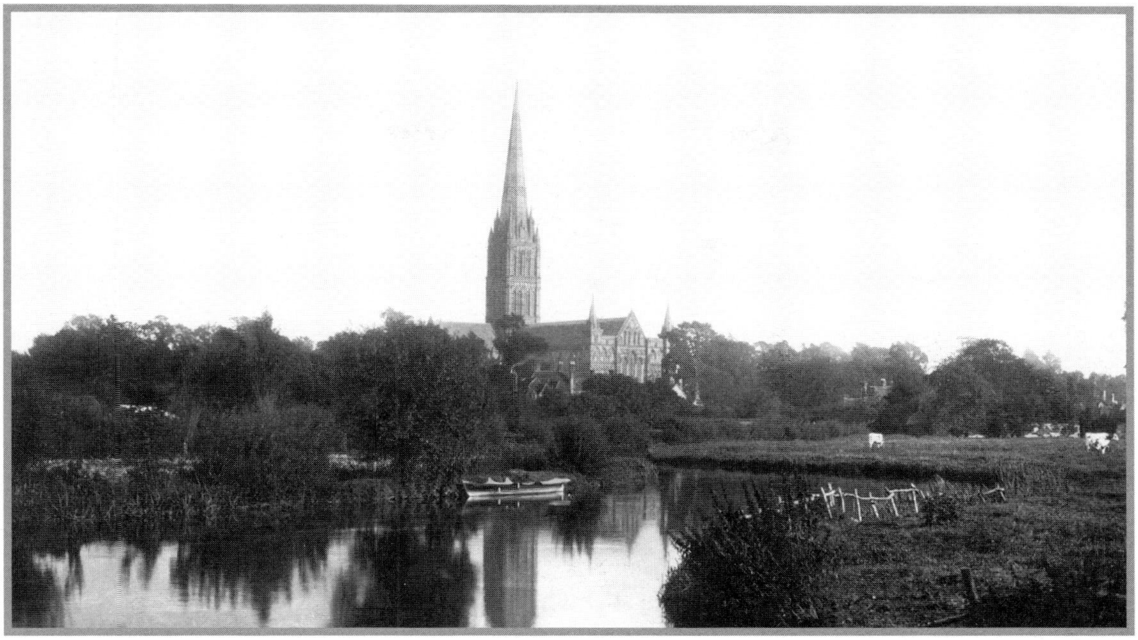

Salisbury, The Cathedral from the River 1887 19730

The tower and spire of Salisbury Cathedral nestle comfortably by the meandering river Avon and its historic water meadows. This scene, made famous by John Constable, shows its magnificent 404ft spire - the tallest in Britain - which was added to the tower between 1280 and 1320.

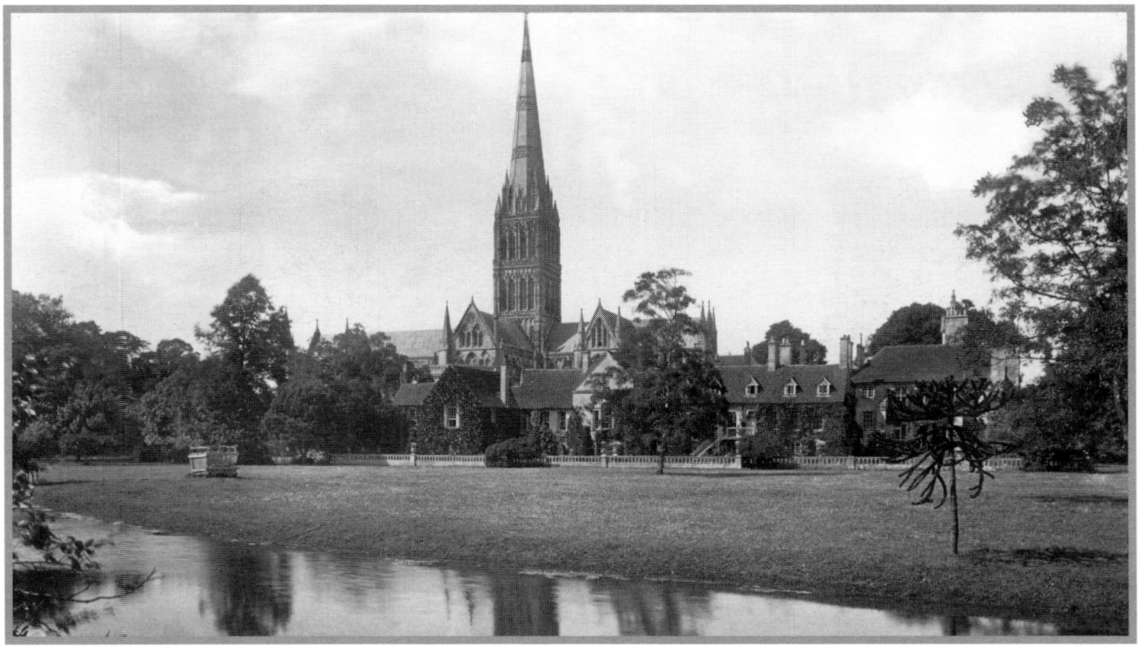

Salisbury, The Cathedral and the Bishop's Palace 1906 56362

The Bishop's Palace, in the foreground, is now the Cathedral School, part of which dates back to the 13th century. This picture reveals how vulnerable the Cathedral is to flooding through the confluence of the rivers Avon, Bourne, Nadder and Wylye; this resulted in a great flood in 1915.

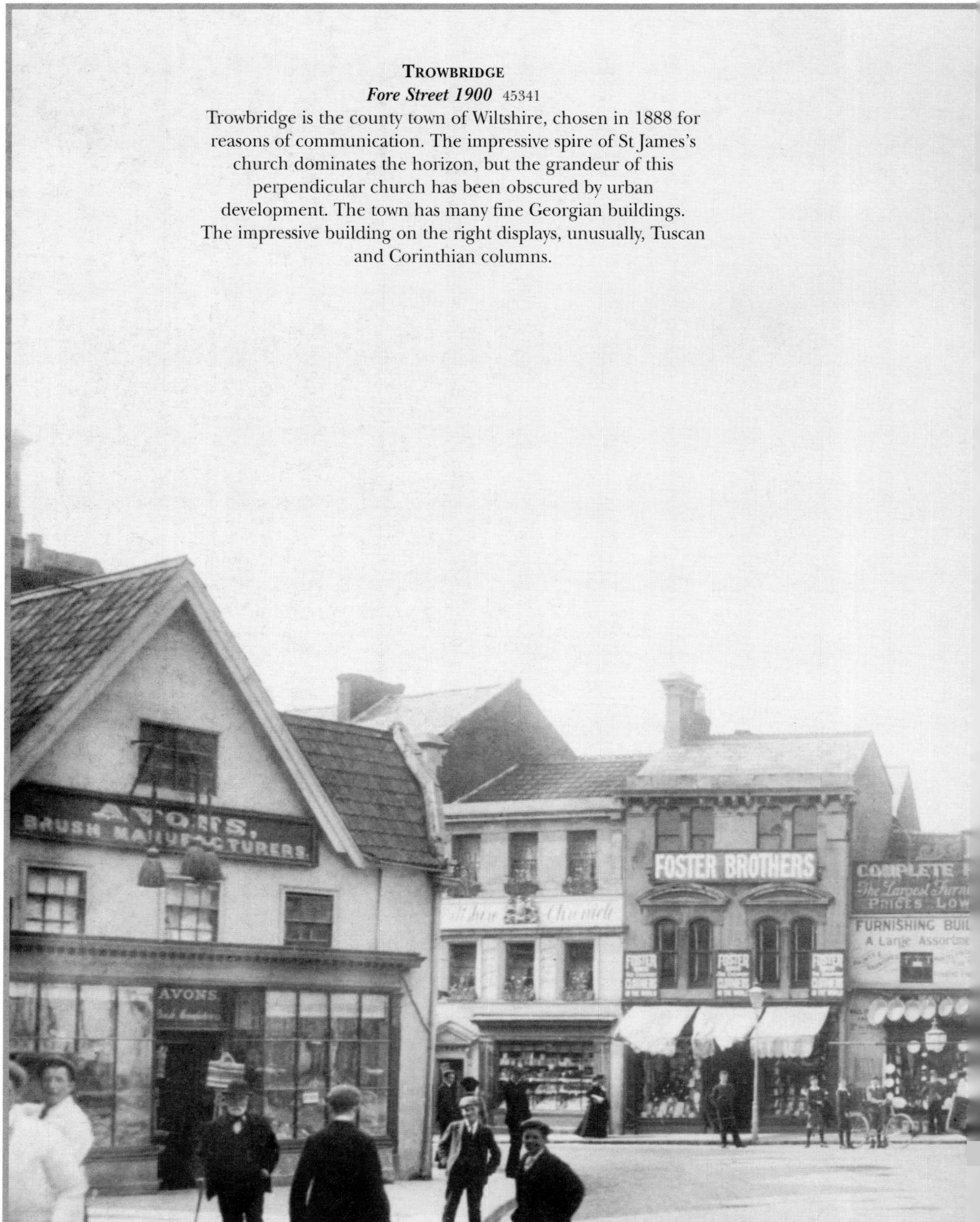

TROWBRIDGE

Fore Street 1900 45341

Trowbridge is the county town of Wiltshire, chosen in 1888 for reasons of communication. The impressive spire of St James's church dominates the horizon, but the grandeur of this perpendicular church has been obscured by urban development. The town has many fine Georgian buildings. The impressive building on the right displays, unusually, Tuscan and Corinthian columns.

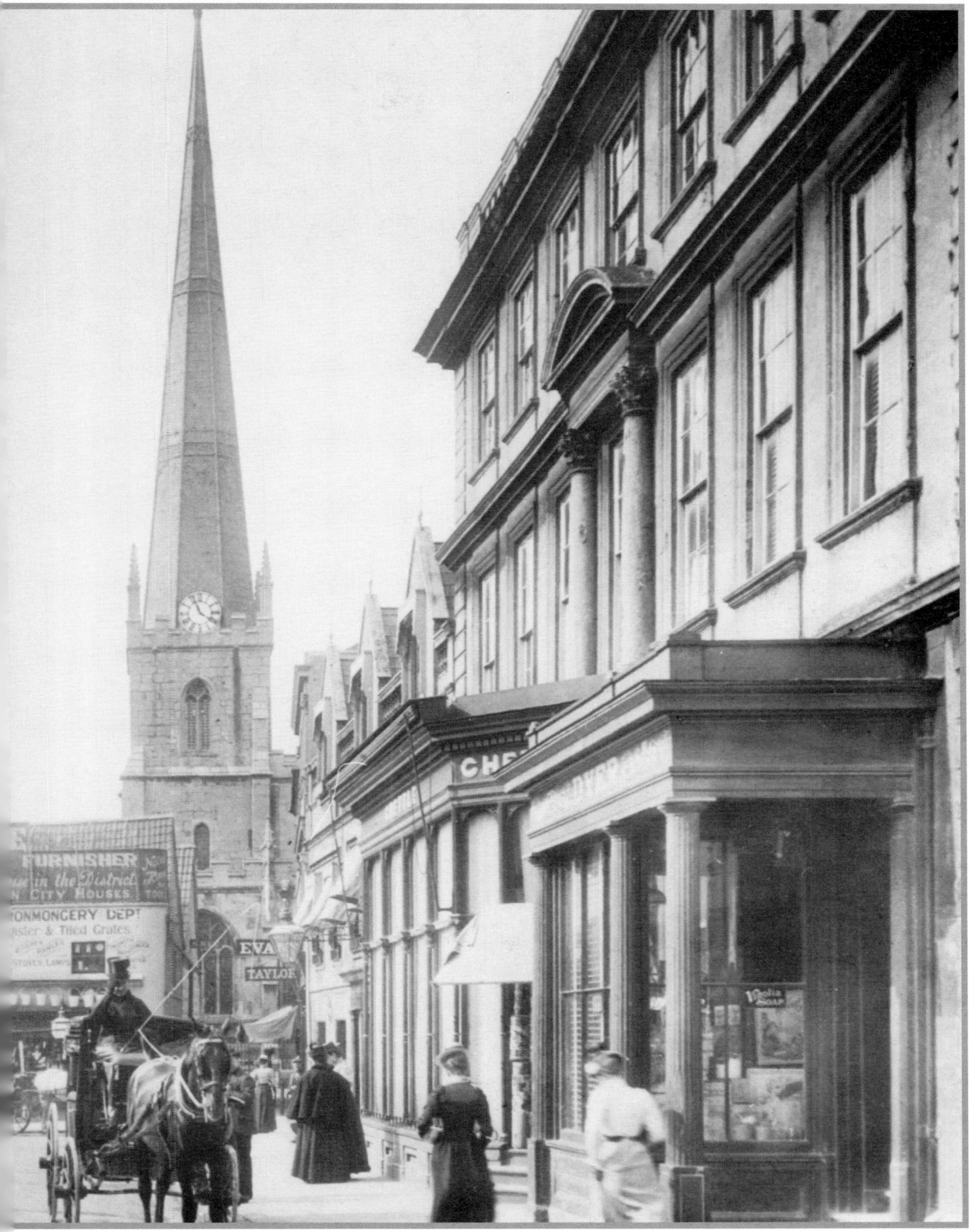
FURNISHER
CITY HOUSES
RONMONGERY DEPT
TAYLOR

Index

Frith Book Co Titles

www.francisfrith.co.uk

The Frith Book Company publishes over 100 new titles each year. A selection of those currently available are listed below. For latest catalogue please contact Frith Book Co.

Town Books 96 pages, approx 100 photos. County and Themed Books 128 pages, approx 150 photos (unless specified). All titles hardback laminated case and jacket except those indicated pb (paperback)

Amersham, Chesham & Rickmansworth (pb)	1-85937-340-2	£9.99
Ancient Monuments & Stone Circles	1-85937-143-4	£17.99
Aylesbury (pb)	1-85937-227-9	£9.99
Bakewell	1-85937-113-2	£12.99
Barnstaple (pb)	1-85937-300-3	£9.99
Bath (pb)	1-85937419-0	£9.99
Bedford (pb)	1-85937-205-8	£9.99
Berkshire (pb)	1-85937-191-4	£9.99
Berkshire Churches	1-85937-170-1	£17.99
Blackpool (pb)	1-85937-382-8	£9.99
Bognor Regis (pb)	1-85937-431-x	£9.99
Bournemouth	1-85937-067-5	£12.99
Bradford (pb)	1-85937-204-x	£9.99
Brighton & Hove(pb)	1-85937-192-2	£8.99
Bristol (pb)	1-85937-264-3	£9.99
British Life A Century Ago (pb)	1-85937-213-9	£9.99
Buckinghamshire (pb)	1-85937-200-7	£9.99
Camberley (pb)	1-85937-222-8	£9.99
Cambridge (pb)	1-85937-422-0	£9.99
Cambridgeshire (pb)	1-85937-420-4	£9.99
Canals & Waterways (pb)	1-85937-291-0	£9.99
Canterbury Cathedral (pb)	1-85937-179-5	£9.99
Cardiff (pb)	1-85937-093-4	£9.99
Carmarthenshire	1-85937-216-3	£14.99
Chelmsford (pb)	1-85937-310-0	£9.99
Cheltenham (pb)	1-85937-095-0	£9.99
Cheshire (pb)	1-85937-271-6	£9.99
Chester	1-85937-090-x	£12.99
Chesterfield	1-85937-378-x	£9.99
Chichester (pb)	1-85937-228-7	£9.99
Colchester (pb)	1-85937-188-4	£8.99
Cornish Coast	1-85937-163-9	£14.99
Cornwall (pb)	1-85937-229-5	£9.99
Cornwall Living Memories	1-85937-248-1	£14.99
Cotswolds (pb)	1-85937-230-9	£9.99
Cotswolds Living Memories	1-85937-255-4	£14.99
County Durham	1-85937-123-x	£14.99
Croydon Living Memories	1-85937-162-0	£9.99
Cumbria	1-85937-101-9	£14.99
Dartmoor	1-85937-145-0	£14.99
Derby (pb)	1-85937-367-4	£9.99
Derbyshire (pb)	1-85937-196-5	£9.99
Devon (pb)	1-85937-297-x	£9.99
Dorset (pb)	1-85937-269-4	£9.99
Dorset Churches	1-85937-172-8	£17.99
Dorset Coast (pb)	1-85937-299-6	£9.99
Dorset Living Memories	1-85937-210-4	£14.99
Down the Severn	1-85937-118-3	£14.99
Down the Thames (pb)	1-85937-278-3	£9.99
Down the Trent	1-85937-311-9	£14.99
Dublin (pb)	1-85937-231-7	£9.99
East Anglia (pb)	1-85937-265-1	£9.99
East London	1-85937-080-2	£14.99
East Sussex	1-85937-130-2	£14.99
Eastbourne	1-85937-061-6	£12.99
Edinburgh (pb)	1-85937-193-0	£8.99
England in the 1880s	1-85937-331-3	£17.99
English Castles (pb)	1-85937-434-4	£9.99
English Country Houses	1-85937-161-2	£17.99
Essex (pb)	1-85937-270-8	£9.99
Exeter	1-85937-126-4	£12.99
Exmoor	1-85937-132-9	£14.99
Falmouth	1-85937-066-7	£12.99
Folkestone (pb)	1-85937-124-8	£9.99
Glasgow (pb)	1-85937-190-6	£9.99
Gloucestershire	1-85937-102-7	£14.99
Great Yarmouth (pb)	1-85937-426-3	£9.99
Greater Manchester (pb)	1-85937-266-x	£9.99
Guildford (pb)	1-85937-410-7	£9.99
Hampshire (pb)	1-85937-279-1	£9.99
Hampshire Churches (pb)	1-85937-207-4	£9.99
Harrogate	1-85937-423-9	£9.99
Hastings & Bexhill (pb)	1-85937-131-0	£9.99
Heart of Lancashire (pb)	1-85937-197-3	£9.99
Helston (pb)	1-85937-214-7	£9.99
Hereford (pb)	1-85937-175-2	£9.99
Herefordshire	1-85937-174-4	£14.99
Hertfordshire (pb)	1-85937-247-3	£9.99
Horsham (pb)	1-85937-432-8	£9.99
Humberside	1-85937-215-5	£14.99
Hythe, Romney Marsh & Ashford	1-85937-256-2	£9.99

Available from your local bookshop or from the publisher

Frith Book Co Titles (continued)

Ipswich (pb)	1-85937-424-7	£9.99
Ireland (pb)	1-85937-181-7	£9.99
Isle of Man (pb)	1-85937-268-6	£9.99
Isles of Scilly	1-85937-136-1	£14.99
Isle of Wight (pb)	1-85937-429-8	£9.99
Isle of Wight Living Memories	1-85937-304-6	£14.99
Kent (pb)	1-85937-189-2	£9.99
Kent Living Memories	1-85937-125-6	£14.99
Lake District (pb)	1-85937-275-9	£9.99
Lancaster, Morecambe & Heysham (pb)	1-85937-233-3	£9.99
Leeds (pb)	1-85937-202-3	£9.99
Leicester	1-85937-073-x	£12.99
Leicestershire (pb)	1-85937-185-x	£9.99
Lincolnshire (pb)	1-85937-433-6	£9.99
Liverpool & Merseyside (pb)	1-85937-234-1	£9.99
London (pb)	1-85937-183-3	£9.99
Ludlow (pb)	1-85937-176-0	£9.99
Luton (pb)	1-85937-235-x	£9.99
Maidstone	1-85937-056-x	£14.99
Manchester (pb)	1-85937-198-1	£9.99
Middlesex	1-85937-158-2	£14.99
New Forest	1-85937-128-0	£14.99
Newark (pb)	1-85937-366-6	£9.99
Newport, Wales (pb)	1-85937-258-9	£9.99
Newquay (pb)	1-85937-421-2	£9.99
Norfolk (pb)	1-85937-195-7	£9.99
Norfolk Living Memories	1-85937-217-1	£14.99
Northamptonshire	1-85937-150-7	£14.99
Northumberland Tyne & Wear (pb)	1-85937-281-3	£9.99
North Devon Coast	1-85937-146-9	£14.99
North Devon Living Memories	1-85937-261-9	£14.99
North London	1-85937-206-6	£14.99
North Wales (pb)	1-85937-298-8	£9.99
North Yorkshire (pb)	1-85937-236-8	£9.99
Norwich (pb)	1-85937-194-9	£8.99
Nottingham (pb)	1-85937-324-0	£9.99
Nottinghamshire (pb)	1-85937-187-6	£9.99
Oxford (pb)	1-85937-411-5	£9.99
Oxfordshire (pb)	1-85937-430-1	£9.99
Peak District (pb)	1-85937-280-5	£9.99
Penzance	1-85937-069-1	£12.99
Peterborough (pb)	1-85937-219-8	£9.99
Piers	1-85937-237-6	£17.99
Plymouth	1-85937-119-1	£12.99
Poole & Sandbanks (pb)	1-85937-251-1	£9.99
Preston (pb)	1-85937-212-0	£9.99
Reading (pb)	1-85937-238-4	£9.99
Romford (pb)	1-85937-319-4	£9.99
Salisbury (pb)	1-85937-239-2	£9.99
Scarborough (pb)	1-85937-379-8	£9.99
St Albans (pb)	1-85937-341-0	£9.99
St Ives (pb)	1-85937415-8	£9.99
Scotland (pb)	1-85937-182-5	£9.99
Scottish Castles (pb)	1-85937-323-2	£9.99
Sevenoaks & Tunbridge	1-85937-057-8	£12.99
Sheffield, South Yorks (pb)	1-85937-267-8	£9.99
Shrewsbury (pb)	1-85937-325-9	£9.99
Shropshire (pb)	1-85937-326-7	£9.99
Somerset	1-85937-153-1	£14.99
South Devon Coast	1-85937-107-8	£14.99
South Devon Living Memories	1-85937-168-x	£14.99
South Hams	1-85937-220-1	£14.99
Southampton (pb)	1-85937-427-1	£9.99
Southport (pb)	1-85937-425-5	£9.99
Staffordshire	1-85937-047-0	£12.99
Stratford upon Avon	1-85937-098-5	£12.99
Suffolk (pb)	1-85937-221-x	£9.99
Suffolk Coast	1-85937-259-7	£14.99
Surrey (pb)	1-85937-240-6	£9.99
Sussex (pb)	1-85937-184-1	£9.99
Swansea (pb)	1-85937-167-1	£9.99
Tees Valley & Cleveland	1-85937-211-2	£14.99
Thanet (pb)	1-85937-116-7	£9.99
Tiverton (pb)	1-85937-178-7	£9.99
Torbay	1-85937-063-2	£12.99
Truro	1-85937-147-7	£12.99
Victorian and Edwardian Cornwall	1-85937-252-x	£14.99
Victorian & Edwardian Devon	1-85937-253-8	£14.99
Victorian & Edwardian Kent	1-85937-149-3	£14.99
Vic & Ed Maritime Album	1-85937-144-2	£17.99
Victorian and Edwardian Sussex	1-85937-157-4	£14.99
Victorian & Edwardian Yorkshire	1-85937-154-x	£14.99
Victorian Seaside	1-85937-159-0	£17.99
Villages of Devon (pb)	1-85937-293-7	£9.99
Villages of Kent (pb)	1-85937-294-5	£9.99
Villages of Sussex (pb)	1-85937-295-3	£9.99
Warwickshire (pb)	1-85937-203-1	£9.99
Welsh Castles (pb)	1-85937-322-4	£9.99
West Midlands (pb)	1-85937-289-9	£9.99
West Sussex	1-85937-148-5	£14.99
West Yorkshire (pb)	1-85937-201-5	£9.99
Weymouth (pb)	1-85937-209-0	£9.99
Wiltshire (pb)	1-85937-277-5	£9.99
Wiltshire Churches (pb)	1-85937-171-x	£9.99
Wiltshire Living Memories	1-85937-245-7	£14.99
Winchester (pb)	1-85937-428-x	£9.99
Windmills & Watermills	1-85937-242-2	£17.99
Worcester (pb)	1-85937-165-5	£9.99
Worcestershire	1-85937-152-3	£14.99
York (pb)	1-85937-199-x	£9.99
Yorkshire (pb)	1-85937-186-8	£9.99
Yorkshire Living Memories	1-85937-166-3	£14.99

See Frith books on the internet www.francisfrith.co.uk

Frith Products & Services

Francis Frith would doubtless be pleased to know that the pioneering publishing venture he started in 1860 still continues today. A hundred and forty years later, The Francis Frith Collection continues in the same innovative tradition and is now one of the foremost publishers of vintage photographs in the world. Some of the current activities include:

Interior Decoration

Today Frith's photographs can be seen framed and as giant wall murals in thousands of pubs, restaurants, hotels, banks, retail stores and other public buildings throughout the country. In every case they enhance the unique local atmosphere of the places they depict and provide reminders of gentler days in an increasingly busy and frenetic world.

Product Promotions

Frith products are used by many major companies to promote the sales of their own products or to reinforce their own history and heritage. Frith promotions have been used by Hovis bread, Courage beers, Scots Porage Oats, Colman's mustard, Cadbury's foods, Mellow Birds coffee, Dunhill pipe tobacco, Guinness, and Bulmer's Cider.

Genealogy and Family History

As the interest in family history and roots grows world-wide, more and more people are turning to Frith's photographs of Great Britain for images of the towns, villages and streets where their ancestors lived; and, of course, photographs of the churches and chapels where their ancestors were christened, married and buried are an essential part of every genealogy tree and family album.

Frith Products

All Frith photographs are available Framed or just as Mounted Prints and Posters (size 23 x 16 inches). These may be ordered from the address below. From time to time other products - Address Books, Calendars, Table Mats, etc - are available.

The Internet

Already twenty thousand Frith photographs can be viewed and purchased on the internet through the Frith websites and a myriad of partner sites.

For more detailed information on Frith companies and products, look at these sites:

www.francisfrith.co.uk
www.francisfrith.com
(for North American visitors)

See the complete list of Frith Books at:
www.francisfrith.co.uk
This web site is regularly updated with the latest list of publications from the Frith Book Company. If you wish to buy books relating to another part of the country that your local bookshop does not stock, you may purchase on-line.

For further information, trade, or author enquiries please contact us at the address below:
The Francis Frith Collection, Frith's Barn, Teffont, Salisbury, Wiltshire, England SP3 5QP.
Tel: +44 (0)1722 716 376 Fax: +44 (0)1722 716 881 Email: sales@francisfrith.co.uk

See Frith books on the internet www.francisfrith.co.uk

TO RECEIVE YOUR FREE MOUNTED PRINT

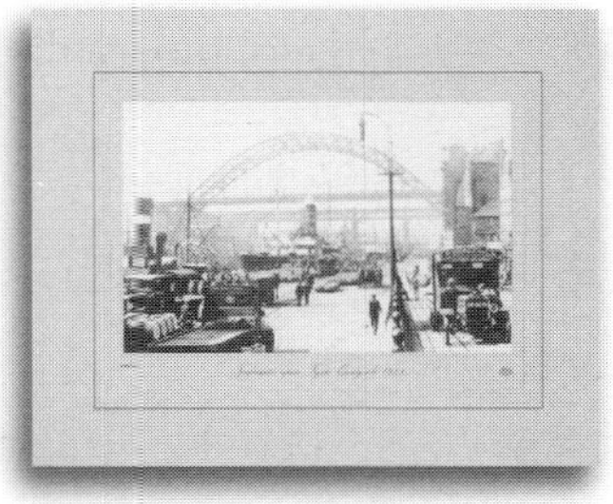

Mounted Print
Overall size 14 x 11 inches

Cut out this Voucher and return it with your remittance for £1.95 to cover postage and handling, to UK addresses. For overseas addresses please include £4.00 post and handling.
Choose any photograph included in this book. Your SEPIA print will be A4 in size, and mounted in a cream mount with burgundy rule line, overall size 14 x 11 inches

Order additional Mounted Prints at HALF PRICE (only £7.49 each*)
If there are further pictures you would like to order, possibly as gifts for friends and family, purchase them at half price (no additional postage and handling required).

Have your Mounted Prints framed*
For an additional £14.95 per print you can have your chosen Mounted Print framed in an elegant polished wood and gilt moulding, overall size 16 x 13 inches (no additional postage and handling required).

*** IMPORTANT!**
These special prices are only available if ordered using the original voucher on this page (no copies permitted) and at the same time as your free Mounted Print, for delivery to the same address

Frith Collectors' Guild

From time to time we publish a magazine of news and stories about Frith photographs and further special offers of Frith products. If you would like 12 months FREE membership, please return this form.

Send completed forms to:
The Francis Frith Collection, Frith's Barn, Teffont, Salisbury, Wiltshire SP3 5QP

Voucher for FREE and Reduced Price Frith Prints

Picture no.	Page number	Qty	Mounted @ £7.49	Framed + £14.95	Total Cost
		1	**Free of charge***	£	£
			£7.49	£	£
			£7.49	£	£
			£7.49	£	£
			£7.49	£	£
			£7.49	£	£

Please allow 28 days for delivery — *** Post & handling** **£1.95**

Book Title .... **Total Order Cost** **£**

Please do not photocopy this voucher. Only the original is valid, so please cut it out and return it to us.

I enclose a cheque / postal order for £ ....
made payable to 'The Francis Frith Collection'
OR please debit my Mastercard / Visa / Switch / Amex card
(credit cards please on all overseas orders)

Number ....
Issue No (Switch only) .... Valid from (Amex/Switch) ....
Expires .... Signature ....

Name Mr/Mrs/Ms ....
Address ....
....
....
.... Postcode ....
Daytime Tel No ....

Valid to 31/12/03

The Francis Frith Collectors' Guild

Please enrol me as a member for 12 months free of charge.

Name Mr/Mrs/Ms ....
Address ....
....
....
.... Postcode ....

Free Print - see overleaf

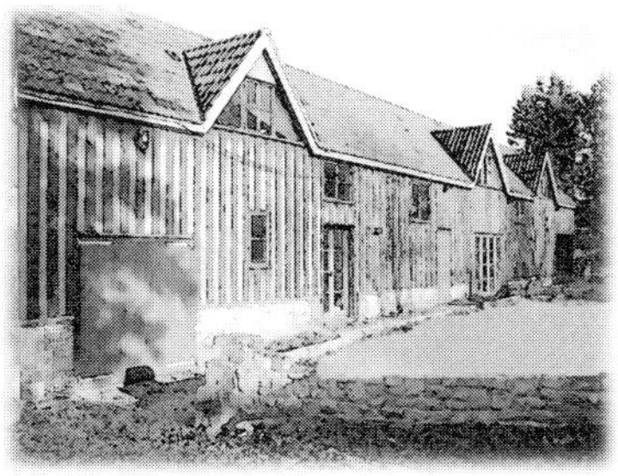

Would you like to find out more about Francis Frith?

We have recently recruited some entertaining speakers who are happy to visit local groups, clubs and societies to give an illustrated talk documenting Frith's travels and photographs. If you are a member of such a group and are interested in hosting a presentation, we would love to hear from you.

Our speakers bring with them a small selection of our local town and county books, together with sample prints. They are happy to take orders. A small proportion of the order value is donated to the group who have hosted the presentation. The talks are therefore an excellent way of fundraising for small groups and societies.

Can you help us with information about any of the Frith photographs in this book?

We are gradually compiling an historical record for each of the photographs in the Frith archive. It is always fascinating to find out the names of the people shown in the pictures, as well as insights into the shops, buildings and other features depicted.

If you recognize anyone in the photographs in this book, or if you have information not already included in the author's caption, do let us know. We would love to hear from you, and will try to publish it in future books or articles.

Our production team

Frith books are produced by a small dedicated team at offices in the converted Grade II listed 18th-century barn at Teffont near Salisbury, illustrated above. Most have worked with the Frith Collection for many years. All have in common one quality: they have a passion for the Frith Collection. The team is constantly expanding, but currently includes:

Jason Buck, John Buck, Douglas Burns, Heather Crisp, Lucy Elcock, Isobel Hall, Rob Hames, Hazel Heaton, Peter Horne, James Kinnear, Tina Leary, Hannah Marsh, Eliza Sackett, Terence Sackett, Sandra Sanger, Lewis Taylor, Shelley Tolcher, Helen Vimpany, Clive Wathen and Jenny Wathen.